Culture House Editions vol. 2

The Manuscripts of Iceland, originally published as Handritin, accompanying an exhibition by the Árni Magnússon Institute in Iceland, which opened in the Culture House, Reykjavík, October 5, 2002

Book design: Helga Gerður Magnúsdóttir

Translation of book: Bernard Scudder, except article by Mats Malm (pp. 101-7) transl. from Swedish by Keneva Kunz, and article by Andrew Wawn (pp. 131-142) originally written in English
Citations are taken from the following sources: Grágás on pp. 10-11 from Andrew Dennis, Peter Foote, Richard Perkins (Laws of Early Iceland, University of Manitoba Press, 1980); Njál's saga on pp. 74-75 from Robert Cook (The Complete Sagas of Icelanders III. Leifur Eiríksson Publishing, 1997); Marie de France on p. 74 from Robert Cook (Strengleikar. Norrøne tekster 3, 1979); Jónas Hallgrímsson on pp. 110-111 from Dick Ringler (Bard of Iceland. Jónas Hallgrímsson, University of Wisconsin Press, 2002

Exhibition design: Gísli Sigurðsson and Steinþór Sigurðsson
Exhibition committee: Hersteinn Brynjúlfsson, Jóhanna Ólafsdóttir, Ólöf Benediktsdóttir, Rósa Þorsteinsdóttir, Svanhildur Gunnarsdóttir and Vésteinn Ólason

Installation: Sviðsmyndir ehf.
Exhibition rooms: Íslandssmiðjan ehf.
Procurement of illustrations: Rósa Þorsteinsdóttir
Photography of exhibits from the Árni Magnússon Institute: Jóhanna Ólafsdóttir
Image processing: Merking ehf.
Sound: Baldur Már Arngrímsson
Lighting: Ögmundur Þ. Jóhannesson
Film editing: Hjálmtýr Heiðdal
Danish translation of exhibition texts: Pétur Rasmussen
English translation of exhibition texts: Bernard Scudder

Authors of the website "Handritin heima" at www.am.hi.is: Laufey Guðnadóttir and Soffía Guðmundsdóttir
Computer graphics: Hugrún Hrönn Ólafsdóttir
Hosts of website www.europeoftales.net: Kroma Production OY Finland

Ink production: Ágúst H. Bjarnason
Tools in scriptorium: Bjarni Þór Kristjánsson and Páll Kristjánsson
Scribe: Kristín Þorgrímsdóttir

Special thanks: Icelandic National Broadcasting Service, Jón Egill Bergþórsson, Íslendingasagnaútgáfan, Hið íslenska fornritafélag/The Icelandic Literary Society, Edda - Publishing, Bókaútgáfan Skjaldborg, Leifur Eiríksson Publishing, Mál og menning bookstores, Búi Kristjánsson, Elisabeth Ward, Örnólfur Thorsson

Front cover: From The Words of the High One (Hávamál) in the Codex Regius manuscript of the Edda poems, GKS 2365 4to. Árni Magnússon Institute in Iceland

ISBN 9979-819-88-X

THE MANUSCRIPTS
OF ICELAND

Editors: Gísli Sigurðsson and Vésteinn Ólason

Árni Magnússon Institute in Iceland
Reykjavík 2004

The Manuscripts of Iceland

VÉSTEINN ÓLASON

"Bring the manuscripts home" was the unanimous slogan of the Icelandic people last century. Three decades after the first manuscripts were returned by the Danish government, people still say: "We want to see the manuscripts." This is a familiar phrase to the staff at Árnastofnun (The Árni Magnússon Institute). It is interesting that we should so often refer to "the manuscripts" with the definite article, even though we are not always talking about the same ones. The exhibition *The Manuscripts of Iceland (Handritin)*, which opened at the Culture House in Reykjavík in the autumn of 2002, features 15 manuscripts and is probably the largest exhibition focusing on medieval Icelandic manuscripts ever staged. The Árni Magnússon Institute houses almost 2,000 manuscripts. Hundreds of Icelandic manuscripts are preserved in museums outside Iceland, and tens of thousands at the National University Library, National Archives, National Museum and other museums all around the country, not to mention those which are privately owned. So how can we possibly display a handful of manuscripts and give the exhibition this name? The explanation is that the term "manuscripts" as used here refers to a concept rather than specific items. There are historical and ideological justifications for this which this exhibition and publication are intended to elucidate.

Written on calfskin, medieval Icelandic manuscripts are at one and the same time the repository of medieval Icelandic culture and its visible symbol. They are not the only visible relics, nor do they preserve everything that was committed to vellum, because much has been lost, yet they do contain invaluable treasures. Paper manuscripts from later centuries fill many gaps from the ancient books, and of course also embody the cultural heritage of their own time. Iceland's medieval literary culture was unique, and gave rise to some notable classics, but to a certain degree such a culture is always abstract and intangible. For this reason, it is invaluable to have tangible and visible objects which at the same time embody what is intangible and offer beautiful exam-

Left: The opening section of Christian Law from the *Arnarbælisbók* manuscript of *Jónsbók*, AM 135 4to. Árni Magnússon Institute in Iceland.

ples of the craftsmanship of centuries past; we feel in a sense that we see and perceive better the culture where our roots lie when we have a book in front of us, for example the manuscript of the *Poetic Edda* (*Eddukvæði*), *Egil's Saga* (*Egils saga Skallagrímssonar*), *Njal's Saga* (*Njáls saga*) or *The Book of the Icelanders* (*Íslendingabók*).

Towards the end of the sixteenth century, word of the old Icelandic Sagas began to spread to the European academic world, and interest in the Icelandic manuscripts was awoken. The influence of Old Icelandic literature in Northern Europe then gained momentum until the Romantic era in the nineteenth century. In the twentieth century much of the ancient literature was translated into other languages, and research advanced by leaps and bounds. Each age links the heritage of the past with the interests of its own time.

It is invaluable for a small, impoverished nation to know it has a heritage which is admired by other nations, and the ancient literature soon became Iceland's main source of pride in relation to the rest of the world. Today Iceland is a wealthy country and can be proud of much more than its ancient literature, not least its contemporary literature and other arts, and also other aspects of the cultural heritage. Nonetheless, there is still a special enchantment about the ancient literature and its visible representation in the manuscripts. We wish to preserve this enchantment without allowing it to blind us to other things that are worth seeing.

When Iceland had recovered a great part of the ancient manuscripts that had been kept in Danish libraries for centuries and it had established an institution dedicated to preserving and propagating this treasure, it was only natural for the nation to take an interest in seeing them. The Árni Magnússon Institute staged an exhibition in its constricted premises, where several manuscripts could be seen. Schools in Iceland have eagerly taken advantage of this and many travellers from abroad have also visited the exhibition. Since October 2002 the Institute has had access to exhibition space in the old National Library premises, now the Culture House, widely regarded as the most beautiful and dignified building in Reykjavík. The present exhibition is staged in the rooms that for several decades housed the National Library's manuscript collection, also the premises of the original Manuscript Institute before it moved to Árnagarður on the university campus. There the manuscripts are kept under optimum conditions, with the space to provide visitors with a wealth of information about the culture in which the manuscripts came into being, and about the influence of medieval Icelandic literature on latter-day culture.

Although this collection of essays has been published to coincide with the exhibition, it is in effect an independent resource. In particular it is aimed at exhibition visitors who want to learn more about and gain a better understanding of the story that the exhibition tells. In these essays, scholars and authors tackle their subject from independent and personal approaches without confining themselves to the material on exhibit. The book opens with a description of the oral lore which characterized the culture of the pioneer generations in Iceland and served as the source of the most distinctive features of its literary culture. Next comes a discussion of the Church and the culture of writing which it introduced following the adoption of Christianity. These basic preconditions having been established, an examination follows of the social structures that took shape in Iceland, their evolution, and how literature and the main literary genres flourished in Iceland until the Golden Age of book production, the fourteenth century. Bookmaking skills are a prerequisite for literary culture, and the next chapter describes bookmaking in the Middle Ages, how the material was prepared and how the books were written and put together. Next comes a discussion of writing and scribal styles and their development from the earliest fragments to the nineteenth century. The next essay focuses on the scribes and their role in literary creation and re-creation. As far as the post-Reformation history of the manuscripts is concerned, no single person played as monumental a role as Árni Magnússon. A separate essay describes his life, manuscript collecting and scholarly work.

The exhibition and this book attempt to inform the reader about how the literature contained in the manuscripts was received by later generations, about its value and the way it was understood, misunderstood and even misused. There are essays on its reception in Scandinavia, nineteenth-century Iceland, Germany and the English-speaking world of Britain and the USA. Another chapter describes the status of the ancient literature, especially the Sagas of Icelanders, in twentieth-century Iceland, dwelling in particular on public disputes which arose in the 1940s concerning control over how they should be presented in print. Another essay outlines the influence of the literary heritage on Icelandic visual art.

To many people, the return of the manuscripts represented the final phase in Iceland's campaign for independence, insofar as such a campaign can ever end. There is a description of the background to and main events in the recovery of the manuscripts, followed by the edifying story of one book, not a very old one, but one containing old material. It "went west" (to America) at the end of the nineteenth century, as people used to say in the first half of the twentieth century, but returned more than a century later.

The final chapter discusses the value of ancient literature and ancient books for Icelanders past and present. It reflects upon the fate of the manuscripts, giving rather freer rein than elsewhere in the book

Right: Illuminated initials from *Flateyjarbók,* GKS 1005 fol.
Árni Magnússon Institute in Iceland.

to the passionate and irrational love which we feel for this unique phenomenon.

The authors and subjects in this essay collection were selected with reference to the exhibition "The Manuscripts" which opened in the Culture House in Reykjavík on October 5, 2002. The illustrations are to a large extent taken from the exhibition, which has been curated by Gísli Sigurðsson from the Árni Magnússon Institute and designed by painter Steinþór Sigurðsson. Nonetheless, this book is an independent work which aims to inform and interest readers whether they have seen the exhibition or not. The Árni Magnússon Institute received a generous grant from the Treasury to set up the exhibition and produce this companion to it. We would like to thank the Government of Iceland and the Culture House for their excellent cooperation on this project.

Vésteinn Ólason
Director, Árni Magnússon Institute, Iceland

MANUSCRIPTS ON DISPLAY AT THE OPENING OF THE EXHIBITION ON OCT 5 2002

Codex Regius: Poetic Edda, GKS 2365 4to (see pp. 2-6, 174).

Codex Regius: Prose Edda, GKS 2367 4to. Mid-14th century (see pp. 2-4).

Flateyjarbók, GKS 1005 fol. (see pp. 35-37, 174).

Stjórn: AM 227 fol. (see p. 23).

Grágás: Staðarhólsbók, AM 334 fol. (see pp.9-11, 29).

Jónsbók: Skarðsbók, AM 350 fol. (see pp. 11, 29).

Egil's Saga: fragment, AM 162 A, fol. (see pp. 39-40).

Egil's Saga: Ketilsbók, AM 462 4to (see p. 40).

Möðruvallabók: Sagas of Icelanders, AM 132 fol. (see pp. 38, 76-78).

Njal's Saga: Kálfalækjarbók, AM 133 fol. (see p. 40).

The Book of Settlements: Hauksbók, AM 371 4to (see p. 31).

The Book of the Icelanders, AM 113 b fol. (see pp. 29-30).

The Life of St. Margaret, AM 432 12mo. C. 1500.

A Book of Magic, AM 434 d 12mo. 17th century.

Melsted's Edda, SÁM 66 (see pp. 179-184).

Contents

… reif hundar vápndœyr vegr ʒ̄ dug, blinde ę bet …
… rende te nýtr mangi nas. Sonr ę bet þot ſe ſíþ oꝛ al …
… þt genginn gva. ſialdan bacar ſteinar ſtanda bꝛauto n …
… ea reiſt nıþ ar nıð. Tveir ro eins hiar rugo ę hafꝛ …
… anı ę m̄ þeim hvn handar vein. not vꝑ ꝼꝛegín ſa ę …
… tir ſcámar ro ſcıpſ rar hꝩb ę haſt gına ꝼꝛialþ v vıð …
… gr vꝑ aꝺ̛ laıdꝛꝩ aptꝛ ꝩ ę audıgr anan o audygr ſeylıt ha …
… rtca vaꝛ. Deyr ꝼ e deyıa ꝼꝛændꝛ deyr ſialfꝛ ıt ſama. e …
… x tıꝩ deyr aldꝛegı hveı eꝛ ſer goðan getꝛ. Deyr ꝼe ꝺ ꝼ …
… e veıt eınn at aldrı deyr dōꝛ v dædꝛan hıꝩ. ſ vllaꝛ grı …
… a ec ꝼ ꝼꝛꝩwngſ ſonō nv ba þr vanar vol. Iva ę aꝺꝛ ſ …
… ꝩga bragð h eꝛ valtaſtꝛ vına. Oſnotꝛ ꝩ eꝼ eıgnaꝛ getꝛ …
… ę eꝼ ꝼ:ꝉıoſſ mvnoð. metnaða hō þaꝛ eꝩ manvıt aldꝛe …
… m getꝛ h drıvgꝛ ıdvl. Þ ę þa reynıt ę þv at rvnō ſ …
… nō regın hvꝩō þeı eꝛ gœðo gınregın. oc ꝼaðı ꝼꝛımbvl …
… a heꝼ. h baꝛo eꝛ h þegır. At gldı ſꝛ dag leyꝙa kona …
… rreıð ę rıekı ę reynıa ę mey eꝛ geꝙ eꝛ 1ſ eꝛ yꝙ hōꝛ a …
… drottıe ę. Ivmor ſꝛ vıð harō vedrı alıo roa myrkꝛ hıe …
… pıalla mœg eꝛa dagſ eongo aceıp ſꝛ ſcrıðar oıea eꝩ aꝼeıeı …
… hlıꝛar mıokı haꝼſ eꝩ mey ę koſa. Gıð eld ſꝛ avl dreet …
… aıſı ſcrıða magran mar cvpa ę rıekı ſaꝛgan hervı …
… eſt ꝼetta eꝩ hvnō abvı. Qhoyıar adō ſcylı mangı v …
… e þın eꝛ qvede kona. þat ahꝩꝛanda hveb v þeı hıe …
… cvpıð bꝛıgð ıbaﬆ v lagꝛo. Breﬆanda boga breꝩand …
… oga gınanda vbꝛ galandı krako rycanda ſvını roꝛ …
… om vſoꝛ varanda vagı vellanda buⱦlı. ꝉ hꝛꝩ̄anda rıeı …

Oral sagas, poems and lore

GÍSLI SIGURÐSSON

Long before the days of books, people used to tell stories and recite
poems to depict their environment and emotions. Historical lore and
social ethics were incorporated into the stories and transmitted from
one generation to the next, century after century, with continual
changes, additions and omissions as time went by and external circumstances demanded. Religions and holy rites were formed around
the word, be it verse or prose, spoken, sung or recited. Public affairs
were carried on without any paperwork. People learned the law,
brought cases and passed sentences without writing a single word.
They could trace their families and pass on their knowledge of astronomy and distant continents with oral narrative. Wherever people gathered, stories might be told and poems recited, reviving memories of
ancient champions and heroes for the purpose of building up the
courage for battle, or simply for entertainment. People told stories to
reflect their own lives, gained control over reality through narrative art
and fashioned their thoughts into poetry. Sagas and poems enabled
people to express their views, set forth ideas and pass them on to others – all of this without books.

People came together to pass on this heritage and keep it alive
through reiteration and innovation. No knowledge was available apart
from the spoken word. There was no place to look anything up –
except in the memories of wise men and women. And if they dis-
agreed, there was no way to decide who was right. Once something
was forgotten it could never be reclaimed.

The first attempt to handle this intellectual heritage and make it
visible in permanent form can be seen in pictures from prehistoric
times, at first in simple cave and stone carvings and later in more elab-
orate visual art portraying characters and events from myths and legends. The cultural function of such art is obscure now, but we assume
that it served a purpose when these stories were told, at sacred rites or
in connection with customs and practices where specific myths were
important. Images in churches were later used in this way, to give
visual form to biblical stories and to present and interpret them. It is
not unlikely that highly evolved visual art such as that which has been
preserved on Viking Age stones in Gotland testifies to the same function of preserving and conveying stories, in this case pagan legends.
Many of the rune stones are beautifully wrought works of art, and

Left: From *The Words of the High One* (*Hávamál*) in the *Codex Regius*
manuscript of the Edda poems, GKS 2365 4to.
Árni Magnússon Institute in Iceland.

Evening reading from the sagas. Painting by August Schiött, 1861. National Museum of Iceland.

some have poems and fragments of verses carved on them. The best known verse of this sort is a skaldic (*dróttkvæð*) verse – the oldest known example of this metre – on the Karlevi stone which was erected in Öland in Sweden around AD 1000 in memory of Sibbi Foldarson, and a memorial to Vemod (Vémóður) in the *fornyrðislag* or eddic metre, carved by his father Varinn on the Rök stone in East Gotland in Sweden and telling of King Theodoric (Þjóðrekur). But although runes were used to carve single verses and inscriptions in stone and wood, there is nothing to suggest that long stories or poems were written in runes.

A cosmogony and system of ethics were incorporated into stories about characters who were known throughout the Germanic cultural world. The forces of nature and a variety of human characteristics were personified in the gods, while the heroic legends presented models for human behaviour. The myths mirror the lives of heroes, and in them gold, power struggles, love and jealousy are the primal forces determining human fate.

Much of the ancient visual art can only be explained with the help of the eddic poems from the *Codex Regius (Konungsbók),* which was written in Iceland around 1270, and the prose accounts of the *Snorra Edda* (1220-30), in which the ancient heritage of stories and poems was systematically recorded for the first time. These two books, which together form a systematic exposition of the mythology and poetry, are by far the most important sources for belief in the North in the pagan era. Images carved in stone in Gotland, for example, can now be read with the help of the written Eddas. The bottom half of one of the best known stones gives a good impression of the weaponry, sails and prow of a Viking ship, while the upper half is thought to show Odin on his eight-legged horse, Sleipnir. He is being greeted by a woman holding a chalice, which corresponds closely with notions of the valkyries in Valhalla and the function of drink in the initiation of kings. "Gunnlod gave to me/on her golden seat/a drink of the precious mead", as Odin says in the *Words of the High One (Hávamál)* in the *Codex Regius*, and Sigurd the Dragon-Slayer (Sigurður Fáfnisbani) is afforded the same kind of reception from the valkyrie Sigurdrifa in the same book. Sigurdrifa picks up a horn full of mead and gives Sigurd a drink when he has cut away her armour. In many cultures, an important component of myths about royal initiations is that the king-to-be accepts his mandate when a woman, the symbol of the land and the nation (cf. the Maid of the Mountains in later Icelandic poetry), gives him a drink of a special mead. The initiation is then confirmed with their intercourse.

The eleventh century images carved on a stone in Ramsundberg,

Sweden, provide another instance where the meaning of a picture is elucidated by written accounts of the episodes it depicts. On one part of the stone Sigurd is shown stabbing the dragon Fafnir and on another he roasts its heart on a spit. The birds warn Sigurd of Regin's treachery and Sigurd's horse, Grani, is carrying a chest of gold on its back, while Regin the Smith lies decapitated among the tools of his trade. More images testify to the widespread knowledge of the story of Sigurd the Dragon-Slayer throughout Northern Europe, a legend well known from the eddic poems in *Codex Regius*, as well as from the *Snorra Edda*, *The Saga of the Volsungs* (*Völsunga saga*), *The Saga of Thidrek of Bern* (*Þiðreks saga*) and the Middle High German *Nibelungenlied* from about 1200. Allusions to the saga are also found in the Old English *Beowulf*, and Richard Wagner used the Icelandic Eddas as a basis for his operatic cycle the *Ring of the Nibelungs*.

Interestingly, one minor detail in the description by Snorri Sturluson (1178/9-1241) in his *Snorra Edda*, of Thor's fishing trip with the giant Hymir when he used an ox's head as bait to catch the Midgard Serpent, was unexpectedly corroborated by an illustration on a stone found in 1918 in a cemetery in Altuna, Oppland, some 40 km west of Uppsala, one of the most sacred sites of Nordic paganism. The image is thought to be from the eleventh century and its style can be traced to the rune-master Lifstein, whose disciples, Bal(l)i and Freystein, are named on the stone. Thor's foot is shown as going through the bottom of the boat; the *Snorra Edda* says he pierced the boarding with both his feet when straining to haul the Midgard Serpent aboard. This detail is not mentioned in the skaldic poetry preserved about this episode, so the picture provides important proof that Snorri Sturluson used ancient Nordic oral tradition when he wrote the myths in his *Edda*. Images associated with this myth are also found in Cumbria in England, Jutland and Gotland.

From time immemorial, people in the North had recited poetry similar to the eddic poems which constitute one of the two main branches of ancient Nordic verse, alongside skaldic poetry. The eddic poems are anonymous, mostly in the *fornyrðislag* metre, while their versification and diction had become established early among the Germanic peoples, as can be seen from the Old German *Hildebrandslied* and the Old English *Beowulf*. The eddic poems are divided into mythological poems about Odin, Thor, Freyr and other gods, and heroic poems. Although they relate incidents from the world of the gods, many of the mythological poems reflect human circumstances. They have no parallels among other Germanic nations, and it has been fiercely disputed whether they are reliable accounts of pagan viewpoints or whether they reveal a Christian interpretation of the myths. Snorri Sturluson unhesitatingly used the mythological poems as sources for his *Snorra Edda*.

The heroic poems, on the other hand, portray real characters from the fourth and fifth centuries, such as Attila the Hun, although these works have lost all historical value since being incorporated into a narrative world which obeys its own laws. The main heroes, Helgi Hundingsbani and Sigurd the Dragon-Slayer, for example, are only known from fiction. Most of the heroic poems describe the history of the gold which Sigurd won from the dragon Fafnir and the curse that accompanied it. The story of Gudrun (Guðrún Gjúkadóttir) links up the poems: she marries three times and at the end has lost all her husbands, brothers and descendants. The eddic poems often present different viewpoints on the same action, because the poems were kept alive by being recited for many centuries during which they were constantly subject to reshaping by their performers, as is common with anonymous, orally transmitted poetry. The main manuscript of the eddic poems is *Codex Regius* from the second half of the thirteenth century; most of the poems are preserved only there.

The *Codex* opens with the *Sibyl's Prophecy* (*Völuspá*), which is the chief poem of old Nordic literature and the introduction to the entire work. It is spoken by a prophetess who describes the creation of the world and the state of peace in plenty among the gods. Gullveig arrives from the world of the giants and instils in men and gods the lust for gold, spawning ill feelings which lead to murder and breaking of oaths. Then the prophetess describes how she acquires the vision that the prophecy presents, by sitting in the open when Odin appears to her. She saw then how Balder the good god will be killed and how the enemies of the bewildered gods will grow in might until the divine and human worlds are destroyed at the "doom of the gods." But the Earth will arise a second time, and the unblemished will live there and enjoy its delights.

After the *Sibyl's Prophecy* comes the *Words of the High One*, which preserves ancient ethical precepts attributed to Odin. These stress individualism, wisdom, moderation and friendship, while wealth and power are dismissed as transitory. Two didactic poems follow: the *Words of Vafthrudnir* (*Vafþrúðnismál*), which presents a large amount of mythological material in the form of a contest in wisdom between Odin and the giant Vafnthrudnir, and the *Words of Grimnir* (*Grímnismál*), which describes Odin's visit to King Geirrod (Geirröður). Their dialogue enshrines many of the oldest ideas about the Nordic cosmogony and its relation to the world of gods and spirits. The *Words of Skirnir* (*Skírnismál*) describes the courtship of the fertility god Frey, while the *Lay of Harbard* (*Hárbarðsljóð*) compares Odin and Thor and clearly reveals what each consider to be his qualities:

Royal reception. Stone carving from Gotland. Antiquarian Topographic Archive, Stockholm.

Thor boasts of his battle with trolls and giants, while Odin is proud of his own shrewdness and attractiveness to women. In *Loki's Slanging Match* (*Lokasenna*), the evil god Loki disrupts Aegir's feast and is thrown out, only to return to insult the gods with scathing sarcasm: the goddesses for nymphomania, adultery and promiscuity, and the gods for cowardice, homosexuality and sorcery. Loki himself is accused of lying, homosexuality and drunkenness. Another comic verse, the *Lay of Thrym* (*Þrymskviða*), describes how Thor had to dress up in bridal costume in order to recover his hammer Mjöllnir from the giant Thrym.

The heroic poems first account for Helgi Hundingsbani and Helgi Hjorvardsson, then Sigurd the Dragon-Slayer and the fateful events set in motion by the gold from Gnitaheidi. In addition to Sigurd, this tale features most to the most famous heroes of the Germanic people: Gunnar and his brother Hogni and sister Gudrun (who was the wife of Sigurd and later of Attila the Hun), as well as Brynhild, who was Gunnar's wife and Attila's sister.

In *The Lay of Helgi Hjorvardsson* (*Helgakviða Hjörvarðssonar*), Helgi marries the valkyrie Svava, who has previously given him the only name that would attach to him. Helgi's brother Hedin falls in love with his sister-in-law Svava but Helgi forgives him and, fatally wounded, asks her to love Hedin, who promises to avenge Helgi's death. There are two poems about Helgi Hundingsbani, both revolving around his love for Sigrun. The couple are thought to be Helgi and Svava resurrected, and in the *Poem of Kara* (*Káruljóð*), which has not been preserved, it is said that they would be reborn as Helgi and Kara.

Most of the subsequent heroic poems relate the tale of the gold won by Sigurd from Fafnir on Gnitaheidi and the curse accompanying it. The introduction to the story is found in the *Prophecy of Gripir* (*Grípisspá*), which summarizes the heroic poems that follow, just as the *Sibyl's Prophecy* does for the mythological poems. Sigurd visits his maternal uncle Gripir who tells him the future. The slaying of Fafnir is described in the *Lay of Regin* (*Reginsmál*) and the *Lay of Fafnir* (*Fáfnismál*), and the encounter between Sigurd and the valkyrie Sigurdrifa in the *Lay of Sigurdrifa* (*Sigurdrífumál*). In the middle of that poem a hiatus in the *Codex Regius* begins. It can be inferred from *The Saga of the Volsungs* and other sources that this would have contained a poem describing how Sigurd asked for the hand of Brynhild (Brynhildur Buðladóttir), and Sigurdrifa could be an alias for her. However, Sigurd marries Gudrun Gjukadottir instead and deceives Brynhild into marrying his brother-in-law Gunnar. Brynhild finds out the truth, makes Gunnar and his brothers slay Sigurd, and then kills herself with him. The brothers are then killed by Brynhild's brother, Attila the Hun, whom Gudrun is forced to marry after Sigurd's death.

Thor's fishing trip with Hymir the Giant. Swedish stone carving.
Antiquarian Topographic Archive, Stockholm.

Audience for an Icelandic court poet. Illustration by Steinþór Sigurðsson.

Gudrun then murders Attila and their two sons, and marries king Jonak (Jónakur). In the last episode, Gudrun loses Svanhild, her daughter by Sigurd, when King Jormunrek (Jörmunrekur) has her trampled to death by horses. Gudrun sends her sons by Jonak to take vengeance but they are killed, and at the end of the story she is left on her own, lamenting her life.

In the tale of Sigurd the Dragon-slayer it is gold which gives rise to evil deeds, in the same way as in the *Sibyl's Prophecy*. Loves, broken oaths and revenge become intertwined into the story, but its root can still be traced to greed. This prompts us to consider how the material is arranged in the *Codex*. In the *Sibyl's Prophecy* with which it opens, the story of the gods is told with constant allusions to men, pointing out parallels between the development of the two races. The *Sibyl's Prophecy* therefore presents the division between the world of the gods and world of the men which characterizes the *Codex Regius*. Gold – the origin of which is traced to the world of the gods in the *Lay of Regin* – bridges these two realms and the heroic poems relate the effect that it has in the world of men. Men kill each other to acquire gold without ever enjoying it, and then the conflicts begin to hinge on something different: the gold that started everything lies neglected on the bed of the Rhine while the humans eradicate themselves. Thus the heroic poems may be regarded as an elaboration upon the hint given in the *Sibyl's Prophecy* that man's fate mirrors that of the gods.

At the beginning of the Viking Age the complex art of skaldic poetry came into being. It flourished among the Icelanders, who enjoyed a virtual monopoly as court poets for Scandinavian chieftains. It might be said that poetry was one of Iceland's oldest exports. The skaldic poems are attributed to named authors who composed in metres which are unknown among other Germanic peoples, but have parallels in ancient Irish verse. They were first composed around the time that Nordic people became acquainted with Irish and Scottish culture in the British Isles and an influence from that source cannot be ruled out. Skaldic poems generally describe recent events and most of them are eulogies or elegies to noble chieftains, although many single verses have also been preserved on a variety of subjects ranging from love and nature to slander. Skaldic poetry is mainly known from Icelandic sources although several rune carvings have been found in Bergen with verses in this mode from around 1300.

There are accounts of the oral transmission of skaldic poetry from as far back as the ninth century, and the *Ode to Ragnar* (*Ragnarsdrápa*) by Bragi the Old is considered the earliest work in this genre. Sources mention verses by Norwegian poets from the first half of the tenth century, but most of the skaldic poets who are known by name came from Iceland. They travelled among the courts of Nordic kings and lived by their art; Egil Skallagrimsson (Egill Skallagrímsson) was the best known Icelandic composer of eulogies of kings. One of the most remarkable poets of the tenth century as well as a man of outstanding strength, Egil was the eponymous hero of a saga written in the first half of the thirteenth century. The saga tells that he made four trips from Iceland, including a visit to king Athelstan of England. Sagas were also told at the courts of the kings of Norway, and one source relates how Thorstein the Story-Wise provided entertainment at the court of King Harald the Stern of Norway (around the middle of the eleventh century) by telling stories about Harald's own voyages abroad, which he had learned at the Althing (assembly) in Iceland from Halldor Snorrason. Another tale describes how Sturla Thordarson entertained the court of King Magnus the Lawmaker in Norway in the late thirteenth century by telling *The Saga of Huld* (*Huldar Saga*).

People not only told stories at the Althing; young poets would make themselves known there too. *Egil's Saga*, for example, describes Einar Skalaglamm, who "began to compose poetry when he was young and was eager to learn. One summer Einar went to Egil Skallagrimsson's booth and they began talking and their conversation soon turned to poetry. Both of them enjoyed discussing that topic." They swapped stories, and Einar later gave Egil a shield which he had received as a reward for his poetry from Earl Hakon. The shield "was adorned with ancient stories," and Egil understood this gesture as meaning that he should compose a poem about the shield describing the illustrations on it.

Icelandic historians, especially Snorri Sturluson, considered skaldic poetry to be a reliable historical source and alluded to it widely in their writings. Some of the main characteristics of skaldic verse are its poetic diction, extensive use of kennings and epithets (*heiti*), and the art of breaking up the conventional word order in the service of the form, rhythm, internal rhyme and alliteration. The kennings of skaldic poetry are largely based on the myths, and *Snorra Edda* is written in part as a manual on how to form kennings from the myths and use the metres. After 1300, skaldic poetry went into decline. However, some of the poetic diction lived on in Icelandic devotional verse, ballads and other poetry until the twentieth century.

Snorra Edda is divided into three main parts: the *Deluding of Gylfi* (*Gylfaginning*), which presents a survey of Nordic mythology; *Poetic Diction* (*Skáldskaparmál*), which explains the kennings and *heiti* through their underlying myths; and the *List of Metres* (*Háttatal*), with 100 examples of metres with explanations. A preface describes the creation of the world, and the origin of the ancient religious belief and the gods (Aesir) who came from Asia and were later venerated. Snorri has adapted the framework surrounding all this lore from medieval scholarly writings – for example the *Deluding of Gylfi* is presented in a question–and–answer form like the *Elucidarius*, a handbook on the Christian faith which was translated in the twelfth century. However, the core, the material itself, he learned from poets and storytellers, wise old men and women.

Sources have been preserved from the earliest times about the Icelandic custom of entertaining by telling stories, both recited from memory and read aloud from books. The oldest account of such entertainment is *The Saga of Thorgils and Haflidi* (*Þorgils saga og Hafliða*) in *Sturlunga saga*, in a description of a wedding at Reykjaholar in 1119 where stories were told about Vikings and ancient heroes. At that feast, Hrolf from Skalmarnes told a story which he himself had composed "about Hraunvid the Viking and Olaf, King of the Warriors, Thrain's mound-breaking and Hromund Gripsson, with many verses." Ingimund the Priest also told "The Saga of Orm the Poet of Barra and many verses and a good *flokkr* (ode) at the end of the story" which he composed himself as well.

Manuscripts were read out loud in the Middle Ages, and as book ownership became more common in later centuries this custom continued, even after printing had begun. In his description of Iceland from 1590, Oddur Einarsson says that farmers in Iceland entertained and delighted their guests by reading for them for hours from the sagas. In the eighteenth century it was still the main form of leisure in the evenings to read the old Icelandic Sagas and recite ballads, a custom which continued into the twentieth century. It was more common for women than men to tell stories – adventures, ghost stories, stories of hidden people, or "stories of all things, dead and alive, between heaven and earth," as Ingibjörg Lárusdóttir (1869-1949) described the subjects told by an old woman from the Húnavatn district in the northwest. People also retold printed stories, Icelandic and foreign, and itinerant travellers could find work at farms as storytellers.

The Althing was established at Thingvellir in 930 and met for two weeks a year in mid summer. Lawspeakers were elected at this assembly for a term of three years. They recited the laws in the presence of those attending and also ruled on legal disputes – the laws were only preserved in people's memories.

In the beginning of the twelfth century, writing had not yet become part of the training for being well versed in law. This can be seen from Ari the Wise's account in his *Book of the Icelanders* about the assembly in summer 1118. Lawspeaker Bergthor Hrafnsson had spent the previous winter at Breidabolstad with Haflidi Masson, taking part in recording the section of the law on the treatment of homicides (*Vígslóði*) "and many other things in law" which were "read in the Law Court by clerics the following summer." The laws of the Commonwealth were later named *Grágás* (Grey Goose), and are preserved in several early manuscript fragments and two vellums which were written around the time that the Commonwealth came to an end, in 1262.

From the perspective of cultural history, it is a major step when written books take over from the human mind as the main repository for public knowledge. In Iceland this was a lengthy process and even after writing had been introduced it took a long time to reach the stage where people began to regard a text as better preserved in book form than in the human mind. Around 1300, for example, oral tradition was still trusted as much as written books, as shown by Hauk the Lawspeaker's *Book of Settlements* (*Landnámabók*) – when he put together his version of this work, he added a great deal of material that he could not have obtained except from orally preserved sources. But was this step taken without a struggle?

After the adoption of Christianity, people began making books and afterwards were able to use writing in areas where oral preservation had previously been the norm. The Church's authority was based on trust in the written word and written culture extended at first only to religious life. General education and secular affairs remained unaffected by the technical innovations of book culture. Children and young people continued to acquire knowledge and absorb the community's ethical values from oral stories and poems about earlier times, and Lawspeakers continued to preserve the laws in the traditional fashion,

Egil Skallagrimsson. AM 426 fol. Árni Magnússon Institute in Iceland.

by reciting them at the Althing and ruling on legal disputes without referring to books. Men who were versed in law needed to keep their knowledge afresh, which was not possible except by training a new generation of people who were skilled at law and by passing on that knowledge by the only method available: reciting it. Formal confirmation of an act of law can only be made "in the presence of an audience" when the authority of books cannot be cited.

We must assume that the office of the Lawspeaker was considered a position of authority and respect. But unlike the Church, the Lawspeakers did not derive their authority from books, but rather from the knowledge that they had acquired from other learned people. And it must not be forgotten that knowledge of the law was necessary to all chieftains in order for them to be able to bring legal action. Nor can the importance of oratory ever be overestimated in a society which is not based on writing and which, out of political and social necessity, uses stories and poems as a repository of knowledge. Under such conditions, authority and influence invariably go hand in hand with language skills. We can take as an example the Sturlung family in the thirteenth century, which included both Lawspeakers and prominent writers of secular sagas and poetry such as Snorri Sturluson in Reykholt. They displayed a remarkable combination of knowledge of the conventional oral lore of society (law, poetry, genealogy and sagas) and writing skills.

So we can try to imagine how the Lawspeaker Bergthor felt when he stood at Thingvellir in the summer of 1118 and could not read the text which he had taken part in having written down the previous winter. To do that, clerics were needed. Would he have been much impressed by this technological innovation, and would it perhaps have crossed his mind on that summer day at Thingvellir that all his oral knowledge would eventually become superfluous – and he himself with it? We may ask: what was the role of the Lawspeaker when he had committed his knowledge to books, thereby affording clerics easy access to it; clerics who now *read* out the *written* laws? There is no reason to assume that Bergthor ever learned to read, and there is no evidence that any book of law accompanied the office of Lawspeaker later. *Grágás* even contains a provision that when law books contradict each other, the incumbent of Skalholt, i.e. the bishop, shall rule upon the matter. Previously this power was vested in the Lawspeaker, judging from the section in *Grágás* about them:

> "It is also prescribed that the Lawspeaker shall recite all the sections so extensively that no one knows them much more extensively. And if his knowledge does not stretch so far, then before reciting each section he is to arrange a meeting in the preceding twenty-four hours with five or more legal experts,

those from whom he can learn most, and any man who intrudes on their talk without permission is fined three marks, and that case lies with the Lawspeaker." (188)

(Laws of Early Iceland, University of Manitoba Press, 1980
Transl. Andrew Dennis, Peter Foote, Richard Perkins)

Had this provision been in effect before the Age of Writing, we can see how much authority it would have conferred upon a group of men who were versed in law, since it was not possible to look up doubtful matters in a book; they themselves could rule upon queries as to what was the law and what was not.

The writing down of the law in Breidabolstad in the winter of 1117-18 was therefore the first step taken by men of the Church towards encroaching upon this area of the Lawspeakers' secular authority, an area where the Church would make its presence firmly felt later.

It is not known that Lawspeakers had any serious difficulties in preserving the laws in their memories before the Age of Writing. People would not have missed what they did not know: the possibility of writing down an article of law in order to remember it or of sending an order written on calfskin. People could not learn whole books of law when there were no books, nor were they eager to divest themselves of the burden of their memories and write down the laws – as people today are tempted to think. There is much more reason to assume that Lawspeakers were not impressed by the laws being read from vellum. Such men were proud of their knowledge and regarded oral skills and legal knowledge as a necessary part of the education of aspiring men of law.

The laws themselves and all legal functions were completely transformed after Iceland swore allegiance to King Hakon the Old of Norway in 1262-64. His son Magnus, nicknamed the Lawmaker, set new laws for the Icelanders with *Jónsbók*, which is preserved in hundreds of manuscripts. It is clear that these were owned by men of secular authority and legal experts who often made great efforts over their production, having them lavishly illustrated and allocating ample space for the text on the pages. With *Jónsbók* and the bureaucracy that was ushered in by royal power, the culture of writing can be said to have established itself for once and for all in secular administration in Iceland – some three centuries after it first came into the society along with a new religion.

hlutt skulu kuztu men ap
hapa iduligha gad þyr oll
her hauir snut er ver hau

The Church and written culture

SVANHILDUR ÓSKARSDÓTTIR

Christianity is based on events attested to in the Scriptures, which reveal God at work in the world. From the outset, therefore, Christianity was in a certain sense already a literary faith and people regarded the Scriptures as the word of God. The importance of the Scriptures in Christian belief is very evident in the structure of the mass, a large part of which is devoted to serving the word by reading texts from the Bible and expanding upon them. In Christianity the book takes pride of place, the Bible is the book of books, and all books partake in its glory.

Because faith is built upon the word in this way, it is important that the text of the Scriptures does not become corrupted, and also that it is correctly understood. It falls to the priest to interpret the word for the congregation and from early on the Church emphasised the basic education of the priesthood as well as attempting to ensure that a reliable text of the Bible was always available. With regard to the latter, a major step was taken when Jerome (c. 331–419/420) produced a standard version of the Bible in Latin. Known as the Vulgate, this was the biblical text used in the Middle Ages, even though many variations of the text evolved through widespread distribution and copying.

The medieval educational system was a legacy from the ancient Greeks and Romans, and involved schooling in the seven liberal arts (*septem artes liberales*). These were divided into the *trivium*, comprising grammar, rhetoric and dialectic, and the *quadrivium*, consisting of arithmetic, geometry, astronomy and music. All the branches of the *trivium* concerned the arts of language, and that language was Latin, the tongue of the Roman Empire and Catholic Church, which remained the *lingua franca* of educated Europeans until the eighteenth century and even beyond. People who received an education learned to read and understand Latin and express themselves in it according to the rules of classical rhetoric.

Education of priests varied widely in early times, but became more

Left: Secular chieftains took advantage of writing. *Svalbarðsbók*, AM 343 fol. Árni Magnússon Institute in Iceland.

standardized during the reign of Charlemagne, partly through the work of Alcuin of York, a scholar who counselled the emperor on educational matters. The kingdom of the Franks expanded under Charlemagne's rule and on his death in 814 it embraced the greater part of western Europe. The basic education of the priesthood was essential if Christianity was to be maintained in the kingdom. The Carolingian educational system was based on the existing framework of monastic schools, while other schools began to develop at the cathedrals. Novices were given instruction in reading, writing, music and the elements of grammar and chronology. Many novices received no more schooling than this, but those who did then studied the seven liberal arts. This educational system remained in effect throughout western Europe more or less until the end of the Middle Ages. The curriculum was also standardized in various respects and certain books were used universally, some of them schoolbooks from Roman times (for example Donatus's grammar, written in the fourth century). The chief aim of study was, of course, to prepare students to read and interpret the Bible, so the Scriptures formed an important part of the curriculum. It was common to begin with the Psalms, which served as a kind of reading primer. But Latin was also studied through secular literature, for example the poems of Horace, Virgil and Ovid and the historical works of Sallust and Lucan, because the classical authors were considered good models for language and style. Despite the emphasis given to the study of the classics, much of the ancient scholarship was only available to students in anthologized form, particularly in encyclopaedias which incorporated the learning of the ancients into a Christian world view. Among the most widely read encyclopaedias was the *Etymologiae* of Bishop Isidor of Seville (c. 560–636), which contained brief accounts on all manner of topics, conveniently arranged according to the seven liberal arts.

Charlemagne's reforms and harmonization of writing made a crucial contribution to the success of his educational policy. The script was simplified, making it easier for students to acquire a command of reading and writing. The script found in the earliest Icelandic manuscripts is a Carolingian variant, derived from the style which evolved as an offshoot of the ambitious pedagogical policies of Alcuin and his collaborators at the Emperor's court.

Iceland became part of the Roman Catholic Church when it adopted Christianity, and was thereby linked to the educational system which had evolved within its institutions, both cloisters and cathedrals. The literary culture of the Church gave Icelanders access to a heritage the roots of which stretched back to classical times, and at the same time opened new ways for them to present their own knowledge and verbal artistry. The Latin alphabet, scribal techniques and book pro-

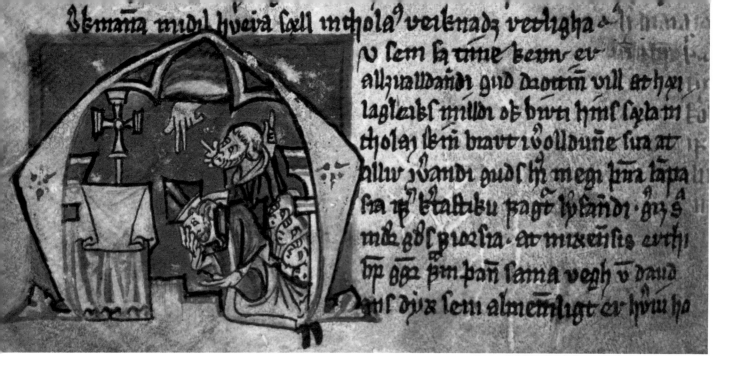

The finger of God. *Helgastaðabók*, Perg. 4to no. 16. Royal Library, Stockholm.

duction revolutionized Icelandic cultural history on a scale that was unparalleled until the advent of modern media almost a thousand years later.

Revolutionary as the introduction of the Latin alphabet may have been, the Icelanders were in fact already acquainted with writing. The oldest records of the Norse language are found in runic inscriptions in many parts of Scandinavia and in Britain, some of which can be traced back to the fourth century. These runes are found either on gravestones and other memorials, or on utensils and ornaments, most often denoting their owner or craftsman. One could be forgiven for assuming that the carving of runes was discontinued shortly after Scandinavians had learned to use the Latin alphabet, but archaeological discoveries in recent decades have demonstrated that both alphabets survived side by side for a very long period, from the eleventh century until c. 1400. Runic inscriptions from this period, including many discovered in excavations in the harbour area in Bergen, Norway, give the impression of being momentary messages and not conceived of as permanent documentation. Generally carved in wood, on tablets, sticks or pins, runes convey diverse messages ranging from confessions of love to orders for goods. They were apparently used as an everyday form of writing, since it was easier to carve a few letters with a knife than to procure vellum, ink and a pen. On the other hand, because it is difficult to commit a long text to rock or wood, most runic inscriptions are limited to just a few words. Very few runic inscriptions have been preserved in Iceland. The oldest is inscribed on the Valþjófsstaðir door from c. 1200. Some of the inscriptions found in Norway have, however, been traced to Icelanders. The oldest of these are dated to the twelfth century, which makes them contemporaneous with the earliest manuscript fragments that have been preserved in the Latin alphabet. Even though nothing would have precluded the writing of runes on vellum using a quill, there is no evidence that this was practised. Use of the runic alphabet remained confined to specific areas of private life, and short texts. The written culture ushered in by Christianity, on the other hand, expanded far beyond the ecclesiastical needs on which book culture originally established itself.

So how did books gain a foothold in Iceland? Records of educational activity during the first decades after the adoption of Christianity are scanty. It is known that itinerant bishops from Britain and Saxony visited Iceland. The Icelandic Church was initially under the authority of the Archbishop of Bremen, and at least some of the missionary bishops who worked in Iceland were sent under his mandate. They were responsible for religious services, teaching and running the churches in the newly Christianized country, but powerful families in Iceland were apparently quick to send boys from their own ranks to be educated abroad in order to gain preferment within the church. Gissur the White, one of the chieftains who was instrumental in the adoption of the new faith, sent his son Ísleifur (1006-1081) to study in the nunnery of Herford, Saxony, south of Bremen. Children of the Saxon nobility received their schooling in the nunnery – education was the privilege of the wealthy there just as it was in Iceland. Ísleifur studied for the priesthood, returned to Iceland and settled in Skálholt, becoming bishop in 1056. His son Gissur followed in his footsteps and studied in Saxony, in all likelihood at Herford too, while Sæmundur Sigfússon the Wise (1056-1133) is said to have gone to France: a name that may refer to another area than it does today, an area that could have extended as far as the Rhine. These men were all from chieftain families in the south of Iceland: Gissur and Ísleifur from the people of Haukadalur and Sæmundur from Oddi. It seems most likely that organized schooling in Iceland began under the auspices of these families, and that the education they provided was modelled upon that received by Ísleifur, Gissur and Sæmundur in their schools abroad. In his *Book of the Icelanders*, Ari the Wise says that on Ísleifur's return, the chieftains sent their sons to him to study. Ari himself was fostered by Hallur Þórarinsson in Haukadalur, where he probably received tuition from Teitur the Priest, Bishop Ísleifur's son.

One of the boys taught by Ísleifur in Skálholt was Jón Ögmundarson (1052-1121). He became the first Bishop of Hólar in north Iceland, ordained in 1106 by Archbishop Özur of Lund, where an archbishopric for all of Scandinavia had been established two years earlier. Jón set up a school at Hólar, undoubtedly modelled in part on Ísleifur's, and brought in a teacher from Gotland, Gísli Finnason, to run it. In *Jón's Saga*, the bishop is said to have provided Gísli with ample funds

> ... both to teach the novices and further the holy Christian faith ... as he was able in his teachings and sermons. And whenever he preached to the people he had a book in front of him and took from it what he talked about to them, doing so with most circumspection and humility; since he was young in years, those who heard him thought it was noteworthy that they could see him taking his teachings from sacred books and not from his own intuition alone."
>
> (The Sagas of the Bishops (*Byskupa sögur* I, pp. 163-4))

This is a lucid illustration of the view that reliable interpretation of the word of God is to be had from books. The book was regarded as the backbone of teaching and of teachings; without books it was impossible either to provide schooling or sing mass. Scholars who went abroad from Iceland to study doubtless brought back books with them, and it is conceivable that Latin books continued to be imported on some scale even when domestic book production gradually gained momentum. We have no records about bookmaking for much of the initial period, although we can presume that the emphasis would have been on use in schools and holy mass. While very few Catholic missals have been preserved in Iceland, church inventories give some idea of the books which once adorned their pulpits. Not only did the clergy need a text of the Bible and other books to read from during the service; they also needed breviaria with instructions on the liturgy and antiphonals for the parts of the mass which were sung. All these books were in Latin and occasional references to Latin as *bókmál* ("book language") show the close association in people's minds between language and medium.

However, Icelanders seem to have been quick to use their own language in writings. The work known as the *First Grammatical Treatise* (*Fyrsta málfræðiritgerðin*), thought to be written around the middle of the twelfth century, states that writing in the vernacular, laws and genealogies and sacred works, had already been practised for some time, and the First Grammarian also mentions "the wise lore that Ari Thorgeirsson has compiled with his reasoned mind." To this list may be added computational and astronomical works found in one of the oldest extant Icelandic manuscripts, GKS 1812 4to. These references give some impression of the kind of information people saw fit to commit to writing once they had mastered the technique. Laws, genealogies and Ari the Wise's history represent domestic learning. Computus, astronomy and sacred texts, on the other hand, are connected with ecclesiastic activities. Chronology was an important element in the education of priests, who needed to be able to calculate the date of Easter and other "moveable feasts." Arithmetic and astrono-

The Icelandic Homily Book. Written c. 1200. Perg. 4to no 15. Royal Library, Stockholm.

my, two of the *quadrivium* of the liberal arts, were therefore a necessary discipline for ordinands, and computus was an essential part of all manuals for priests. The *Grammatical Treatise* itself bears witness to original scholarship in the vernacular, the direct product of acquaintance with Latin and efforts to use the new medium of writing for extensive documentation of domestic material. The author's aim is to adapt the Latin alphabet to Icelandic phonology, whereby each sound is represented by a different letter: a harmonized orthography makes reading and writing simpler.

We have no evidence that the directions given by the First Grammarian were followed "to the letter," but his proposals do appear to have played some part in determining the spellings used by Icelandic scribes. At seats of learning where groups practised reading and writing consistent scribal customs gradually developed. In addition to the educational seats in south Iceland and cathedral schools at Skálholt and Hólar, the establishment of monasteries saw more centres of bookmaking emerge. The monastery at Þingeyrar in northwest Iceland was the first to be established in the country, in 1133. In one sense the monastery was an offshoot of the school at Hólar, because Bishop Jón Ögmundarson prepared the way for its establishment and some of its monks were educated at Hólar. This was a Benedictine cloister, and three others from that order would later be established in Iceland: a monastery at Munkaþverá in Eyjafjörður (1155) and convents at Kirkjubær á Síðu (1186) and Reynistaður in Skagafjörður (1295). Some sources indicate an initial relationship between the Þingeyrar monastery and others in England, but a clearer example of an association between Icelandic and foreign centres of learning is given by the life of Þorlákur Þórhallsson, prior of the first Augustinian house in Iceland and later bishop. Born in 1133, the year that the Þingeyrar monastery was established, Þorlákur received his first schooling at Oddi from Eyjólfur, the son of Sæmundur the Wise. He then spent six years studying abroad, first in Paris and then in Lincoln, England. In 1168 he took charge of a new cloister at Þykkvibær which was established under the Augustinian order. This order was intended for canons and was an influential force in intellectual life in France and England; presumably Þorlákur came into contact with it during his student years. When the archepiscopal see of Niðarós, Norway was established in 1153, Iceland became part of its jurisdiction. The Augustinian order exerted significant influence within that sphere, since two of the first archbishops had connections with the religious community of Saint Victor in Paris, one of the main Augustinian centres of learning in northern Europe. Four years after the establishment of the Þykkvibær community, an Augustinian house was set up on the island of Flatey in Breiðafjörður, then transferred to Helgafell in Snæfellsnes 1184. In the course of time three more houses of this order were established: on Viðey island (1226), at Möðruvellir in Hörgárdalur (1296) and at Skriða in Fljótsdalur (1493).

Monastic life revolved around prayer and offices, and these depended on books. With time many monasteries acquired quite impressive libraries. An inventory of books from Möðruvellir, compiled in 1461, includes missals and an assortment of other liturgical works such as graduals, antiphonals and books of sequences, lectionaries containing epistles and gospels, psalters, processionals, records of feast days, etc. – around seventy books in all, counting only the part of the library which was used for services. It is likely that missals were copied from early times in monasteries to meet the need for books, while demand for them must also have grown as the number of churches in Iceland increased. Furthermore, the monasteries had to own some schoolbooks for teaching the children they sometimes took in. The Benedictine order also stipulated a reading from saints' lives or other acceptable works at mealtimes, for the edification of the sisters or brethren of the community. Many such books are listed in the Möðruvellir inventory, both in Latin and Icelandic. Saints' lives are among the oldest works preserved in Icelandic and it can be assumed they were some of the first to have been translated from Latin. We can also mention sermons, fragments of which are found on two leaves of vellum from the mid-twelfth century, thought to be the oldest preserved writings in Icelandic. The sermons reveal how Icelanders interpreted the word of God in the vernacular. Although in church the readings from Scriptures were in Latin, parts of the Bible were soon translated for other uses. The oldest extant Bible translations into Icelandic have been dated to the thirteenth century, but the manu-

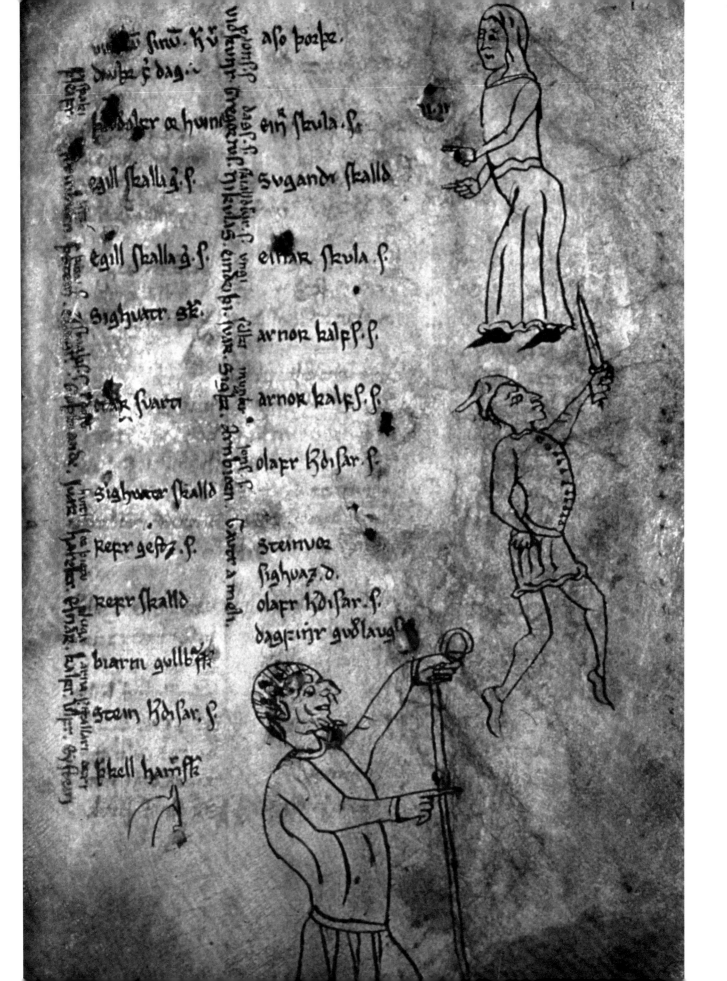

... sinū. k̄ v̄

dauða ī dag. ꞏ꞉ꞏ

hœðaler œ humē

egill skalla g̅. s.

egill skalla g̅. s.

sighuatr sk.

... suarti

sighuater skalld

refr gestz. s.

refr skalld

biarni gullbꝛ...

stein ... kolsar. s.

skell harmski

also þorke.

ein skula s.

sugandi skalld

einar skula s.

arnor kalps. s.

arnor kalfs. s.

olafr kolsar. s.

steinuor
sighuaz. d.
olafr kolsar. s.
dagfinr guðlaugꝛ

scripts containing them are somewhat younger, most of them from the fourteenth century. Among them is one of the greatest achievements of Icelandic bookmaking in the Middle Ages, *Stjórn* (AM 227 fol.), containing passages from the Old Testament with a commentary.

Monks and nuns did not confine themselves to copying missals and translating biblical texts, however. The cloisters engaged in the writing and dissemination of vernacular literature from early on, as may be seen from the writings of three monks from Þingeyrar monastery, Oddur Snorrason, Gunnlaugur Leifsson and Abbot Karl Jónsson, around 1200. Both Oddur and Gunnlaugur wrote a *Saga of King Olaf Tryggvason* of Norway, while Gunnlaugur also wrote a Latin life of Bishop Jón Ögmundarson and translated *Merlin's Prophecy* from Geoffrey of Monmouth's *Historia Regum Britanniae*. Abbot Karl is credited with writing *The Saga of King Sverrir Sigurdarson* of Norway, and one of the first contemporary sagas of Icelandic events, *The Saga of Gudmund Dyri* (*Guðmundar saga dýra*), is thought to have been written in the vicinity of Þingeyrar or even in the monastery itself. As time went by the cloisters became literary institutions which produced books on a fairly wide variety of subjects, although their literary activity must always have revolved around the essence of monastic life: the word of God which was the beginning and the end of all things, *alpha et omega*.

myskun a giora vtan giptingar m̄ uilie þira ha iafnræde þa ma hun
giptaz mz añara skynsama frænda sina rade ef þm lizt iafnræde
edr betur og megu þ þ mz eide sinu sana og a þo ad leim þılla ad v
giptingar mañ. En gipting m̄ e þad e brod sameddr þar nest
mod skilgeingũ ef hun er til þa er barlñ ruhigr edr elldre sa sem
næstur er erfdum eft þa konu er giptizt. En sa sem slikt dugizt gia
llde fullrette giptingar m̄ eft xij mana dome edr þe vtlegr af þm
fiordunge nema andrũ frændũ vndizt iafnræde vera. Eckia ma gip
ta sig sialf huñ o hin uill mz nordurb frænda rade. En konur þer
sem hazt til þs ad locka til slikt edr añars samlifis born m̄ e frænd
konur og uðr þ uitnisfast þa bæte eft xij m̄ dome penningu su o þe
tiek̄ til en hm hafe refsing epter dome.

þ dætur verda fraudr sins arfar modr edr brodr edr huskis arf
þær verda sumar giptar en sumar ogipt þa su þær o ogiptar
eru taka suo mikid fie af oskiptũ arfe o þær hofdu er henñar
voru gipt. En þo allar sie henñgipt og er e skipt henñanfylgiu r iaf
nað fra z millũ þa taki þær af oskiptũ arfe iafnmikit fie sem su er
mest hafde henñar er mz fie vmzt til. En ef fie edr arfr vinzt e
legge aptr til iafnad nema e uære meira henñangiefid en slikr fice
me þa o hurar hlut. Grip þr allir o hedn e til henñanfylgiu og
eru metin og mynd z hendr hm o konu þer og a hin þa iafnheimila
o þad edr mod hete henñanfylgia. En ef hm seig ad hn liede e til þs
fra gripa þa suie hn eins eide barl m̄ o kona og sæke til iafnmils gipt
ingar mañ konuñar og skerdi þ til gioz hã eft neme til raulu. Engin
mær sl haya forræde fiar sins fyr en hun e xx vetra gomul þo ad vnd
ha hafe bornd nema hun sie gipt mz frænda rade og a sa er hã þar þær
bæde forræde þ fie og penningu hã. Hu o gipting m̄ er rettr ad konu

Society and literature

VÉSTEINN ÓLASON

The settlers arrived in Iceland full of knowledge about the world they had left behind and its past, and they also had firm ideas about the correct and practical way to live in this world. On the basis of these ideas they forged a society in their new country. It was not exactly the same as the one they knew before, because conditions were different, but many of its fundamental elements were the same, and these appeared in the laws. The dispersed population and the obstacle of crossing the Atlantic removed the need to organize defences against invasion by enemy armies, nor were military leaders necessary. For this reason, the settlers felt no need to have a king, and in any case no one laid claim to the realm. However, they needed methods for solving the disputes which inevitably arise when interests clash in the routine business of life. Laws and courts were necessary to resolve these disputes.

Iceland's new settlers had inherited the religion of their forebears, and although our knowledge is limited, it can be seen from laws and accounts of times past that the legal system is rooted in what may be called the sacred realm of life, linked to higher forces. Religion revolves around an awareness of such powers and an attempt to ensure their protection. The life of the individual was sacred, sacredness (*helgi*) encompassed people's households and was the rule for the duration of assemblies. This is shown by terms such as *mannhelgi* (the inviolability of the individual), *örskotshelgi* (immunity as far as an arrow shot from one's household) and *þinghelgi* (immunity during the assembly). Religious rites themselves, the feasts or sacrifices, were naturally sacred too, and the same men, the godis (*goðar*) were in charge of both the communal feasts and assemblies. The function of the godi was a hereditary office and the division of Iceland into quarters was in some way connected with the sanctity of this office. The godis performed a key role at the assemblies and in the judicial system, since one of their functions was to nominate men to sit on judgement panels and on the Law Council at the annual general assembly (*Althing*) at Þingvellir, where new laws were passed or older ones interpreted. By law, a farmer had to support a particular godi at the assembly and share in the cost of holding it. Farmers were effectively the backbone of society, as a landowning class with clearly defined rights. The godis were farmers, but by virtue of their leadership they had more authority and responsibility than others. Women and labourers were free by law but

Left: Riding to a wedding, from the *Reykjabók* manuscript of *Jónsbók*, AM 345 fol. Sixteenth century. Árni Magnússon Institute in Iceland.

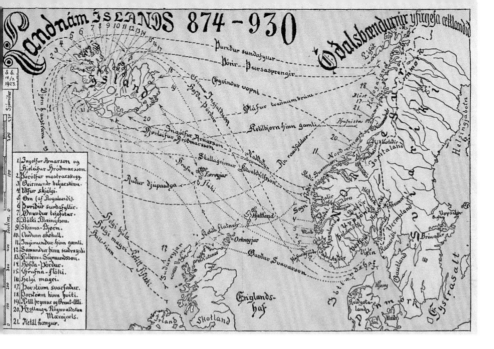

Postcard by Samúel Eggertsson showing the settlement of Iceland, 874–930.

enjoyed few rights, since these were vested with the farmer and his godi. Slaves were not free, but owned by farmers.

Although the sacred right of all freeborn men was defined by law and by rulings passed on it in courts which enjoyed the immunity of assembly, it was the responsibility of each individual to ensure or defend his rights. A man's right was at the same time his honour and that of his family, and it was dishonourable or shameful not to be able to defend either. There was no official punitive or executive power to appeal to. This served to strengthen solidarity among members of a family and secured the bonds with the godis, who were obliged to safeguard the rights of their *thingmen* or supporters. It was vital for the godis and society as a whole to maintain a certain balance of power, but this was highly prone to disruption, and conflicts were both commonplace and inevitable. When the balance was upset it could take a long time to restore, not least because of the strong duty to avenge misdeeds against kinsmen, and the fact that parties to disputes rarely agreed upon how to assess misdeeds and vengeance for them. From this developed protracted disputes and cycles of revenge and counter-revenge, which became the narrative material for sagas. Such forces of discord were counter-balanced by the judicial system, and by the everyday needs of people to earn their livings in peace. Many of the main secular works of medieval Icelandic literature appear to have been specifically intended to assert the importance of social order.

The Church ushered in a completely new social force and new jurisdiction over spiritual affairs. Secular and religious matters interacted in many ways in pagan times, so it came as no surprise that the Church gradually became a decisive secular force as its property and influence grew. Its power was fairly weak at first, but grew when native Icelanders acquired the education they needed to establish their leadership of it. The turning point was reached when Ísleifur Gissurarson, from the Haukadalur family, was ordained bishop in 1056. He donated his land, Skálaholt (now Skálholt), to the Church and it served as an episcopal seat for almost 750 years. After the bishopric was established, the Church gradually consolidated its position.

During the first centuries of Christianity in Iceland the most influential clerics inevitably came from the ranks of the chieftains. No other class had the means to have people educated abroad, and the recipients of such education automatically became influential figures within the Church. The first whose names we know, Ísleifur Gissurarson and his son Gissur Ísleifsson, both bishops of Skálholt, were from a wealthy noble family, the people of Haukadalur. Páll Jónsson from the Oddi family, who was Bishop of Skálholt from 1195-1211, had also studied abroad. There were instances of learned clerics who enjoyed the patronage of chieftains, generally their relatives, even if they were not from wealthy families themselves. Such a man was Þorlákur Þórhallsson the Holy, a beneficiary of the Oddi people, educated in Paris and Lincoln, who was Bishop of Skálholt from 1178-1193. Secular and spiritual leaders were thus linked by close bonds and it is not surprising that the former soon saw reason to have something more than Christian knowledge committed to vellum. In a well known account in his *Book of the Icelanders*, Ari the Wise describes how the laws were written down at Breiðabólstaður in Vesturhóp in the winter of 1117-1118. The *Book of the Icelanders* itself is another example of the need that was felt early on to record secular material, in this case, historical lore. Such documentation began no later than 1120-1130. There is much to suggest that the first version of the work later known as the *Book of Settlements* was produced in the beginning of the twelfth century, perhaps even pre-dating the *Book of the Icelanders*. Gradually this secular aspect of literature expanded as books became a stronger cultural force in Iceland. Literacy spread within the chieftain class as its members came to realize the power of the written word.

It is important not to forget that secular literature was an offshoot of the ecclesiastical book culture, but drew its nourishment and subject matter from lore which had been kept alive by oral tradition. In the creation of secular literature two worlds meet, just as two languages had met in the translations organized by the Church, and from them a new world emerged which preserved the old and created new lore, regenerating the forms of popular narrative art and transforming its character.

Why did people begin committing laws and history to writing? There had to be abundant justification for such a radical and at the same time expensive innovation. Foreign models probably played some part. Men of the Church were familiar not only with religious writings but also historical works in Latin, including accounts of the ori-

Genealogy from Ari the Wise's *Book of the Icelanders* (*Íslendingabók*),
AM 113a fol.

gin of nations and probably also ecclesiastical law and related material. The Old Testament abounded in stories of kings and heroes, battles and legal wrangling, and recounted the history of the Jews from the very beginning. People would have sensed in such accounts an affinity with various aspects of their own history. The Church emphasised the word. The word was of course transmitted orally to the public, while what the priests preached was founded on the Scriptures, to which reference was made in cases of disputed interpretation. The idea that it would be useful to have a written book of law to rely upon and cite in disputes would have been obvious to powerful men who enjoyed a close relationship with the Church. Of course, other chieftains may not have been much impressed by this innovation, due to both conflicts of interest and conservatism. However, very few of them probably realized the immensity of the revolution that had begun.

It is not unlikely that the association between the pre-Christian religious and worldly functions of the godis was instrumental in the swiftness with which the Icelandic chieftain class took the book into its service. The account in the *Book of the Icelanders* about the adoption of Christianity and the ruling delivered on the new faith by Þorgeir, the godi of the people of Ljósavatn, bears all the marks of an act of arbitration and compromise. Nonetheless, from a modern point of view, the pagans apparently received quite a raw deal in purely religious terms. They were allowed to worship the heathen gods in private, eat horsemeat and expose infants. On the other hand, there is no mention of the fact, although this is implied in the *Book of the Icelanders* and other sources, that the heathen godis retained their secular functions, power and influence, and as it happened they were also assigned some religious role as the owners and custodians of churches. Undoubtedly this was the crucial factor in the compromise struck when Christianity was adopted. The godis' links with the Church later provided them with a good source of income after the introduction of the tithe which largely accrued to those who were in charge of churches. Thus the strengthening of the Church at the same time strengthened the chieftains' authority, and it was an obvious step for them to adopt the same instruments that the Church used: writing and the producing of vellum manuscripts.

In later centuries the name *Grágás* referred to the laws of the Icelandic Commonwealth, but in the Middle Ages it was the name of a Norwegian law-book. The legal code that was written down at Breiðabólstaður in 1117-18 at Hafliði Másson's farm has been called *Hafliðaskrá*, but this book is no longer extant, nor is any other Icelandic lawbook from such an early time. A fragment of the laws of the Commonwealth from around or before 1200 has been preserved, but our main records of these laws are two large codices from the third quarter of the thirteenth century. It is clear from an examination of these two that not all collections of law were identical, that they were augmented and gradually altered from the first writing down to the end of the Commonwealth, when the two codices, *Codex Regius* (GKS 1157 fol.) and *Staðarhólsbók* (AM 334 fol.), were produced. These books should be regarded as private compilations of law rather than official law codes. It is interesting to note that they were written around the time that the Commonwealth was collapsing. It is conceivable that both books were intended to have a role in dealings with the Norwegian crown: the *Codex Regius* as an attempt to consolidate the position of the ancient law and written before 1260, while *Staðarhólsbók*, which does not contain the section relating most closely to the system of government itself, was written around 1270 after Iceland became subject to the king of Norway, with the intended function of ensuring that as much of the Icelandic legal tradition as possible would be taken into account while the king was having new laws drawn up in the books known as *Járnsíða* (in effect 1271-1281) and *Jónsbók*. *Járnsíða* is preserved in *Staðarhólsbók*, appended to the laws of the Commonwealth but written in another hand and probably somewhat later. *Jónsbók* took effect in 1281 and was the law in Iceland for centuries; a number of articles from it are still in effect today and occasionally referred to in court cases. There are numerous manuscripts of *Jónsbók* and some of them rank with the most beautiful Icelandic manuscripts, especially *Skarðsbók* (AM 350 fol.), named after the farm Skarð on Skarðsströnd, in the west of Iceland, and written around 1363.

The *Book of the Icelanders* is only preserved in late paper manuscripts. Two copies which the Reverend Jón Erlendsson from Villingaholt (d. 1672) made around 1650 at the request of Bishop Brynjólfur Sveinsson (AM 113 a and b fol.) are of importance in establishing the text. These are carefully made copies, and judging from their spelling and scribal forms, the original would have been written around or even before 1200. As its preface shows, there were two versions of the *Book of the Icelanders*. At some time during the period 1122-33 Ari Þorgilsson (1067-1148) composed a book the original version of which is lost, while the one preserved has been altered somewhat, especially by shortening, and was presumably not finished until after 1133. Ari's preface shows that the book was written at the instigation of the bishops of Iceland and in consultation with Sæmundur Sigfússon the Wise from Oddi (1056-1133), a widely travelled man of learning and a leading cleric. The *Book of the Icelanders* describes the settlement of Iceland and the four main families of settlers, the establishment of assemblies and law, the chronology of important events and the calendar, and the discovery of Greenland and Vinland. There is also a detailed account of the adoption of

Christianity, followed by the history of Iceland, especially of the Church and the first bishops of Skálholt until just before 1120. Ari's account is concise and enumerative, apart from his description of the introduction of Christianity. It is not likely that he had any native model for vernacular narrative, so it is not surprising that some influence from Latin writings can be discerned. Since the work was compiled in Icelandic it was undoubtedly intended for a lay audience, and might possibly have been read out at the Law Rock during the Althing. One important feature is the detail in which Ari explains the provenance of his book, both in the preface, which describes its background and editing, and in the main text where he cites a large number of oral authorities for individual topics, such as Christianization and the Lawspeakers. The list of Lawspeakers forms his main chronological reference point, together with the foreign events he cites, namely the death of Saint Edmund, King of England, in 870 and the death of King Olaf Tryggvason of Norway in 1000. Ari clearly used some foreign works of reference, especially annals.

The *Book of the Icelanders* shows all the signs of having been written to define and establish the position and rights of the dominant class and institutions in Iceland. Its account of the settlement confirms entitlement to the land that had been claimed, and the leadership of certain families. Descriptions of the composition of courts and assemblies confirm the legitimacy and sanctity of these institutions, and last but not least the account of the adoption of Christianity and the first bishops confirms the importance and rights of the Church and episcopacy. The book is not written from a narrow ecclesiastical perspective, however; it also displays a deep-rooted interest in the origin and evolution of the secular society.

The *Book of Settlements* confirms the entitlement of landowners to their land, describing settlements throughout Iceland, large and small alike. Mainly dealing with settlements and genealogies, it is of course much more detailed on these points than the *Book of the Icelanders*. The preserved versions mention around 430 settlers (male and female), while numerous other persons are named in the narrative passages and genealogies, as well as place names. Some kind of association or accord among secular leaders must surely underlie the composition of this work. However, the *Book of Settlements* does not appear to have institutional connections in the way that the *Book of the Icelanders* clearly does, although a conception of the land and people as a single entity underlies both.

Details about the families that formed the backbone of secular society are a prominent feature of the *Book of Settlements*, and information about people and genealogy appears in the oldest sources describing what the Icelanders were writing as early as the twelfth century.

What we have of the *Book of Settlements*, however, derives entirely from versions composed in the thirteenth and fourteenth centuries, greatly augmented in terms of subject matter and even differently structured and conceptualized from the work about the settlement which was written at the beginning of the twelfth century. Consequently the transmission of the *Book of Settlements* is not as easy to trace as that of the *Book of the Icelanders*. The most complete of all the medieval versions is *Sturlubók*, named after the Lawspeaker and historian Sturla Þórðarson (1214-1284), although it is preserved only in copies from later times, the best and fullest being AM 107 fol., written by the Reverend Jón Erlendsson from Villingaholt. Another version is found in *Hauksbók* (AM 371 4to), which was compiled during the first years of the fourteenth century by Haukur Erlendsson (d. 1334). Born into the Icelandic chieftain class, Haukur was a legal officer first in Iceland and later in Norway. Part of his version of the *Book of Settlements* is preserved in its original form and part in copies, while other parts are lost. Haukur's main source was *Sturlubók*, although like Sturla he also drew upon the version, now lost, written by Styrmir Kárason the Wise (d. 1245), as well as other sources. Two calfskin pages have been preserved with the text of *Melabók*, which is named after Melar in Melasveit, in the west of Iceland, and was probably composed around 1300, but these are of later date, from the early fifteenth century. Somewhat more of the *Melabók* text is preserved in a paper manuscript from the seventeenth century. All these versions are very much altered and augmented from the earlier ones. *Melabók* would have been closest to the original version, but the extant text is not a good one. The history of the transmission of *The Book of Settlements* testifies to the interest that its contents aroused; older versions were lost through repeated use and because they were not considered as interesting as the much longer, later ones, partly because these were augmented with material from written sagas and oral tales. In effect the evolution of the versions of *The Book of Settlements* provides an excellent example of how thirteenth- and fourteenth-century authors recorded and reworked historical information and incorporated it into increasingly larger wholes.

Icelandic society underwent major changes in the thirteenth century, although of course to some extent these had early beginnings. Several chieftain families gained control of large parts of the country and began to vie for power and wealth with increasing vigour. The Church took part in this rivalry and had both allies and opponents among the chieftains. Then the king of Norway began to exert influence, since the chieftains considered his favour worth courting. All this served to upset the balance which was the underlying principle for the social structure during the first centuries of the Commonwealth.

Ship illustration in an illuminated initial from a fourteenth-century manuscript of *Jónsbók*, GKS 3269a 4to. Árni Magnússon Institute in Iceland.

The concentration of wealth into few hands, however, was what made it possible not only for the Church but also for secular leaders to afford to have books written for themselves. After Iceland swore allegiance to the king of Norway in 1262-64, its political structures stabilized and it began to resemble other European nations more closely. The flourishing of Icelandic literature in the thirteenth century was undoubtedly linked with the great upheavals taking place in the country at that time. Conflicts not only involved wealth and power but were also ideological in character. The ancient ethic of heroism and vengeance gradually and reluctantly gave way to the combined forces of the Church and crown which wanted to establish a centralized society where punishment would replace revenge, and compensation for crimes would be paid either to the king or to the Church, depending upon their nature.

When we talk about literature flourishing in the thirteenth century, we are thinking primarily about the large number of exceptionally original works composed then, too numerous to list here although we might mention the sagas of kings attributed to Snorri Sturluson and those in *Morkinskinna*; as well as *Snorra Edda, The Saga of the Volsungs, Egil's Saga, The Saga of the People of Laxardal, Njal's Saga* and many other *Sagas of Icelanders*, Sturla Þórðarson's *Saga of Icelanders* and an abundance of others. To the thirteenth century goes the credit for making copies of eddic poems and the collection of them found in *Codex Regius*, GKS 2365 4to. Literature continued to flourish in the fourteenth century, albeit of somewhat different character. More Sagas of Icelanders were written then, sagas of kings were incorporated into increasingly larger units, and numerous legendary and chivalric sagas were put down on vellum; furthermore, in both the thirteenth and fourteenth centuries a great amount of religious prose and poetry was written. As far as preserving and transmitting texts is concerned, the fourteenth century was the golden age of Icelandic manuscript production, when the most important of all the extant calfskins, apart from the *Codex Regius* of the eddic poems and the two manuscripts of *Grágás*, were made. These include the three main manuscripts of the *Snorra Edda, Möðruvallabók, Stjórn*, the *Skarðsbók* text of the *Jónsbók* law code and another *Skarðsbók* containing *Lives of the Apostles*, numerous other saga manuscripts, law books and collections of other material, and last but not least, towards the end of the century, *Flateyjarbók*.

There is reason to ask why such intense literary activity should have arisen among a tiny impoverished nation far out in the ocean, and what led people to devote so much time and financial resources to making books. The likelihood that more medieval manuscripts have been lost than preserved makes the question even more poignant. Various explanations have been offered, but there are no clear answers.

This essay has made the claim that the close relationship between the Church and several prominent families induced many leaders of society to attain a high standard of education and an interest in books, while their secular interests then called for the writing of sagas in the vernacular. Another theory has been that this nation of immigrants to a new country paid particular attention to cultivating its ancient heritage, so that the arts of storytelling and poetry were in a certain sense spawned by homesickness. Nor should it be forgotten that many settlers did not arrive directly from Scandinavia but spent long periods in the British Isles, became acquainted with the culture there and mixed with the local population. There is no doubt that the settlers brought a large number of Irish or Gaelic speakers with them, probably many more women than men; scholarship, storytelling and poetry were all flourishing in Ireland at that time. It is not unknown for island nations that consider themselves as somehow at the extremity of the world to foster poetry and bookmaking, and Ireland is indeed one example. As far as book production is concerned, it has been suggested that since a great deal of calfskin was a by-product from the type of farming practised in Iceland, the cost of materials was not as great as might have been expected, even bearing in mind that a hundred calfskins were needed to produce *Flateyjarbók* alone (admittedly the largest Icelandic

From the *Reykjabók* manuscript of *Jónsbók*, AM 345 fol. Árni Magnússon Institute in Iceland.

vellum). While such theories are little more than speculation supported by arguments of varying credibility, the facts still speak for themselves: in the Middle Ages Iceland acquired a richer literature than any
other Nordic country.

It is clear that the tradition of sagas, poems and other lore which has
been preserved and kept alive in peoples' memories furnished the
most important material for the literature written in Iceland in the
Middle Ages. Nonetheless, it should not be forgotten that books
invariably derive much of their content, ideas and models from other
books. From the challenge of fusing divergent materials into a unified
whole, new and sometimes significant works are born, not least when
elements of radically disparate origin are successfully integrated.

Among the material that the Icelanders probably kept stored in
their memories for centuries, and possessed in ample measure at the
time people began to realize the advantages of vellum for preserving
ancient knowledge, were old and more recent skaldic (*dróttkvæð*)
poems which poets from Iceland, and initially from Norway too, had
composed about the kings and earls of Scandinavia. These poems had
been handed down, together with memories and legends about
remarkable events from earlier times. Once Nordic clerics had
achieved a good command of the art of writing, it seemed a good
idea to set down in books this knowledge about kings, not least to
give fixed form to the chronology of kings' lives. Latin was the language of writing and the oldest historical works of the north were
written in it, including the lost work of Sæmundur the Wise and
extant ones by the Norwegian Theodoricus on the kings of Norway
and by Saxo Grammaticus on the history of the Danes. An earlier version of the *Book of the Icelanders* included "lives of kings," and Ari was a
pioneer in vernacular writing. As the twelfth century progressed the
writing of kings' sagas gained impetus in Iceland, doubtless drawing
for source material upon the known poems about kings and the stories accompanying them. These works are now only preserved in later
versions, rewritten and augmented from the originals. By 1200 the
Icelanders can be described as having taken the lead in writing vernacular sagas about the Scandinavian rulers. These include sagas about
the Norwegian kings from around 1000, sagas of twelfth-century
kings and claimants to the throne, and also sagas of the ancient kings
of Denmark and earls of Orkney. In the first three decades of the thirteenth century, three major chronicles about successive Norwegian
kings were written, later to be known as *Morkinskinna*, *Fagurskinna* and
Heimskringla. While their subject matter is linked in a variety of ways,
they differ widely in style and technique. These sagas gradually
increased in length, not only with the addition of orally transmitted

material and poetry, but also because authors made efforts to lengthen them and augment them from other writings. Material from the oral tradition and the storytelling tradition itself influenced the authors, endowing these writings with a character that distinguishes them from European historical works from the same time. Of course, diverse signs of influence from European literary tradition can be found, in varying amounts, in both their style and arrangement. The kings' sagas by Snorri Sturluson, *Heimskringla*, have their own distinctive character, contain the most material and have been the most admired in later centuries.

Although the sagas of kings and saga cycles are said to have been written in a specific period before 1240, in the overwhelming number of instances the text is preserved only in fourteenth-century manuscripts or copies of them, so that it is hard to distinguish old material from later. *Kringla*, the beautiful manuscript containing the text which we now call *Heimskringla*, was somewhat older, written around 1260. *Kringla* was destroyed in the great fire of Copenhagen in 1728, but one page still exists and is now kept at the National and University Library of Iceland. Most of the main manuscripts of the sagas of kings are preserved outside Iceland. Some were sent to Norway as early as the Middle Ages, others to the Royal Library in Denmark or Árni Magnússon's collection, or to Sweden in the seventeenth and eighteenth centuries. When the manuscript collections in the Arnamagnean Institute and the Royal Library were divided (see pp. 171-177), the manuscripts of the kings' sagas remained in Denmark, except for the largest and most splendid of them all, *Flateyjarbók* (GKS 1005 fol.), which went to Iceland. The core of this book, which was copied in 1387-94, consists of stories of the kings Olaf Tryggvason, Olaf Haraldsson, Sverrir Sigurdarson and Hakon Hakonarson the Old. The sagas of Magnus the Good and Harald the Stern were added later. This list of kings only tells half the story, however, because the producer of this book clearly wanted it to be as long as possible and therefore included an assortment of material associated in some way with their lives and reigns. This includes *The Saga of the Greenlanders* (*Grænlendinga saga*), *The Saga of the Orkney Islanders* (*Orkneyinga saga*), *The Saga of the Faroe Islanders* (*Færeyinga saga*) and *The Saga of the Sworn Brothers* (*Fóstbræðra saga*), as well as many shorter tales. Tales of Icelanders had already been incorporated into this genre, even from the earliest days of writing kings' sagas in the vernacular. Much of the material in *Flateyjarbók* is now preserved nowhere else, but had been written long before its inclusion there. *Flateyjarbók* was made for a chieftain from north Iceland, Jón Hákonarson from Víðidalstunga. It is not unlikely that the various rich sources for it were largely found at the monastery at Þingeyrar and that the book was written there. *Flateyjarbók* is not only the largest of all medieval Icelandic manuscripts,

almúning e̅ ok v̅ i þm̅ rínc ... hr nema naud ꞩyn haꞇu. J almungi
þat era almening er at þornu ... fl hual ꞩka hur ꞩem uill. ok hit þær
h̅ uiꞇ. Sæꞇr ma hur til gma er ... a huart ꞩem uill a ꞩkipi edr eykium
þm almening eu. eꞇ þ uill þar ... eñ þ̅ er þa um þu ꞩem a̅ iüꞇ, hit þlu
ꞩma i ꞩunnar ꞩeꞇr. eꞇ ꞩ er eu hurziaꞇ ... tr ꞩem adr ꞩkilt. Eñ eꞇ ꞩkaꞇ bruꞇ i
gengi. Eꞇ ij til ganga i ema ꞩattu ba ... hual þm. þa ꞏ ꞩa iüdueꞇꞇa iarnhua
dur ꞩen. hazi bad þ er þr ꞩa. En eꞇ þ ... er næꞇr byr. Hꞟu breꞇ til ꞩætr ial
a ꞩkilꞇ eu huak þra þri orꞇi a. hazi ... mingi. ueidi. hin edr arundurku þ ꞩe
ꞩa ꞩiꞇ mal er ꞩakar i̅; emeidi uea ... þar er. þa ꞩekiz ꞩa er þ gir iij. moz
hꞟu berdi uetta iuioꞇi. þiꞏki uoꞇni doll ... kum uid Ꞃg. eñ tiu gildi þm er h
i almungi e̅ allun iazn heimil. þ eig ... brendi þ̅. þat ꞩama aptr iazngo
u̅ m at taka þiꞩka ok þugla. Eugiꞟ ... ꞇꞇ. ok rett hn eu rzan ept laga domi.
ꞩ̅ þetta i almeninngi þra kroꞩ oꞇ a uak ...
ok til baꞇolz uaku. þar eiga m at ꞇu ... þ byri hꞟn eu til lagbok. e̅ hei
lgia uid. ok þæra til ꞩkipꞩ edr bud ei ... ꞇ reka þam. ok ꞩ þꞏt u̅ morcka
ok er þa uidan heilagr. Hꞟu koma þ ... ok hual reka
til a̅dꞏu ꞩkipi. ok þat a̅ þin eu ꞩiꞇ ꞩki ...
eñ hui haza meik eñ þm ꞩinu ꞩkipi ...
huart ꞩem þ e̅ uidr edr hualr. þa er ...
rett at þr taki þm ꞩinu ꞩkipi. eñ bæ ...
ti hinum þ ꞩtarþ ꞩin. R. B. E̅. R. Ecki ...
eu iord iuidi þm er þiuꞇꞇr er eu alu̅ ...
ettungi uea þ hei lengr en lag ueꞇꞇ ...
a. Hꞟu kemr hualr þa er itꞏe i alu̅ ...
etungi. þa ꞩ bod upp ꞩka ꞩa e̅ næꞇr ...
biꞏr. ok laꞇa þa alla uega ꞩem dag ...
eudꞏr. ꞩekr er h ui. aurum v̅ Ꞃg eꞇ ...
h̅ ꞇkr a̅ bod upp. eñ eyri hur er þel ...

hur til eu reka alla ... þ läh ꞩinu uidar ... ok huala. Zela et ... þiꞩka. ꞟngla ok ... þara. nema i̅; ... logum ꞩe þ koꞇ ... eꞇ uid rekr eu þioꞇu manz. þa ꞩ h̅ ... tika uidar marki ꞩinu. þ ꞩem adr ... heþ h̅ ꞩyꞇr u̅ grꞟꞩu ꞩinun. Eigi ... er logmark ella. Reꞇ er hm at ... uada til. ok marka þ uidꞟu eꞇ h̅ ... kemr a̅ eu zloedar mah eꞇ þ er v ... þa þiou h̅ꞩ er þeꞩta uiꞏ reka eu but also of the most lavish with beautifully illuminated initials and all manner of embellishment. The scribes were two priests, Jón Þórðarson and Magnús Þórhallsson; the latter was also its illustrator.

It was the Church which initially exerted authority over writing and could be expected to preserve for its own people material from the Scriptures and stories of saints and its other loyal servants. As mentioned earlier, a sizable part of the Old Testament was translated into Norse or Icelandic at an early date, along with exegesis by foreign theologians, as preserved in the beautiful manuscript of *Stjórn*. Stories about holy martyrs and Church leaders who had vigorously affirmed their faith through their conduct were familiar in other Christian countries. Even before 1200 there was a tendency in Iceland, among ordinary people and clergy alike, to regard worthy domestic Church leaders as saints, most patently in the case of Bishop Þorlákur Þórhallsson, because shortly after his death stories began to circulate about miracles worked under his agency. Soon afterwards, the see of Hólar began trying to identify saints among its bishops and stopped at the first one, Jón Ögmundsson (1106-21). Clerics started to write the lives of these holy men, supplementing them with accounts of their posthumous miracles. The need was soon felt to record the lives of other bishops than simply those who were considered holy, thereby spawning a large branch of literature, the sagas of bishops (*Byskupa sögur*), which like the kings' sagas continued to become longer and more diverse well into the fourteenth century. The sagas of bishops who were regarded as saints obeyed general hagiographical rules, and all of them obviously have a Christian point of view, since their main purpose was to enhance the reputation of the Church and its servants. But the sagas of bishops also contain a wealth of historical knowledge, both ecclesiastical and political. Often they present glimpses of the lives of the common people, their tribulations and joys, not least in accounts of miracles, because holy men serve the poor no less than the rich. Thus these sagas from books combine a narrative art derived from the folktale with rhetorical literary art.

From as early as the twelfth century, cultural activities flourished among certain chieftain families, such as the people of Oddi and Haukadalur. In the thirteenth century the Sturlungs joined the ranks of those in command of the art of writing when Snorri Sturluson made his home in Borgarfjörður, after he had been educated at Oddi. Around this time, secular leaders began writing or commissioning stories about their forebears which on first impression are quite unlike Christian literature. These have since gone by the name of the "Sagas of Icelanders" – the name refers particularly to the sagas which tell the lives of people from the Age of Settlements towards the middle of the eleventh century. Around the same time, in fact, the first contemporary sagas were written, to be collected into *Sturlunga saga* shortly after 1300. The origin of the secular sagas is somewhat obscure: some are closely related to the kings' sagas, others totally independent of them. *The Book of the Icelanders* and *The Book of Settlements* show that in the twelfth century a wide range of orally transmitted knowledge was recorded about people and events, but continuous accounts of the lives and conflicts of farmers and their leaders could hardly have been written until some time after 1200, when kings' sagas as well as bishops' sagas might have provided models, and perhaps also translated chivalric sagas and saints' lives. The oldest manuscripts of the *Sagas of Icelanders* are all lost and only a handful of fragments now extant may be assumed to date from before 1300. These are fragments from *Egil's Saga* and *The Saga of the People of Laxardal*. Dating from around 1300 are a fragment from *The Saga of the People of Eyri* (*Eyrbyggja saga*) and several fragments from *Njal's Saga*, along with the oldest complete manuscripts of that saga. Many manuscripts and fragments of Sagas of Icelanders have been preserved from the fourteenth century. The largest and most significant is *Möðruvallabók* (AM 132 fol.), written close to the middle of the century and containing eleven Sagas of Icelanders: *Njal's Saga, Egil's Saga, The Saga of Finnbogi the Strong* (*Finnboga saga ramma*), *The Saga of the Confederates* (*Bandamanna saga*), *Kormak's Saga* (*Kormáks saga*), *Viga-Glum's Saga* (*Víga-Glúms saga*), *The Saga of Droplaug's Sons* (*Droplaugarsona saga*), *Olkofri's Saga* (*Ölkofra saga*), *The Saga of Hallfred* (*Hallfreðar saga*), *The Saga of the People of Laxardal* (*Laxdæla Saga*) and *The Saga of the Sworn Brothers* (*Fóstbræðra saga*). Substantial amounts are missing from some of them where pages have been lost from the manuscript.

Neither the Sagas of Icelanders nor the manuscripts in which they are recorded contain a single word about their author or their inception, and given the circumstances of their preservation it is obviously very difficult to give a precise account of their age or when the writing of such sagas began. Opinions have differed, but it is now generally believed that the writing of the Sagas of Icelanders commenced in the early thirteenth century, and that the majority of them were written before 1300, although many not until the fourteenth century and some possibly even later.

The Sagas of Icelanders are written like historical accounts. Characters are introduced, their family backgrounds and places of residence are explained along with the time of the action, and in some cases their lineage is traced onwards to the twelfth or thirteenth centuries. But how reliable are such accounts in historical terms, and what kind of connection do they have with life as it was lived in Iceland from the Age of Settlements until the Age of Writing? This has long been a controversial point. The Sagas are so well told that the reader is tempted to believe every word, as people in Iceland actually did for centuries, although scholars began early on to doubt the veracity of these stories. The first scholar to voice such doubts, long before anyone else, was Árni Magnússon, who felt that much in the sagas was exaggerated and untrue and the Icelanders absurdly idealized, with the author of *Njal's Saga* the most shameless of all in this respect. Such a critical standpoint, however, remained remote to most saga readers. In the nineteenth century ideas began to emerge that the sagas had originated as oral accounts shortly after the events they describe, and were subsequently preserved almost unchanged from one generation to the next until they were written down. Later studies of the preservation of folktales revealed little probability that such long stories could ever have come into being or been preserved in such a way, and gradually the view has gained acceptance that the sagas are the work of authors who shaped them and put them into words, while relying for both their subject matter and narrative stylistic models on the storytellers who related these old tales. Oral preservation is no guarantee for veracity, however, since storytellers alter their stories both deliberately and unconsciously, merge them and create new material. The model for the form itself – the long story which frequently begins with the settlement or describes its background and then traces the conflicts and fate of one generation or more until the main action is over – must surely be written stories, lives of kings or church leaders and saints. Such literature also provided authors with a source of diverse material to enrich what they took from oral tradition.

Egil's Saga must rank with the oldest Sagas of Icelanders and has even been claimed to be the first of them all. Certainly, one of the

Detail from the *Reykjabók* manuscript of *Jónsbók,* AM 345 fol. Árni Magnússon Institute in Iceland.

extant manuscript fragments, AM 162 A ϑ fol., was written around 1250, and two other leaves are thought to have been written in the second half of the thirteenth century and around 1300, respectively. Most scholars agree that the saga was written by Snorri Sturluson, giving it a *terminus ad quem* of 1241, the year that Snorri was assassinated. The best and most complete medieval text of *Egil's Saga* is found in *Möðruvallabók*, even though two pages are missing from it. The saga is also in another vellum book from around the mid-fourteenth century, preserved in Wolfenbüttel in Germany; quite a number of pages are missing from this manuscript. There is also a paper manuscript from the seventeenth century, *Ketilsbók* (AM 462 4to), named after its scribe, the Reverend Ketill Jörundarson (grandfather of Árni Magnússon), who copied a now lost medieval manuscript which was independent of the other two. Some later paper manuscripts also contain texts deriving from lost medieval versions of the saga, including several very late ones from Eyjafjörður, preserved in the National Library, and related to the version found in the ϑ-fragment. *Egil's Saga* is related to the kings' sagas insofar as it describes dealings with kings and its main conflicts take place outside Iceland, especially in Norway and England; the hero is a farmer's son, the offspring of a family of settlers from Norway who wage a running battle with the monarchy there. The main character, Egil, is one of the most memorable in world literature: a farmer and a Viking, a courtier and a rebel, a tough and obstinate thug but also an emotional man who loves his wife and children passionately. Above all he is a poet, and the poetry which forms part of his saga is diverse, colourful and vigorous, just like the man himself, and lends depth and forceful expression to his feelings. Three long poems are attributed to Egil in the saga: "Head Ransom", "Loss of his Sons" and "Ode to Arinbjorn". All are magnificent poetry and "Loss of his Sons" is also one of the most powerful elegies ever composed in Icelandic. Many scribes omitted Egil's poems from their manuscripts, or else the poems were not written in their entirety in the original version. Thus "Loss of his Sons" is preserved only in *Ketilsbók* from the seventeenth century, and it is one of the miracles in the history of preservation that it should not be lost to us forever.

Njal's Saga is the most monumental and famous of the Sagas of Icelanders, amply and securely preserved in manuscripts from the Middle Ages. A strong case can be argued that the saga was written in 1275-90, and the oldest of its quite numerous manuscript fragments are thought to be from around 1300 or first quarter of the fourteenth century. Dating from the same time are *Reykjabók* (AM 468 4to), a manuscript with very little missing, and *Gráskinna* (GKS 2870 4to), an old and tattered manuscript which is lacking many more pages. Slightly later are *Möðruvallabók* and *Kálfalækjarbók* (AM 133 fol). There are 20 manuscripts or fragments of *Njal's Saga* from the period 1300-1600; no other Saga of Icelanders has been so well preserved from medieval times. Whether measured in terms of preservation, later critical acclaim or admiration by readers from all manner of cultural backgrounds, *Njal's Saga* represents the pinnacle of the old Icelandic narrative art. The reasons are simply too many to discuss in detail here. Its characterization is memorable and extremely diverse, the style is concise and the saga itself is a moving human tragedy. *Njal's Saga* is a solid memorial to the thirteenth century and its splendid culture of writing, its ideological and political conflicts. There is no question that it was a great artist who crafted *Njal's Saga*, but it would never have assumed such a form had it not been for the ancient narrative art and wealth of oral tradition which provided the author with its subject and inspiration. In this saga written culture, nourished by oral narrative art, has reached its peak, and the saga glorifies an ancient heroic world which is gradually disappearing from view. Grand heroes lose their lives through adherence to old and obsolete virtues, and eventually people settle for a less contentious and less colourful world, dominated by the Christian spirit.

A number of excellent Sagas of Icelanders were written in the fourteenth century, reaching their summit with *The Saga of Grettir the Strong* (*Grettis saga Ásmundarson*). Legendary sagas also flourished then, as did chivalric sagas and religious literature. By this time there was no longer any tension between centralized ecclesiastical authority and dispersed secular authority. The king was now the fount and focal point of the secular power structure, and the world picture was simpler. Literature in the fourteenth century often appears to have become divorced from external reality, but at the same time it offers more opportunity for perceiving the magical and supernatural as symbols of the inner world of man, of the life of the soul and the emotions. Much of this literature resembles the world of the folktale, bringing literary evolution full circle.

The advantage of the book is that it binds together and preserves products of the mind which otherwise would be transitory and either partly or completely lost, or altered by each new generation. But the book and the symbols it contains are also prone to destruction. In our manuscripts we often find nothing more than the ruins of ancient creations of the mind, but when these ruins, together with the monuments that have been preserved intact, are examined as a whole, they provide unique insights into the thinking and culture of centuries past.

Overleaf: The *Króksfjarðarbók* manuscript, AM 122a fol, of *The Saga of the Sturlungs* (*Sturlunga saga*). Árni Magnússon Institute in Iceland.

oc þa hvervr kirkia þa i. ... hest z ... e ek
gör huart ... nanu... er ... mæðr ... laufan
... oc ef tim e ... nacquar t
... þa við ... oc vera ef ek mega hefna ...
... er ... vel ... ek urnu ... er ... fylgi sialfr ...
... þ placha meðum til fullungs ... oc en var
... a ... en læt ti ept i hafsa ... þa ... e land
... laut ... oc ... ar viðo riða t þig iuns
... sem coðkar ... þa ... er ... villa fylgia ...
... kup ... e þ þ... dænglig · Oc ... þegar
... z riða ... ofan ... cauð kluft · en engi
... apt huat þeg · þg · riðt þtu · ht sem a áð
... hauð ...

N ... ar segia ... þm bardi · oc ... ar
... riða ... at ... z ... þ .aða
... up imot · oc ... þen vel at þ at
... þus · þat ... þ ... baðvaðr al
... guðmða ... s · magn ... z ...
... vel · c · maña · B · frem b · at z ...
... ne ... vel · c · maña · B · frem b · at z æela
... en barðe · F · B · riðr af þginu · oc ... þ þhg
... ei megin · er ... villðu heyra ... lagr
... ef þa hafa ... talar of ... þa riða þa · b ·
... oc alle þ til e þa ... ofan a vollu ar
... hafr · oc ... þm vel fagnat · er þ at
... villu darh a þm ... þa ... ht þa
... er segia af ... þ ... þoline þa · C ·
... ... dal ...
... þolinetie · oc þa rome ... i mot ...
... oc þm ... þ bonað þg reiðin · oc ht
... at ... þghelgina · en þg ... mða
... hauð þ þm ... þa en ...
... vðu ... · Oc er ht ... aftr comu ...
... ... þa e ... villu ... z ... namu
... ... z ... raða ... ... up ...
... · Oc riðr ... þa e þa villu ...
... til buða · oc ... ...
... þm ... · Oc ... segia ht audu allan ...

... oc hu þa ... kom allu ...
... þa ... at ... ...
... þ þ ... ...

Quiða ... hanu ... þg und ...
...elli · z otran stoða at þ ... þa ...
... beðr · oc segia þg · alle ... varir ...
... at þ at buðm ... oll þm er ... · þa ...
... þ e ... tslics · s · h · at ht spar ... hende ...
... hefna · enda ... þ e ... at ... þur ...
... kyni · nacið fleira at villa ... up bubira ...
... þ þ at nu klara oll ... oc tok at ...
... ahlifin · þa ... nu vnð er þ oi þa ...
... at þg ... raða ar ... þa ...
... z ... · Asvnar oll vera ... arasprungandi ...
... segiar ... hins giella · ... þlogu verða ·
... z munu ... · s · þg · eigi at ... · oc ...
... sem ...

Se tvei ... saugu þm · þa e þp harða ...
... ... laða ... þa gengr ...
... ... ht · er ... · Ertu nu hapt ...
... at ... engis ... oc ... ne villa ...
... · Se þ ... · þa ... þp · þa munu ...
... hai ol ... · Oc af þ velldr e guð ...
... þa ... at buða alle oc leosa ...
... ti gar ... · oc hve at ...
... en ... arætu þp gar ...
... man oc ... ... at ... z ...
... en ... · Sva ... þm oc ...
... heyði · oc ... ...
... oc ...
... ...
... við guð · oc ...
... ... oc þu er ... ...
... ht þat þ at ...
... þ · ... oc ...
... ... en ... þ ... þar ...
... daglangt ef ... ...

Book production in the Middle Ages

SOFFÍA GUÐNÝ GUÐMUNDSDÓTTIR AND LAUFEY GUÐNADÓTTIR

Books today are public property in many countries of the world and in general are easily accessible. A wide selection of books is available in many places, in shops and on the Internet, and anyone who can afford them has no problem in buying them. In centuries past the mere act of making books was completely different from today. The necessary materials required much labour and were expensive, and few people had the means to acquire books. They were entirely handmade and no two were identical; each one was a unique object. In the course of time papermaking and printing superseded the old techniques and industrialization ushered in mass production in place of craftsmanship. The following is a discussion of both the materials and techniques used for book production in the Middle Ages.

Books and vellum

When the Age of Writing began in Iceland, books were made from animal skins. Some 4,500 years ago, a technique was devised for curing skins to produce suitable material for writing on. Known as parchment (pergament) or vellum, it can be made from the skins of sheep, goats and calves. Vellum differs from leather insofar as instead of being tanned after the wool or hair is removed, the skin is stretched and then dried. Stretching changes the properties of the skin, making it extremely durable if kept under the right conditions, neither too dry nor damp.

Initially, vellum was cut into rectangular shapes which were then sewn together and rolled up, as was done with Egyptian papyri. Several centuries into the Christian era the first books appeared. Instead of sewing together lengths of skin, pages cut into standard shapes were placed together and bound into books. It was far more convenient to locate a certain passage by paging through a book than by turning a scroll, and the book soon achieved popularity.

Vellum was more expensive than papyrus and more complicated to

Left: Many medieval illustrations provide detailed insights into the craft of bookmaking. These illustrations from a German manuscript from the second half of the twelfth century show all the stages of book production: treating the vellum, cutting the vellum and styli, preparatory writing on wax tablets, and the writing itself. Bookbinding is also shown: the completed quires are sewn together, wooden covers are prepared, and the bindings and warps are attached to the book. From Patr. 5, fol. 1r, State Library, Bamberg, Germany.

Vellum was cured by scraping a stretched skin with a crescent-bladed knife. From Amb. 317 fol. 34v, State Library, Nuremberg, Germany.

produce, but by virtue of its much greater durability it soon became widespread. On reaching northwest Europe with Christianity, vellum became the most common material for book production in the Middle Ages. Beginning in the fourteenth century the use of paper spread throughout Europe, especially with the advent of printing, while in Iceland paper gradually replaced vellum as a material for books in the sixteenth century.

Medieval book production was a major undertaking. First the skin had to be procured and cured, then the surface had to be prepared for writing, ink made and quills trimmed. Then the writing could begin. Once the text had been copied, pigments were mixed and used for chapter headings and sometimes illustrations. Finally the book was bound, and then it was ready for use.

From calf to book

The first step in book production was to turn the skin into vellum. Although no extant Icelandic records describe medieval book production and skin curing, some impression of how vellum was made can be gained from two sources. One is descriptions of medieval book production in Europe, where the techniques which were introduced to Iceland originated, and the other is the appearance of Icelandic books and the vellum in them.

The curer's first task was to remove the wool or hair from the skin. Liming was the most common technique, which loosened the hair sufficiently to make it easy to scrape off. After careful cleansing the skin was stretched on a frame, scraped and dried; drying under tension is an important and characteristic feature of the vellum curing process. The length of time it took to dry the skin varied, but the quality of the vellum depended upon how well this process was handled. In warm climates, efforts were made to delay drying by dampening the skin, while in colder countries powdered chalk was applied to the skin to speed up the process. When the skin was beginning to dry in the frame, dry chalk was applied to it to dissolve residual fat and moisture, then it was scraped with a curved knife. Good vellum had to be thin and strong, and at the same time supple and smooth.

Vellum production in Iceland

Medieval Icelandic vellum manuscripts are generally much darker than those from elsewhere in Europe. To a large extent this is because they were much used for centuries and kept in sooty, damp turf-built farmhouses. Icelandic manuscripts that have been preserved in Norway under different conditions are lighter and in a much better state than those that remained in Iceland. Nonetheless, there seem to have been some differences between curing of vellum in Iceland and elsewhere in Europe, because the Icelandic type has slightly different properties.

In the absence of descriptions of medieval Icelandic vellum production it must be assumed that the craft was broadly similar to that practised in northern Europe. However, it has been noticed that European vellum is different, as a result of other methods, raw materials and the intended use of the product. Geographical isolation and expensive materials presumably taught Icelanders to utilize what nature offered them. It is possible that they used geothermal water and various types of volcanic ash for removing the hair. The climate, especially the short summer, probably also influenced the methods for producing vellum.

The main difference between vellum production in Iceland and the rest of Europe apparently involved techniques for removing the hair; in other countries the skins were usually limed or soaked in a calcium solution. A lighter vellum resulted, because the skin absorbed the chalk and was coloured by it. The lack of chalk in Iceland may have affected the appearance and the nature of Icelandic vellum. Although no medieval descriptions are available, later accounts of skin curing in Iceland mention three techniques for removing the hair, all of which may go back to the earliest times, and none of them involves liming.

Sources relate that hides were sometimes shaved but another method of removing the hair, and possibly more common, was known as rotting. The skins would be soaked with urine, then stacked and left to rot until the hair or wool came loose. The third method was to tie newly flayed skins to the back of a heifer, with the hair side down. After twenty-four hours the hair would have worked itself loose. It is thought that most Icelandic vellums were made from calfskin. This hypothesis is supported by the handful of studies of Icelandic vellum that have been made, as well as by the fact that rearing cattle was very common in early Iceland. Skins from animals with light or reddish hides probably yielded whiter vellums, which were more desirable for book production.

Margin illustration of a cow from *Heynesbók*, AM 147 4to. Another scribe has added cows on either side of the original illustration.
Árni Magnússon Institute in Iceland.

Book production

The fully cured vellum was removed from the frame before the next stage of production began. First, the skins were trimmed into rectangular shapes of equal size, if the sheets were all intended for the same book. After the size of the book was decided, vellum was selected for it and then cut to fit.

A sheet folded once produced two leaves or four pages for writing

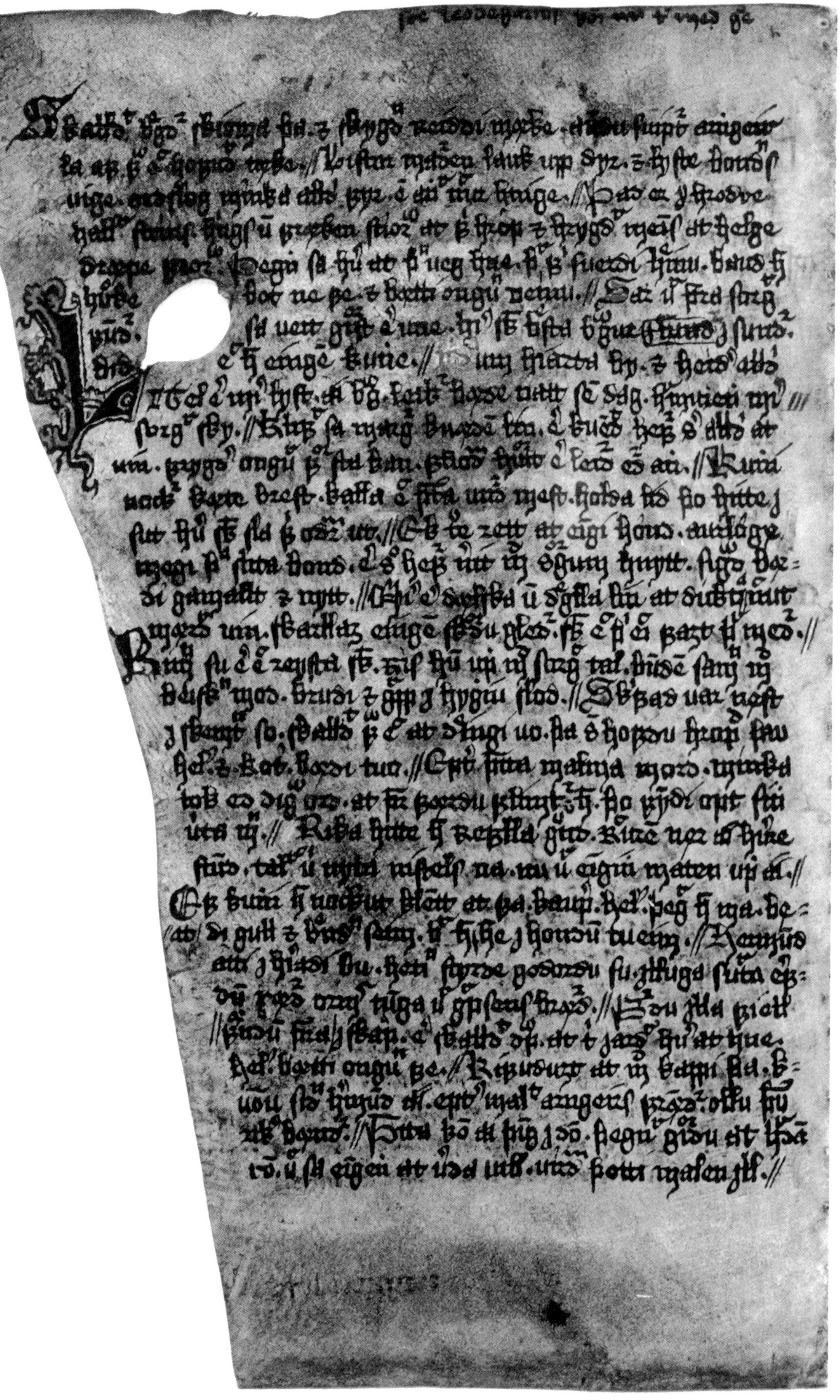

Left: Resourceful use of a leaf from AM 604 4to - the text fits the shape of the skin and is wrapped around the hole in it.
Árni Magnússon Institute in Iceland.

Above: Manuscript sizes: folio, quarto, octavo and duodecimo.
Photograph: Jóhanna Ólafsdóttir. Árni Magnússon Institute in Iceland.

on, known as a folio. The next size down was quarto (4to), for which the sheet was cut in half before each sheet was folded, yielding four leaves or eight pages. The third size was made by cutting the sheet in four before each piece was folded, and was known as octavo (8vo), with 16 pages. Duodecimo (12mo) with twelve leaves or twenty-four pages was the smallest size, made by cutting each sheet in six. Modern paper sizes are comparable to those of skin books. Roughly speaking, one sheet of folio corresponds to one A3, 4to corresponds to A4 and 8vo to A5. References to manuscripts generally cite the leaf rather than the page, and then add r(ecto = right) for the front or v(erso = left) for the back.

Libraries usually classify manuscripts according to size, even though manuscripts within the same classification are not always exactly the same size. The common explanation is that the margins were trimmed when the book was bound or its binding renewed. A possible reason for doing this could be that the sheets had become torn at the edges or were cut to fit an existing cover. Also, manuscripts of different sizes but similar in content may have been trimmed in order to match when placed side by side on a shelf. If a marginal figure has been cut away in an illuminated manuscript, it is clear that trimming has taken place.

Before being used, vellum was rubbed with pumice and sometimes chalk to create an even smoother surface, which would absorb the ink most effectively. Afterwards the writing surface was marked out with lines and columns by piercing or perforation at regular intervals on the margins. A ruler was generally used to draw lines between the holes, either by cutting with a knife or using a bone, lead or ink to mark the lines and columns. Markings can still be seen on some vellums.

The leaves were placed together to form a quire, perhaps before the scribe began writing; otherwise he would have to make sure how

Clear markings for lines, columns and margins, from the *Codex Regius* of *Grágás*, GKS 1157 fol, mid-thirteenth century. Árni Magnússon Institute in Iceland.

the leaves would subsequently be arranged. Four sheets were often used for a quire, although the figure is not absolute, and each book consisted of many quires. Since the different sides of the skin had different properties, it was a common principle in much of Europe to arrange the sheets together so that a flesh side and a grain side would not face each other on two open pages. This gave a more pleasing appearance, but the rule was not always followed in Icelandic manuscripts.

Vellum was an expensive material, so it was often used even when there were minor flaws in it. Torn vellum was sewn together and scribes wrote around holes. For the same reason some leaves in manuscripts are of different sizes or irregular shape. All of this shows a determination to use vellum to the full.

Pens, ink and colours

For centuries, pens were made from quills – the Latin *penna* means "feather". Quills were used in Iceland from the beginning of the Age of Writing until the nineteenth century, when steel pens were introduced. They were made from the feathers of large birds such as swans or geese; feathers from the left wing were considered to fit the hand better than those from the right. When quills were made the barbs were cut away from a portion of the shaft and the marrow was extracted. This created a kind of chamber running the length of the quill, comparable to that found in modern pens. When the quill was placed in the inkwell the chamber would fill with ink by capillary action. A scribe would often try to make each filling of ink last for one line in a manuscript.

The point of the quill was trimmed and hardened by heating in a pan of hot sand before being used for writing. Scribes also needed to trim their quills regularly; they need sharpening just like pencils – otherwise the point would wear, making the writing thicker. Quill-sharpening was a delicate task which had to be performed in a specific way. As vellum became the chief material for writing letters and making books, a type of ink was developed which was suitable for writing on it. In medieval Europe, an extract of tannin was most commonly used. This was a mixture of iron sulphate and tannin which was preferably obtained from gall apples, which are knobs formed on oak trees around the eggs that insects lay under the bark. Gall apples are highly rich in tanbark which is easy to process into tannin. In Icelandic they are also known as *blekber* (ink-berries) with reference to this use.

Upper photograph: Materials for making ink: sticks of willow, bearberry and black humus. Photograph: Jóhanna Ólafsdóttir. Árni Magnússon Institute in Iceland.

Lower: Minerals for colouring, powdered dyes and coagulant. Photograph: Jóhanna Ólafsdóttir. Árni Magnússon Institute in Iceland.

Mixing the ink appears to have been a painstaking task. Some letters were black and glossy, others browner, possibly depending on the proportion of iron sulphate in the ink. In the Middle Ages black dye made from soot was sometimes mixed with the tannin ink to turn it dark and thick and raised, but the ink hues could span the whole spectrum from grey to brown or green to black.

Tannin ink contains substances which turn black on contact with oxygen, which is why they are generally darker on the written page than in the inkwell. Ink particles penetrate the fibres of the vellum, making the writing more durable and harder to erase. Under certain conditions over a long period of time the ink may penetrate too far into the skin and be seen from the other side. If the ink was not made properly it could erode the vellum, although no instances of this are found in Icelandic manuscripts. On the other hand, properly made ink lasted well and did not blur into the area around the letters.

Icelandic scribes probably used imported ink when writing was first introduced, but in the course of time they perfected ways of making it from natural materials found locally. Although there are no accounts of ink production in the earliest times, a technique described in seventeenth-century sources is considered old. Bearberry was used for making ink. It was boiled in an iron pot with sticks of unbudded willow, undoubtedly to extract some kind of tannin or resin. A black dye made from humus was added to darken the ink. This was otherwise used for dying clothes and derived its black colour from the presence of iron sulphate. Its surface properties were ideal when a drop placed on a fingernail held its form; this meant it would not spread on the vellum but penetrate well into it. In *The Travel Journal of Eggert Ólafsson and Bjarni Pálsson* (*Ferðabók Eggerts Ólafssonar og Bjarna Pálssonar*, first published 1752-57), Ólafsson describes ink-making:

The green pigment has eroded the vellum (*Svalbarðsbók, AM 343 fol*). Much care was needed in preparing and mixing the colouring. For example, only certain coagulants could be used with green pigment, and the disappearance of the letter "n" could be because an incorrect coagulant caused an erosive compound to form.
Árni Magnússon Institute in Iceland.

Most of the ink used in Iceland is produced from willow, as follows: A brew of bearberry is mixed with black humus and they are boiled together to produce a dye. Some people use only the darkest part of this concoction. Sticks of raw willow are placed in the concoction and left there to soak. Then the brew is boiled until it turns thick and sometimes slightly sticky. When it is so thick that it remains in a round drop if allowed to drip onto a fingernail, the ink is ready for use after filtering. This ink is very black and shiny, but if it contains too much willow sap it is slow to dry and after several years the paper will turn brown, because the ink spreads through it. (*Ferðabók* I (1974), p. 101).

In medieval Icelandic manuscripts, especially from around 1400 and later, the ink differs slightly from that used elsewhere in Europe. The letters are often black and shiny, almost in relief, which makes them easy to read even several hundred years after they were written. Perhaps some kind of gum was added to the ink to make it shine. Rubrics in manuscripts were written with dyes, but calf's blood was never used for writing on skin, as is sometimes claimed. Eggert Ólafsson says of the gum:

> We do not know whether people in other countries use resin or gum. People say, however, that in earlier times it was used in ink for writing on vellum, before paper became commonplace near to the Reformation. All the Nordic peoples probably used it, in particular in winter and spring, when it was most abundant. Gum is the first milk in the udders of young ewes and heifers, before they give birth for the first time. It is yellow, thick and sticky. It is generally known as *klár*, but also *kvoða* (gum), which is properly the name of clear, melted *harpix*, which it closely resembles. Particular dexterity is needed to milk the gum. It is now used to glue books, wood and other objects. It is said that the glowing, relief and rounded letters on old vellums are made from this gum, but the type of dye used is not known. One thing is certain: the gum can retain its shape and gloss. It turns harder than rubber and is better than both that and albumen, which was formerly much used in painting, insofar as it does not run on contact with moisture or water. Not so very long ago, when conveyances of property and other important deeds were still written on vellum, thick-boiled willow ink was used, as described earlier (p. 115).

Colours in manuscript illustrations

Few illustrated vellum books that have been preserved in Iceland are as splendid as those from other countries. The coloration in Icelandic manuscripts is generally not as bright as in European ones, although the difference may stem from the way the former were preserved and their present dark condition. It is not known for certain where Icelanders obtained the pigments for their manuscripts, but they probably used both native plant dyes and imported colours from Europe, mostly in the form of coloured minerals.

Pigments were ground to a fine powder which was then mixed with a coagulant such as egg yolk, albumen or fish glue to make it adhere to the vellum. One method was to whisk the white of an egg and leave it to stand until it turned runny. Then it was easy to mix in the pigment; the mixture adhered well to the skin. A drawback, however, was that this colour was quite soluble in water, so other coagulants may have been added.

The only study of pigments in an Icelandic manuscript was made at University College London, in 1993, using a microscope that allowed non-destructive examination of the book's pigments. The manuscript studied, the *Skarðsbók* containing the *Jónsbók* law code, is one of the most beautifully and lavishly illustrated of all those that have been preserved, and was written in 1363. Six pigments were found in the illuminations on the manuscript: *vermilion* (red), *orpiment* (yellow), *realgar* (red yellow), *red ochre, azurite* (blue) and *bone white*. Other pigments, in particular variant hues of green-blue and blue, were not examined in detail but appear to be a mixture of *verdigris*, produced from copper, and a dark green pigment which could be a mixture of *verdigris* and green earth. The main finding of the study was that the pigments that were firmly identified in the *Skarðsbók* illuminations were not found in Icelandic nature but were imported. They are similar to those used in illustrations elsewhere in Europe.

Scribes and writing

In the Middle Ages, scribes all over Europe were busy copying books. Books were produced mainly in monasteries, which needed to add to and replenish their libraries regularly, but also derived an income by producing books for others. As time went on, a class of professional scribes appeared, independent of the monasteries, especially with the growth of universities after 1200, which brought about a demand for text books in various disciplines: history, law, theology, medicine and philosophy. Administration also proliferated, and the secular authorities needed increasing numbers of scribes to make copies of agreements, proclamations and the like. With the passage of time, scribes found

From the *Skarðsbók* manuscript of *Jónsbók*, AM 350 fol. Árni Magnússon Institute in Iceland.

A scribe at his pulpit, from *Flateyjarbók*, GKS 1005 fol.
Árni Magnússon Institute in Iceland.

work for rich noblemen who wanted to acquire books, and some lay-men learned to do their own writing, especially when paper came into use in the fifteenth century.

Books were copied profusely in Iceland in spite of the small population, but book production was not the domain of monasteries on the scale witnessed in Europe. Although monks and nuns worked as scribes in Iceland, writing is thought to have been more common among laymen than in the rest of Europe, with more scribes coming from their ranks, especially from the class of wealthy farmers. Chieftains had access to education and thereby to literacy, and the great number of preserved manuscripts containing secular material demonstrates that there were people in Iceland who wanted to make copies of these books and were capable of doing so. Furthermore, comparisons with the handwriting in early charters have shown that many hands are those of lay scribes, although clerics too wrote secular books, in particular sagas of kings.

Writing conditions

Scant records are available about the working environment and techniques of Icelandic scribes, but scribal remarks on the margins of manuscripts, especially from the later Middle Ages, may give some idea of their conditions and how they felt. Foreign sources can help to fill in the gaps.

The scribe's task was a difficult one, calling for great precision and patience, and working conditions in the Middle Ages were different from what is customary today. In order not to risk damage to precious manuscripts, the scriptoria of European monasteries were not heated and had no other light than daylight. In Iceland, however, some kind of lighting must have been provided during the darkest period of the year, so that writing could continue all year round.

Nonetheless, book production was in some sense a seasonal activity, and spring, summer and autumn, when it was brightest, were the optimal times of year. The following remark on the margin of an Icelandic manuscript of ballads (*rímur*) might imply that the scribe had to end his work when the daylight ended: "Darkness has fallen, necklace-bearer" (i.e. woman). Another marginal comment in the same manuscript – "It's bad to write in a northwester" – leads us to think that the Icelandic scribes were just as plagued by the cold as their continental colleagues.

Total silence was insisted upon in the scriptoria of European monasteries to ensure the concentration necessary for a task requiring great precision. No one was allowed to enter the room and disturb the scribes with irrelevant remarks. The scribes worked together in scrip-

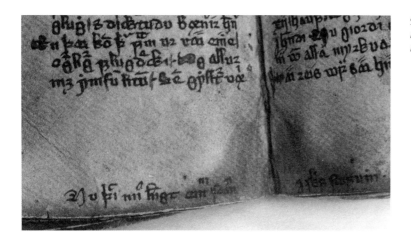

toria or the common rooms of the monastery; it does not appear to have been customary to work in solitude, even when conditions for doing so were at hand.

It is uncertain whether the same is true of Icelandic monasteries, which, in comparison with European monasteries, had few brethren. From jottings in the margins it can be inferred that being a scribe in Iceland was a lonely task: "I feel I have been a long time alone in the scriptorium," is written in a manuscript of *The Life of St. Margaret* (*Margrétar saga*).

Methods and corrections

When a scribe wrote out a text he would either have had in front of him the original from which he copied, or someone would have read the text out to him. Scribes often made errors in copying texts, and sometimes the errors provide clues to their working methods. Some may indicate that the scribe misunderstood what was being read out loud. A common form of error suggests that either the reader or the scribe himself missed a line or jumped over part of the text in the original.

Few materials were available in the Middle Ages to erase or correct the frequent errors that occurred during writing. If the error was discovered immediately the ink could be scraped away with a knife. Scribes also had other methods for correcting texts. For example, dots were placed under superfluous letters to show they were not to be read. An omitted word tended to be written in above the line or in the margin, while superfluous words were often crossed out. A special sign, generally a diagonal mark above the line, indicated that the word order should be changed.

Scribes may have used wax tablets to write a draft in order to preclude errors before they began writing, especially when important documents were involved. Tablets were made by pouring molten wax

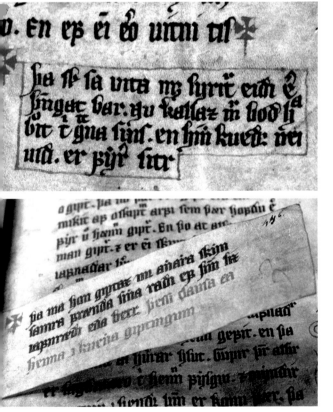

Corrections in the *Codex Regius* of *Grágás*, GKS 1157 fol. Dots under letters and an insertion between the lines.
Árni Magnússon Institute in Iceland.

Upper photograph: An insertion with a red scribal mark, from the legal codex *Arnarbælisbók*, AM 135 fol. The place where text is missing from the manuscript is marked with a red cross. The missing text is written in the margin and enclosed in a red box to make it more easily identifiable.
Árni Magnússon Institute in Iceland.

Lower: An inserted strip of leaf in the same manuscript, *Arnarbælisbók*, AM 135 fol. The scribe has omitted a fragment of the text while copying it. The correction has been made with a vellum strip bound into the book and the place where it should be inserted is marked with a red cross.

into a small wooden frame, leaving it to harden and then writing on it with a stylus. A tablet could be reused by rubbing the wax away and pouring fresh wax into the frame.

Toil and eye strain

Scribes were plagued by various physical discomforts such as backache, as shown by the complaints written at the end of books and in the margins. An anonymous eighth-century continental scribe insists that the users of his book treat it with care and caution, because its production entailed so much suffering: "O, fortunate reader, wash your hands and touch the book by turning the pages gently, keeping your fingers a good distance from the letters. He who does not write supposes it to be no labour. O, how difficult it is to write: it dulls the eyes, presses on the kidneys and torments all the joints. Three fingers write, the whole body suffers." In this light, it is not surprising that writing was sometimes used as a form of penance in European monasteries.

Poor sight was a common ailment among scribes who often needed to read texts closely in poor light. Before the advent of reading glasses, poor sight was uppermost in many scribes' minds, as shown by remarks in the margins of Icelandic manuscripts: "The poor wretch is ill in his eyes" comes from the pen of one who then invokes the Saviour to help him: "Jesus son of Mary, behold the eyes of your slave."

It is not surprising that scribes tired of their work. Writing out a book could take a long time, even several years; a scribe's productivity undoubtedly depended on his comfort, health and working conditions. One Irish scribe is said to have completed a book of 248 pages in twelve days, which was considered fast, though there is no mention of how much text was on each page or how large the book was. His compatriot and colleague Timothy O'Neil was said to write an average of 200 words an hour, but needed to take regular pauses. In the margins are complaints about fatigue and the long hours, and expressions of relief at finally completing a hard task. Some are far from contented with their lot, like the Icelandic scribe who declared "Writing bores me." He was also dissatisfied with his ink: "Poor is the writing for weak is the ink," and he also complains about his badly sharpened quill. Some look forward to being rewarded for their labour, others complain outright about poor pay or their superiors' ingratitude. One Icelandic scribe is disgruntled with his employer and complains of lack of food: "You do me wrong, Dóri, you never give me enough fish." This Dóri can be assumed to have made some kind of contract with the scribe concerning pay, board and lodging, as was customary elsewhere in Europe. The work of copying is likely to have been the most expensive part of the book production process, accounting for more than one-third of the total cost. Judging from foreign sources, in some cases the scribe may have had to provide and pay for his own vellum, but this would doubtless have been stipulated in the contract.

Although scribes generally use the margins of their books to write complaints about physical discomfort, bad conditions or poor pay, as well as devotional reflections, they sometimes vent personal complaints, for example failed love affairs: "All hope is lost that she will love me," it says in the Icelandic manuscript of ballads cited above, which contains numerous scribal comments in the margins.

Despite difficult conditions and various occupational ailments, sources reveal that both learned and lay scribes in Europe regarded their profession as a spiritually noble one, for all their comparisons of it with manual labour. Armed with pen and ink, monastic scribes fought the devil himself when they copied the divine word. But it was not only the scribes themselves who regarded their work as noble; they also seem to have enjoyed respect in society.

Manuscript art

After the text had been written the book was illuminated or decorated, if this was the plan. The scribe would leave sufficient space for titles, illuminated letters and capital letters at the beginning of chapters. Either the scribe or a separate artist would fill in the titles and design and paint the illuminations. Chapter headings or rubrics were almost always written in red irrespective of whether the manuscript was otherwise illuminated. The preserved manuscripts show that scribes and illuminators were highly skilled designers, decorators and illustrators. Like the vellum-makers and scribes, most medieval artists were anonymous craftsmen. The few names that survive in the records suggest that most of them were male. However, there is nothing to rule out that women were involved in this work, as was the case in convents outside Iceland.

Christianity not only introduced writing to Iceland but also opened new possibilities in creative art. The settlers had brought with

A scribe's spectacles, item no. 9231 in the National Museum of Iceland. Photograph: Ívar Brynjúlfsson.

them their native artistic traditions, in the form of carvings, embroidered tapestries, painted shields and other objects of art. Nonetheless, the raw materials available naturally in Iceland played a part in determining the course that art would take, just as it did with other aspects of book production such as curing of skins, ink production and pigmentation. Natural dyes were found in Iceland but not in the variety known from many other countries.

Along with carvings, manuscripts and their illuminations are the best known representatives of medieval Icelandic art. Manuscript illustrations are important not least as indications that ecclesiastical art flourished in Iceland and that churches were originally decorated with painted religious art which has since been lost. Little research has been conducted on Icelandic manuscript art, but the few studies that have been made show that it was influenced from many parts of Europe, especially from England.

Perforations marking the outline of an illustration in the *Icelandic Sketch Book*, AM 673a III 4to. Perforations were probably made around the outline so that the illustration could be copied to another manuscript. Árni Magnússon Institute in Iceland.

Illuminations

The most common forms of manuscript illustration are initial capitals and illuminated letters. The illuminated letters stand at the beginning of a new saga or new chapter of laws and they typically portray the subject of the text or are descriptive of it in some way. Initials, which are much more common, are often embellished or decorated and are smaller than illuminated letters.

Illustrators used such different pictorial styles that virtually every illuminated manuscript has its own characteristics. Many hagiographies and biblical translations are richly illustrated and bear witness to the splendour and wealth of the Church. Law books, which have been preserved in large numbers, are also beautifully illuminated. In some of them, e.g. *Reykjabók* and *Heynesbók*, the margins of almost every page are decorated with diverse and colourful scenes from daily life drawn by talented artists.

Not only religious and legal texts, but also saga manuscripts tend to have ornate initials at the beginning of sagas and chapters, sometimes in colour, although they rarely contain illuminated letters. Virtually the only preserved saga manuscripts containing illustrations are the *Kálfalækjabók* text of *Njal's Saga* (three illuminated letters) and the sagas of kings in the lavishly illustrated *Flateyjarbók*. Manuscripts of ballads and poems are generally not decorated, with a few exceptions such as the ballad manuscript AM 604 4to, in which almost all the illuminations are in ink and generally in the margins. Similarly, a small book containing *The Life of St. Margaret* is decorated with ink drawings, but otherwise small books were rarely decorated.

A remarkable manuscript known as the *Icelandic Sketch Book* (*Íslenska teiknibókin*) contains a collection of originals that medieval artists used when, for example, illuminating manuscripts or painting altarpieces. It is the only book of its kind to be preserved in the Nordic countries and very few parallels have been preserved elsewhere in Europe. On one page, holes have been pierced into the skin around a picture of a man and a dragon to mark the outlines which could then be used as the basis for a new picture.

Illumination styles

In the Nordic countries, particularly Norway, woodcarving was an indigenous art form going back all the way to heathen times. Celtic interlacing was brilliantly blended with the Urnes stave church style. When the Roman garland style, based on woven vines, reached the Nordic countries in the mid-twelfth century a distinct variant developed merging these traditions and remained popular for centuries in Iceland for both carving and filigree. Icelanders also incorporated flo-

ral patterns, oak leaves and rosettes from the Gothic style, notwith-standing their fondness for the Roman garland.

In the earliest period of book production in Iceland, the Roman tradition of illustration must have flourished. At least, it established itself on such a firm footing that it dominated Icelandic manuscript illumination throughout the entire Middle Ages and well into the Reformation period. The basic form of the Roman style is a circular space with a specific pictorial construction inside it, usually with the main subject in the centre. Each element of the picture was static and skilfully arranged.

The Gothic style originated in architecture when the pointed arch began to replace the rounded Romanesque arch. In decoration, sculpture, carving, art and illumination, Gothic influence can be seen in more delicate and less stylized drawing. More emphasis is given to kinetic images, such as more normal folds in clothing, more curved bodies and a more realistic attention to detail.

Bookbinding

Little is known about bookbinding during the first centuries of book production in Iceland, since few medieval manuscripts are preserved in their original binding. Our knowledge can be enhanced by examining bookbinding techniques from other countries, as well as what is said about this craft in Icelandic charters. Ornate books were used in churches in the Middle Ages, often bound in leather-clad wooden covers with blocked decorations, sometimes ornamented with gold, silver or brass, precious stones or carved ivory.

During bookbinding, individual quires first needed to be sewn together with yarn, after which all the quires for the book were either sewn inside a cover of leather or bound in wooden boards. There are instances of binding in sealskin, but cowhide, calfskin and sheepskin were also used. Quires were fastened to the cover with leather thongs, which was the simplest type of binding. The *Gráskinna* manuscript of *Njal's Saga* is a good example of a leather-bound book which could be quite old.

When books were bound in wooden covers the joined quires were sewn, using a strong thread, onto warps – leather thongs or strings of flax – which were spaced at regular intervals across the spine and extending beyond the quires. The ends of the warps were then pulled through holes in the covers and fixed down by various means, for example with wooden pegs, on the inside. Wooden covers were mainly made from oak, beech or pine, and probably often from driftwood. The wood covering was sometimes clad in leather and fitted with clasps or leather straps to keep it shut.

Upper photograph: Illuminated letter from AM 132 4to. The conscious pictorial construction of the circular form with its prominent axe and tree, and the stylized, static human figure are characteristics of the Roman style. Árni Magnússon Institute in Iceland.

Lower: Illuminated letter from *Stjórn*, AM 227 fol. Gothic characteristics include the folds in the clothing, curved bodies and meticulous attention to detail. Árni Magnússon Institute in Iceland.

Obsolete and worn skin books were often refurbished and their leather used, among other things, for binding new ones. With the advent of printing, curers in other countries continued to cure leather for books, but now for binding paper books. After a printing works was set up at Hólar Cathedral in the sixteenth century a primitive bindery was included with it. During this time, it became more common for Icelandic books to be covered with leather, often with embellishments stamped into them and with metal at the corners.

Books with wooden covers could last for centuries but the binding often came under great strain with long use, careless treatment and poor storage. As a result, few vellum books have been preserved to the present day in their original bindings. Most manuscripts are in bindings from later centuries and the process of rebinding old books continues today, often using similar techniques to those that were customary in the Middle Ages.

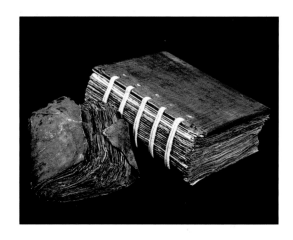

Manuscripts of *Njal's Saga*: *Gráskinna*, GKS 2870 4to, is bound in a seal-skin cover, and *Möðruvallabók*, AM 132 fol, in wooden boards. Photograph: Jóhanna Ólafsdóttir. Árni Magnússon Institute in Iceland.

Annal um fiolda allra
kirkna a Hólum i Hialla=
tadal. Sidan Kristni kom
a Island:

Anno 1000 v. lögtekin kristni a Islndi.
og um þann tima sobþ pyrst kirkiu=
inga byggd ad Hólum oxi hialla=
son Þordson hiallta sonar dalr .. .
.. Þordson skalps .. söpdu fyr
la dal m .. .. Þordson hus .. hiall=
.. sad oxa: a þopi hielldu
.. .. bradi. Þordr polvalldr þa
.. biolmn .. veit þ .. .. .. v ..
.. xij m cpt hiallta dalr m ..
Bod: Bad s .. .. þ .. piol m .. a is=
landi vrid:

oxi liet smida pyrst kirkiu ad
Jans Hóli sygg .. m ad f .. kkia
.. haffi mid v .. gior und trie þa=
bps ki a ollu Islndi. oxi lagdi mid
a .. d .. pi t þ kirkiu liet hana ut
.. bua mg m gh .. .. .. pkria
da t þckia alla m blyi: Enn sw
kkia bran oll upp mg sin þkir .. =
.. var sidan g .. þ uppsmidad

Writing

GUÐVARÐUR MÁR GUNNLAUGSSON

The oldest relics of writing date back more than 5,000 years. The first to employ some sort of letters were the Sumerians in Mesopotamia (modern Iraq) and all Middle Eastern and European letter-forms can be traced to Sumeria. Sumerians wrote on soft clay. Initially they wrote with pictograms, but their writing soon evolved from transparent graphs to a kind of logograph (a single symbol that represents an entire word or phrase) and from that to phonograms where each symbol corresponded to a word, syllable, morpheme or sound. Sumerian cuneiform was a syllabic script. The great majority of surviving Sumerian inscriptions contain accounting records. However, it is believed that phonograms evolved when the need to represent abstract words and thoughts, and to represent personal and place names, caused the graphs to become distanced from their models. The Egyptians probably learned to use writing from the Sumerians but evolved a distinctive hieroglyphic script. Semitic peoples in the area between Egypt and Mesopotamia adopted graphs from the Egyptians or Sumerians and evolved them into phonograms which the Phoenicians, who lived in what is now the Lebanon and nearby countries, developed further into a consonantal writing system in the fourteenth century BC. The Hebrews adopted the Phoenician consonantal alphabet, but added dots below or above a letter to indicate vowels. Arabic and Hebrew are still written in consonantal script, with or without vowel markers. The Greeks learned their alphabet from the Phoenicians but added letters to represent vowels. In turn, the Romans learned writing from the Greeks, adapting the letters slightly but without adding to them. The Roman alphabet is the foundation of the writing later used in Western Europe, i.e. in the sphere of influence of the Roman Catholic Church. Writing spread through the whole of the Roman Empire, where Latin was the *lingua franca*, and farther throughout the continent with the Church in the Middle Ages, since Latin was its main language. Western European colonialism in later centuries spread Latin

Left: Specimen of scribal style from The Annals, a record of the number and age of churches at Hólar in Hjaltadalur since the Christianization of Iceland, in AM 220 8vo which was written in the second quarter of the seventeenth century by Björn Jónsson from Skarðsá. Árni Magnússon Institute in Iceland.

Carolingian script in the encyclopaedic *Rímbegla*, GKS 1812 IV 4to, from the late twelfth century. Árni Magnússon Institute in Iceland.

script throughout the world, with the position of French and English as world languages proving instrumental. Before the Germanic peoples were christianized they used runes, but it is unclear whether the runic alphabet originated from the Etruscan, Latin or Greek scripts.

Carolingian minuscule

The form of writing that reached Iceland in the eleventh century was *Carolingian minuscule*, named after the Emperor Charlemagne who reigned around 800. In his Empire, a new form of Roman script evolved and gradually spread through Roman Catholic Europe during the following centuries, with the exception of southern Italy. Around 1000 it was the dominant form of writing in Central Europe. It was also prevalent in Latin writings in England, but the Anglo-Saxons used *insular script* for vernacular writing until 1100. Icelanders and other West Norse speakers could not use Carolingian script without adapting it, since it lacked letters for the sounds that had to be represented. At first they adopted the letter 'þ' (*þorn*) from the Anglo-Saxons, who had originally taken it from their runic alphabet (in the Nordic languages, the rune was named *þurs*). They also devised the letter 'ǫ' to represent an open o-sound, and many scribes followed the recommendation of the First Grammarian and employed small capitals to represent a double consonant (e.g. 'N' and 'G' for nn and gg). Abbreviations of various kind were also common. Other common letters in the old script which have since disappeared include the tall s ('ſ') and r-rotunda ('(ꝛ)').

The specimen is from *Rímbegla* in GKS 1812 IV 4to (f. 31r), an encyclopaedic work written at the end of the twelfth century. The same scribe also wrote AM 249 l fol which contains a calendar.

manana . nett oc blezat ær harvð synd ær ætingar . ef
þat var heroulega neist oc langlega ráscat . En þav
ge er men gulltov full yanntagi sina . let ħ altozegn yið
ænvr ge . hellðe lagst ħ þav til bess . at þav hiv er yel
þory saman . oc varv gelavs mætti þa hellðe saman .
vera en aðe . oc yrbi þeim þat þa nocgt til sciolf . oc

Protogothic

Protogothic script in a manuscript of *The Life of St. Thorlak* (*Þorláks saga helga*), AM 383 I 4to, from the mid-thirteenth century. Árni Magnússon Institute in Iceland.

Carolingian script gradually became more compressed, and the letters became more slender and taller, until it eventually evolved into *Gothic script*. The intermediary stage between Carolingian minuscule and Gothic script has frequently been defined as a separate hand termed *Late Carolingian* or *Early Gothic*; some palaeographers now call it *Protogothic*. After beginning to evolve in northern France and England at the end of the eleventh century, it spread through the western part of the continent. It arrived in Iceland in the first half of the thirteenth century. Most of the oldest Icelandic manuscripts are written in this hand; only the very earliest ones are in pure Carolingian. As mentioned earlier, the letter 'þ' was adopted from Anglo-Saxon by Norse scribes at the start of the Age of Writing, and later they took 'ð' (with a hook, not a horizontal strike), 'ẜ' (i.e. f) and 'ꝩ' (i.e. v) from the same source.

The specimen is from *The Life of St. Thorlak* (*Þorláks saga helga*) in AM 383 I 4to (f. 2r), written in the mid-thirteenth century or shortly afterwards. The scribe is anonymous – like most in medieval times – but he was clearly experienced and confident.

Gothic Textualis

Carolingian minuscule developed into Protogothic and thence into *Gothic Textualis*. This transformation reflects the formal changes that took place in architecture: Carolingian script can be said to correspond to the Roman architectural style and Gothic script to Gothic architecture. With Gothic, sharp corners became more common, and pointed, angular letters replaced rounded and curved lines. Gothic writing was compressed, the letters taller and proportionally more slender and angular. After appearing in northern France towards the end of the twelfth century, Gothic Textualis spread through virtually

Gothic Textualis in *The Life of the Apostle Peter* (*Péturs saga postula*) in *Skarðsbók* postulasagna, SÁM 1, from the third quarter of the fourteenth century. Árni Magnússon Institute in Iceland.

the whole of western Europe (although it never established itself fully in Italy, where *Rotunda* prevailed, which as its name suggests is more rounded than the Central and Western European hand). Around 1300 or shortly afterwards *Gothic Textualis* reached Iceland and although it had largely been superseded by Gothic Hybrid early in the fifteenth century, it continued to be used until the sixteenth century.

The specimen is from *The Life of the Apostle Peter* (*Péturs saga postula*) in *Skarðsbók postulasagna* (SÁM 1) from the third quarter of the fourteenth century (f. 20r), and is thought to have been copied at the Helgafell monastery. The scribe is unknown but his writing can be seen in several other manuscripts, along with that of his brethren. 'p' does not occur in this manuscript, its use having been discontinued in the first half of the fourteenth century.

Gothic Cursive

The styles of writing described above were primarily bookhand, i.e. used for books but not so suitable for quick taking of notes. Cursive script appeared as early as in Roman times, but it always reflected the prevailing bookhand. No separate Cursive script appears to have developed alongside Carolingian, but when the Gothic influence began to increase, handwriting became more ornate and took correspondingly longer to render. At the same time, European society was becoming more complex and urban, universities were established, and increasing numbers of people learned to read and to express themselves and communicate in writing. *Gothic Cursive* appeared in England at the end of the twelfth century and was confined to documents at first, but as Textualis became more ornate in the fourteenth century, Cursive also began to be used in books. Cursive is lighter with joined letters; some letters extend below the line, which they very rarely do in bookhand, and the tall letters are often looped. This script reached Iceland in the first half of the fourteenth century. In Denmark, the Gothic Cursive period is divided into two parts: earlier (c.1250–1400) and later (c.1400–1550), but the later type was rarely used in Iceland, since Hybrid script was used for most documents by the fifteenth century.

The specimen is from a document, AM dipl isl fasc II 8, written on October 24, 1358 at Kvíabekkur in Ólafsfjörður. It was probably written by Þorsteinn Eyjólfsson, Lawspeaker from Urðir in Svarfaðardalur. 'ð' is not used in this document, having been discontinued in the second half of the fourteenth century. Another document has been preserved in the same hand, written on January 29, 1372 at Hvammur in Vatnsnes.

Gothic Cursive in a charter from 1358, AM dipl isl fasc II 8.
Árni Magnússon Institute in Iceland.

Gothic Hybrid

In the fourteenth century, as Gothic Textualis became more ornate and slower to write, a mix of Gothic Textualis and Cursive developed in the Rhine area. It is known as *Hybrid* or *Bastard*. Textualis and Cursive also merged in Iceland around 1400 and Gothic Hybrid was employed extensively until after the Reformation. Hybrid is more block-shaped than Cursive and the letters do not join as well, but it retains certain characteristics of the latter such as loops on tall letters. Icelandic Hybrid is a separate script and easily distinguished from the Scandinavian version.

Gothic Hybrid in a manuscript of *The Saga of Grettir the Strong* from the end of the fifteenth century, AM 556 a 4to.
Árni Magnússon Institute in Iceland.

New Gothic Cursive, earlier form, in a letter of complaint by Páll Jónsson from Staðarhóll, AM 249 c II 4to, 1558.
Árni Magnússon Institute in Iceland.

Below: AM 220 8vo. Árni Magnússon Institute in Iceland.

The specimen is from *The Saga of Grettir the Strong* (*Grettis saga*) in AM 556 a 4to (f. 46r) from the end of the fifteenth century. The scribe is unknown, but also he wrote AM 556 b 4to which was originally part of the same manuscript, and 556 a. On the final page of the manuscript is a note written at the end of the fifteenth century. Its scribe might have been Jón Arngrímsson; the same hand is found in a document written on May 17, 1494 at Hof in Vatnsdalur.

New Gothic Cursive, earlier form

During the Reformation Later Gothic Cursive evolved in Germany into what has been termed *New Gothic Cursive*. A more personal script, it makes different scribal hands from later centuries easier to distinguish than those from medieval times; one reason is that the position of the hand during writing changed around 1600. Until the Reformation, vellum was used for manuscripts, primarily calfskin. Paper was known in Iceland as early as the fifteenth century, but by the mid-sixteenth century it had become the norm and skin was used progressively less, although it was not discontinued until well into the seventeenth century. New Gothic Cursive arrived in Iceland immediately after the Reformation but was little used before the seventeenth century.

The specimen is from AM 249 c II 4to (f. 1r) from 1558, a draft or copy of a letter of complaint by Páll Jónsson from Staðarhóll in Saurbær (Staðarhóls-Páll) – in his own hand – to Royal Governor Páll Stígsson at Bessastaðir.

Icelandic script

Most Icelanders continued to use Gothic Hybrid after the Reformation, although foreign scribal fashions arrived. Writing continued to evolve and in the second half of the sixteenth century a distinctive form known as *Icelandic Script* appeared; it was used with other scripts until around 1700.

The specimen is from *The Annals*, a record of the number and age of churches at Hólar in Hjaltadalur since the Christianization of Iceland, in AM 220 8vo (f. 1r). It was written in the second quarter of the seventeenth century by Law Council member Björn Jónsson, a prolific copier of manuscripts and a known scholar in his day.

Fraktur

Fraktur evolved in Germany from Hybrid script in the second half of the fifteenth century and spread to the Nordic countries with the Reformation. It was also widespread as a print typeface. Outside Iceland it was rarely used for texts, but extensively in titles. It is common in both Icelandic and other manuscripts to have titles in Fraktur (or Chancery Fraktur which was not considered as sophisticated) but

Fraktur in Ásgeir Jónsson's manuscript of *The Saga of the People of Eyri* (*Eyrbyggja saga*), AM 448 4to, 1687-1688. Árni Magnússon Institute in Iceland.

the actual text in new Gothic Cursive. As the seventeenth century progressed and the wave of medieval manuscript copying began in Iceland, many scribes adopted Fraktur (or Icelandic script) because they did not feel it was proper to copy medieval script using cursive, which was primarily an everyday form of handwriting. Chancery Fraktur was used well into the eighteenth century in copies of earlier texts and titles. 'β' was the general symbol for *f* until almost 1700.

The specimen is from *The Saga of the People of Eyri* (*Eyrbyggja saga*) in AM 448 4to (f. 1r) from 1687-1688 in the hand of Ásgeir Jónsson, one of Iceland's most prolific scribes at the end of the seventeenth century. He was a scribe for the Royal Historian Þormóður Torfason, and he also copied manuscripts for Árni Magnússon.

New Gothic Cursive, later form

New Gothic Cursive evolved and by the mid-seventeenth century it had undergone such great changes that Danish palaeographers distinguish an earlier form until that time and a later form afterwards. The younger script reached Iceland in the second half of the seventeenth century and was used until the latter half of the nineteenth; in Icelandic it has been called *fljótaskrift* or "quick writing". Some German scholars classify new Gothic Cursive into three stages: *Renaissance script* in the sixteenth century, *Baroque script* in the seventeenth and first half of the eighteenth, and the final form used in the second half of the eighteenth and in the nineteenth.

The specimen is from the book of letters by the prolific scribe Jón Ólafsson from Grunnavík in AM 996 4to (f. 83v) from 1738. This letter is to sheriff Jón Benediktsson from Rauðaskriða in Skriðuhverfi.

Humanist Script

In late fourteenth-century Florence, attempts were made to create a new script in an effort to revive the art of bookmaking. The result was known as *Humanist Script*, since it spread through Europe with the

New Gothic Cursive, later form, in a book of letters by Jón Ólafsson from Grunnavík, AM 996 4to, 1738. Árni Magnússon Institute in Iceland.

![Handwritten Humanist script letter in Icelandic]

ðer seinasta ðip þann 12. þ. m., en eg hefi latið þetta dragast hvað eg gat, til þess að ðomast sem minnst í bága. Þú verður því að hafa einhver rað til að hjálpa uppá saðirnar, og það nú na strax; eg segi þer satt, að eg ðkyldi eðði ðvelja þig ef eg væri eðði neyddur til, en her dauðliggur mér á.

þinn
Jón Sigurðsson.

humanism of the Renaissance, and it is broadly based on Carolingian script. Gothic Textualis in its most pointed form never established itself firmly in Italy; the more rounded *Rotunda* was used there instead. Thus the scribal reform in Florence was not as radical a departure as might be assumed from a comparison with northern or central European Gothic Textualis. Humanist Bookhand (*Antiqua*) was mainly used for printing and has changed little in its 500-year history. Humanist Script (and typeface) spread throughout the Catholic world in the sixteenth century and then to England and the Netherlands, but new Gothic Cursive continued to be written in Germany and the Nordic countries until the nineteenth century (and in Germany into the twentieth century, in fact). Nonetheless, Humanist Cursive was used there for writing in Latin and the Romance languages. Latin or French loanwords in vernacular texts were written in Humanist and later so were all proper names, in printing as well as writing. The form of Humanist Cursive that replaced New Gothic Cursive in the Nordic countries in the nineteenth century was taught in Icelandic schools until 1985, when a variant of it, *Italic* handwriting, was introduced.

The specimen is from a letter by independence movement leader Jón Sigurðsson (in his own hand) to Professor Konráð Gíslason, dated May 26, 1856 from Gíslason's collection of letters, KG 32 (no. 228). Here, 'ð' has returned to Icelandic orthography, having been revived at the instigation of the Danish linguist Rasmus Rask in the first half of the nineteenth century.

Fym hundrud Dyra Oꝑ fiörm
tugu sva hygg ek Valhöll vera
atta hundrud einherria ganga ut
einom Dyrū ⸳ þeñ þa er þeir þara
at vitne at vega

heidm heiter geit er stendur hællu a
skapt ker hun fylla skal ins skira
miadar kna at su veig vanaz

heizmdallur

The re-creation of literature in manuscripts

SVERRIR TÓMASSON

Some Icelandic sagas contain signs that they have been rewritten. The younger version of *The Life of Saint Thorlak* (*Þorláks saga*) states for instance that the holy man had not been remembered as he deserved "for the tribulations and misdeeds" he had suffered from "his adversaries, who were committed to damaging the Church in his episcopacy". There is even a reference to the older version, which is called "the ancient presentation of the story". During the Middle Ages there existed at least three versions in the vernacular of the Life of Thomas à Becket, Archbishop of Canterbury (d. 1170). The oldest are probably composed around 1200, with one version seen in a manuscript dating from around 1400. Like the earlier version of *The Life of Saint Thorlak* it has been revised and the preface states outright that new times demand new stories. Both examples show that written narratives were sometimes extensively reworked; stories in books are continually changeable, just like those that are transmitted orally. Indeed, another shared feature with oral tradition is anonymous authorship. Each piece of rewriting therefore also aspires to a new role with a new audience.

One of the clearest examples of such rewriting is *The Saga of the Confederates*. This saga was probably first composed in the last quarter of the thirteenth century, and has been preserved in this form in *Möðruvallabók*, in all likelihood written in the mid-fourteenth century. *The Saga of the Confederates* is a satire on the lust for power and the greed of the chieftain class in the eleventh century. Some scholars have maintained that it accurately portrays Icelandic society at that time, but in fact reliable sources from that time are scarce; the chief authority about the eleventh century, *The Book of the Icelanders*, says little about disputes between individual chieftains and makes no mention of the main characters of *The Saga of the Confederates*, although they are all well known from other sagas. But the satire in *The Saga of the Confederates* is timeless and because the structure of Icelandic society remained largely unchanged for centuries, the saga could refer to the

Left: Two pages from the Long Edda, portraying Valhalla and the Midgard Serpent, AM 738 4to. Árni Magnússon Institute in Iceland.

Arngrímur Jónsson the Learned.

Icelandic society of any time. The writer of the other main version of the saga has taken advantage of this. In this version, which has been preserved in *Codex Regius* (GKS 2845 4to) and was written in the early fifteenth century, the storyteller makes several adjustments. The chief character, Odd Ofeigsson, grows rich from selling stockfish and his wealth is compared with that of the churches, even though such a parallel was only realistic in the fourteenth and fifteenth centuries. Such readings enhance the realism of the saga, while other narrative motifs such as sheep-rustling and avarice were realistic to Icelandic audiences then and in fact right up to the present day.

Marie De France was one of the best known twelfth-century French writers. Her work included a substantial number of poems about love. Some were translated into Old Norse prose in the first half of the thirteenth century under the title *Strengleikar*. In a famous prologue, Marie expects her readers to "explicate in lucid discourse" the words of wise old men of old; in other words to interpret the text, find its sense or meaning:

> It was the custom of wise and well-mannered men in olden days that they should set forth their learning, so to speak, in dark words and deep meanings for the sake of those who had not yet come, that these should explicate in lucid discourse that which their forbears had said and probe with intelligence whatever pertained to the elucidation and correct understanding.

Conceivably, sagas which exist in two versions are a product of this viewpoint: One version could be a new interpretation of old material, and the revised text would represent a different understanding of it which is then passed on to the audience. *Njal's Saga*, for example, exists in at least two versions. The one preserved in *Reykjabók* and *Kálfalækjarbók* contains several more verses than the version in *Möðruvallabók* and presents a somewhat different interpretation of the characters' behaviour. An example is the account of how Unn speaks of her husband Hrut when she tells her father, Mord, about their sex life. In the *Reykjabók* version, she answers Mord with a verse when he presses her to speak forthrightly about the problem between her and Hrut:

Certainly his flesh swells,
Hrut, that peg for rings,   *peg for rings: warrior*
when the spitting snake's bed seeks,   *spitting snake's (= serpent's) bed: warrior, i.e. Hrut*
wild-minded, pleasure's action;
I seek with the dispenser   *dispenser of snake-wounds: warrior*
of snake-wounds to find
our delight's trouble,
O aged profferer of shields!   *profferer of shields: warrior, i.e. Mord*

The verse may conceal a play on words involving "snake", which was certainly not difficult for a thirteenth- and fourteenth-century audience to understand, but it hides what the audience of Möðruvallabók heard said outright in Unn's answer:

> "When he comes close to me his flesh is so large that he can't have any satisfaction from me, and yet we've both tried every possible way to enjoy each other, but nothing works. By the time we part, however, he shows that he's just like other men."

This invites the conclusion that these two versions were written with a specific audience in mind. It is quite conceivable that the group supposed to listen to the *Reykjabók* version of *Njal's Saga* included children, while those who heard the saga from *Möðruvallabók* were accustomed to ecclesiastical vocabulary; "flesh" can hardly be said to be a well-known idiom for the male member in the thirteenth and fourteenth centuries.

It is rare for a textual interpretation to appear in remarks concerning the main text unless these are specially delimited or written in the margin. However, this did occur, with the best known examples being from the *Oddabók* manuscript of *Njal's Saga* (AM 466 4to). There, the enemies of Gunnar from Hlidarendi are called "sons of whores", and after Valgard the Grey has been buried, the scribe adds: "and may the devil take him." Another insertion can be cited from one manuscript of *Egil's Saga*, describing how Kveldulf kills King Harald Fair-Hair's emissary Hallvard Travel-Hard: "He tossed Hallvard into the air like a dog and slung him overboard like he was drowning a cat." Clearly the scribe thought these similes would meet with the approval of the audience.

The Saga of Havard from Isafjord (*Hávarðar saga Ísfirðings*) does not rank among the better known Sagas of Icelanders. It relates how Havard, despite his old age, manages to avenge his son; in effect the hero rises up from senility to dispatch his heroic duties. Transparently relying on few facts, the saga is largely woven according to the traditional pattern of such stories apart from reversing and parodying well known motifs. The point of view is not that of the chieftain, as was otherwise common in the Sagas of Icelanders, but rather of the ordinary man who needs to stand up for himself. It is thought to have been written in the fourteenth century but may in fact be a later work, perhaps even originating from the fifteenth or sixteenth centuries. The saga has only been preserved in seventeenth-century paper manuscripts, one of which says it is copied from "a very old *membrana*", i.e. a vellum book. One of the paper manuscripts (AM 552 o 4to) stands out from the rest, however. It was written by Ólafur Gíslason from Hof in Vopnafjörður, who spent some time in the service of Bishop Brynjólfur Sveinsson. Scholars have not managed to trace the original manuscript from which Ólafur Gíslason copied the saga, nor

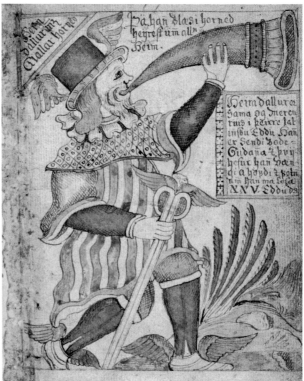

Left to right: Ull, son of Odin, on his skis.
Heimdall corresponds to the Roman Mercury in the Latin version
of the *Edda*.
Odin riding Sleipnir, the greatest of horses.
Thor in his regalia, holding the hammer Mjollnir in his grip of iron.
Loki son of Laufey, with his net.
From *Melsted's Edda*, SÁM 66. Árni Magnússon Institute in Iceland.

has it been demonstrated whether he added material himself or whether he relied on an original, since the version of *The Saga of Havard from Isafjord* in this manuscript differs considerably from the one that has been printed. An attempt was apparently made to correct what were considered to be discrepancies in the text, and make it conform to what was felt to be the truest version.

It is not entirely clear when the Sagas of Icelanders were first used as historical sources. Sturla Þórðarson may have been the first writer to do so in his *Book of Settlements*, and in the sixteenth century Arngrímur the Learned drew upon works such as *The Saga of Bard Snaefellsas* (*Bárðar saga Snæfellsáss*), *The Saga of Gunnlaug Serpent-Tongue* (*Gunnlaugs saga ormstungu*) and *The Saga of Ref the Sly* (*Króka-Refs saga*). He also cites *Flateyjarbók* and other prose literature as historical authorities. In the seventeenth century interest in the sagas as source material began to grow and Ólafur Gíslason's copy of *The Saga of Havard from Isafjord* may be an offshoot of that approach.

One version of *Egil's Saga* which has been preserved in three copies differs radically from the others. Árni Magnússon believed it must have been compiled in the seventeenth century and he favoured attributing it to Gísli Jónsson, a sorcerer from Melrakkadalur in Víðidalur, Húnavatnssýsla. It is uncertain when Gísli Jónsson was born but he is thought to have died in 1670. He is not rated highly by the scholars Páll Vídalín and Jón Ólafsson from Grunnavík, and Árni Magnússon actually labelled him an impostor. In terms of style and vocabulary, this version of *Egil's Saga* is very different from the familiar

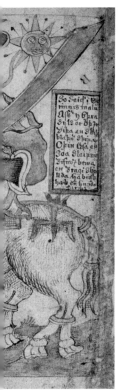

old one; the storyteller has incorporated some material from a metrical romance (*rímur*) by Jón Guðmundsson from Rauðseyjar, but his version also contains late loan-words, which are rare in Sagas of Icelanders. However, it is particularly at the end of the tale that the storyteller diverges significantly from the old plot of *Egil's Saga*. One account is of Egil's last hours; a horse "lay right across the door to the farm at Mosfell." The women there mentioned it, led the blind man to the horse and:

> He took hold of the horse's rear legs and tossed it in one throw out into the yard so that the guts burst out. There was a river running below the meadow. An islet was in the middle of the river with shrub on it. Egil said: "Is there nothing in the way now?" The women said there was not. Egil took hold of the horse's rear legs and threw it across the whole river and on to the bank on the other side. Egil said: "Where did it land?" The women said it had landed on the bank on the other side of the islet. Egil said: "I was aiming for the shrub with it." Egil went to his bed-closet and did not live for long afterwards. He died at Mosfell and was buried in a mound there.

This can be compared with the account from *Egil's Saga* in *Möðruvallabók*:

> The cattle at Mosfell were kept in a shieling, and Thordis stayed there while the General Assembly took place. One evening when everyone was going to bed at Mosfell, Egil called in two of Grim's slaves. He told them to fetch him a horse, "because I want to go to bathe in the pool." When he was ready he went out, taking his chests of silver with him. He mounted the horse, crossed the homefields to the slope that begins there, and disappeared. In the morning when all the people got up they saw Egil wandering around on the hill east of

Left: Eirik the Red in full battledress, from *Grönlandia* by Arngrímur Jónsson the Learned, printed in Skálholt in 1688.
Right: Ingolf Arnarson, first settler of Iceland, from *The Book of Settlements* (*Landnámabók*), printed in Skálholt in 1688.

the farm, leading a horse behind him. They went over to him and brought him home. But neither the slaves nor the chests of treasure ever returned, and there are many theories about where Egil hid his treasure ... In the autumn Egil caught the illness that eventually led to his death. When he died, Grim had his body dressed in fine clothes and taken over to Tjaldanes, where a mound was made that Egil was buried in along with his weapons and clothes.

These passages from the seventeenth-century *Egil's Saga* and *Egil's Saga* from *Möðruvallabók* have only three words in common: *horse*, *meadow* and *mound*.

It is uncertain whether this kind of story-telling began until the seventeenth century, but later on learned men began to write stories in the saga vein, drawing on genealogies and snippets of lore. One of the most prolific practitioners of this craft was the scholar Gísli Konráðsson (1787-1877). His work includes *The Saga of the Cave-Dwellers* (*Hellismanna saga*) which tells of disputes and slayings in the uplands of Borgarfjörður in the closing decades of the tenth century, drawing on *The Book of Settlements* and taking its cue from place names and folktales. The verse in the saga was composed by Gísli Konráðsson himself. He also wrote *The Saga of Helgi the Poet* (*Skáld-Helga saga*), and in the manuscript he says he composed it from the "old *rímur* about Helgi the Poet". He clearly tries to imitate the old sagas as closely as possible, the style is economical and largely free from the exaggeration that could be seen in the version of *Egil's Saga* attributed to Gísli Jónsson from Melrakkadalur. One clear example of this is the account when Halldor, the farmer from Holl in Thverarhlid, thinks Helgi is seducing his daughter:

> Shortly afterwards Halldor complained again about Helgi's visits and they argued fiercely. Helgi said he would determine for himself what he did. Halldor said: "I shall determine, Helgi, that you will never love each other and you will meet more seldom than you have, and thus repay you for the shame you have caused me and my daughter."
> "I shall pay little heed to your words and threats," Helgi said, and at that they parted ways.

Although it is not known exactly when Gísli Konráðsson wrote this saga, he did so before publication of the Sagas of Icelanders began to increase during and after the mid-nineteenth century. Several sagas were first printed in 1756 at Hólar in Hjaltadalur in the series *Some Wise Examples of the Icelanders' Sagas* (*Nokkrir margfróðir söguþættir Íslendinga*). The publication of this work may have prompted the composition of *rímur* based on the sagas. *The Saga of Havard*, for example, was retold in metrical form in the eighteenth century and there are seven *rímur* based on it from the same time or later. The first poet to do so who is known by name was Þorvaldur Magnússon (d. 1740). Prose narratives had been versified from early times, however. These include the *Rímur of Svold* (*Svöldrarrímur*) based on the battle of Svold in Olaf Tryggvason's Saga, *The Rímur of Sorli* (*Sörla rímur*) from *Sorli's Tale* (*Sörla þáttur*) which is preserved in *Flateyjarbók*, *The Rímur of Landres* (*Landrés rímur*) based an episode in one version of *The Saga of Charlemagne* (*Karlamagnús saga*), *The Rímur of Roland* (*Rollants rímur*) from the famous episode in the same saga, and so on and so forth. Prose and sagas were turned into *rímur* well into the nineteenth century and possibly even later. Chivalric and legendary sagas were the most common subject.

The poetic diction of the *rímur* is largely derived from *Snorra Edda* or the copies of it some of which proliferated after Magnús Ólafsson, minister at Laufás, translated *Snorra Edda* into Latin in the first half of the seventeenth century which was printed in a bilingual edition. Well known copies include those in *"The Long Edda"* (*Edda oblonga*, AM 738 4to) and *Melsted's Edda*. Both these books are lavishly illustrated and give a good idea of seventeenth- and eighteenth-century imagination as well as serving as handbooks of poetics.

One of the main influences that seventeenth-century humanism had on poetry was to increase the use of ancient poetic vocabulary and kennings – the diction became more scaldic in character, possibly even more than in earlier centuries. Mythological knowledge appears to have become more widespread; the audience is expected at least to

be as familiar with the old myths as it would have been in the past. Admittedly there is little evidence of the extent of mythological knowledge before the Reformation, apart from the manuscripts containing material from *Snorra Edda*. In many places in the *rímur*, however, the audience would appear to have been familiar with the myths. One example is the following verse that appears in *The Rímur of Sorli*, probably written in the fourteenth century and one of the oldest examples of this genre:

> Fire upon the tarred trees feasts,
> chewing men and swallowing beasts,
> the flame grew hungrier, greedier yet,
> devouring all that it could get.

This verse would have been incomprehensible to an audience unfamiliar with the account of the illusions that Utgarda-Loki used to deceive Loki and Thor when they visited him:

> The first was what Loki did. He was very hungry and ate fast, but the man called Logi was wildfire and he burned the trencher as quickly as he did the meat.

Indeed, the use of the old poetic diction became such a rigid convention in composing *rímur* that one poet would learn from others without necessarily having a handbook of poetics at his disposal. This convention extended well into the twentieth century and has helped to make the ancient poetry more readily comprehensible for modern readers.

More recently, *rímur* have rarely been composed although they are sometimes recited. Occasional attempts have been made to revive the form, with simplified diction. However, even well composed rímur have not achieved widespread popularity. On the other hand the prose works, the Sagas of Icelanders and sagas of kings, are a different matter. These genres are still widely read, although no one has tried to follow in Gísli Konráðsson's footsteps and write in this tradition – with the possible exception of Halldór Laxness, who in his *Happy Warriors* (*Gerpla*, 1952) takes the same approach as Marie de France with a personal interpretation of the ancient learning of *The Saga of the Sworn Brothers* and *The Saga of St. Olaf*.

Above: Grettir Asmundarson the Strong, from a seventeenth-century manuscript, AM 426 fol. Árni Magnússon Institute in Iceland.

Right: Njal Thorgeirsson, from a seventeenth-century manuscript, Lbs 3505 4to. National and University Library of Iceland.

Overleaf: Two elephants from a bestiary, AM 673 a 4to, c. 1200. Árni Magnússon Institute in Iceland.

Niäll.

Árni Magnússon

SIGURGEIR STEINGRÍMSSON

Þorlákur Skúlason and Brynjólfur Sveinsson, the respective Bishops of Hólar and Skálholt, began the extensive copying of Icelandic vellums onto paper before the middle of the seventeenth century. Manuscripts were being collected at that time and they were also sent abroad in some number. *Flateyjarbók* was sent from Iceland in 1656 and in autumn 1662 Thormod Torfæus set off from Engey near Reykjavík to present King Frederik III of Denmark with the *Codex Regius* of the eddic poems and the *Gráskinna* version of *Njal's Saga*. Just over a year after Torfæus left Iceland with the *Codex Regius*, Árni Magnússon was born. His parents were Magnús Jónsson, the minister at Kvennabrekka in the Dalir district, later local prosecutor and sheriff, and Guðrún Ketilsdóttir, daughter of archdeacon Ketill Jörundarson from Hvammur in Dalir and his wife Guðlaug Pálsdóttir. Little is known about Árni Magnússon's childhood and upbringing. He was brought up by his maternal grandparents at Hvammur and received his first education from his grandfather, after whose death in 1670 his maternal uncle, Páll Ketilsson, took over. In 1680 Árni Magnússon enrolled in the Skálholt school, where he spent the next three years. Several of his contemporaries there became his lifelong friends: Björn Þorleifsson, later Bishop of Hólar; Jón Halldórsson, later minister at Hítardalur; and Jón Þorkelsson Vídalín, later Bishop of Skálholt.

Icelandic manuscripts remained in great demand while Árni Magnússon was growing up. Many vellums ended up in the private collections of scholars and collectors in Denmark, often gifts from Icelanders who needed the assistance of respected figures in that country. King Frederik III died in 1670 and was succeeded by his son Christian V. He appointed Hannes Þorleifsson, the son of Þorleifur Kortsson, the magistrate at Þingeyrar, as his Keeper of Antiquities in 1681; his duties were historical writing and the collection of manuscripts for the royal archives. Hannes Þorleifsson went to Iceland in the summer of 1682, collected books there and returned to Denmark

Left: Árni Magnússon. Painting by the Rev. Hjalti Þorsteinsson, 1745.

Memo by Árni Magnússon on the history of manuscript collection.

De fatis Manuscriptorum Islandicorum
(On the fate of Icelandic manuscripts)

Magister Brynjólfur (i.e. Bishop Brynjófur Sveinsson) collected sagas and
    had them copied
Herra Þorlákur imo ante Brynolfum, ut puto
    (Bishop Þorlákur Skúlason likewise before Brynjólfur,
    I believe)
The late King Frederik III received a number of membranas (vellums)
The Swedes had Jón Rúgmann, and later Jón Eggertsson, buy Codices Is-
    landicos.
I, tandem, have collected that which I have been able.

that autumn on the ship from Höfði, taking with him what he had acquired. The ship sank on its way to Denmark, probably off Langanes, northeast Iceland, there were no survivors and nothing on board was recovered. Little is known of how much or precisely what Þorleifsson had managed to acquire during the weeks he spent in Iceland, but when Árni Magnússon later tried to trace what he had been given he was told that it was "a load of parchment book rubbish". The same summer that Hannes Þorleifsson was collecting manuscripts for the Danish king, Jón Eggertsson from Akrar in Skagafjörður was in Iceland too, on the same errand for the king of Sweden. He went about his task energetically and gathered dozens of manuscripts which he took with him to Sweden the following year. Among them were some of the most noteworthy Icelandic vellum books such as the *Homily Book* – the oldest Iceland manuscript preserved in its entirety, thought to date from c. 1200 – and *Helgastaðabók*, a beautifully illuminated fourteenth-century manuscript of *The Saga of St. Nicholas (Nikulás saga)*, which had once belonged to the church at Helgastaðir in Reykjadalur. Jón Eggertsson had intended to take the same ship as Hannes Þorleifsson, but changed his plans at the last moment, spent the winter in Iceland and went abroad in summer 1683.

Árni Magnússon completed the Skálholt school and left for

Copenhagen late in the same summer that Jón Eggertsson went abroad with what he had collected. He accompanied his father, Magnús, who by this time was the sheriff of Dalasýsla and was a member of a delegation going to Denmark to lobby for Icelandic trade interests. Árni Magnússon enrolled at the University of Copenhagen on September 25, 1683. Little is known of his studies in the following years, although he undoubtedly pursued them with his characteristic industriousness and devotion, and in 1685 he received a good degree in theology.

In 1684, the summer after he enrolled at the university, Árni Magnússon started working for Thomas Bartholin Junior. Although only four years older than Magnússon, Bartholin had completed his schooling ten years before him and had already been appointed professor when the Icelander arrived in Copenhagen. That February, Bartholin had been appointed Keeper of the Royal Antiquities after Hannes Þorleifsson and was now collecting and preparing for publication all the main writings of Danish and Nordic interest. On his urging the king prohibited the sale of Icelandic manuscripts out of the Kingdom in 1685. Bartholin had his assistants copy out all manner of writings and documents that he planned to use in his works, and Árni Magnússon joined him in this task alongside his studies.

The summer that Árni Magnússon graduated, 1685, he returned to Iceland to attend to his affairs, after his father's death the previous year. He was also supposed to look for manuscripts for Bartholin. Magnússon spent the summer with his relatives in Dalir. In the autumn he planned to leave on the ship from Rif, but it was wrecked in the harbour by a storm shortly before it was due to depart. All the other autumn ships had left and no passage abroad was to be had. Forced to stay the winter at Hvammur with his uncle Páll Ketilsson, Magnússon spent his time studying manuscripts and methods of copying them. Ketill Jörundsson, his grandfather, was a prolific copier and his uncle had also been a scribe. Árni Magnússon had therefore been familiar with the scholarly activities that were practised in Iceland since his childhood, but his acquaintance with Bartholin and the time spent working for him undoubtedly sharpened his awareness of the importance of collecting everything that could be found about Icelandic history and literature, and of preserving it for posterity. Although he did not bring Bartholin many manuscripts from Iceland after this stay, it is fairly certain that he began collecting privately around this time.

In the summer of 1686 Magnússon returned from Iceland to Copenhagen and resumed his work for Bartholin, which would occupy him for the next four years. As before, Árni Magnússon copied texts from ancient manuscripts and translated quotations from old

Brynjólfur biskup Sveinsson

Icelandic literature into Latin. One product of this work was *Antiquitatum Danicarum de causis contemptæ a Danis adhuc gentilibus mortis*, on the contempt for death shown by the Danes in times of old. Árni Magnússon assisted Bartholin in preparing this work for printing in 1689 and the book is more than 700 pages in length. Much of its content derives from Icelandic sources – sagas, eddic poems and skaldic verse – as well as other medieval writings. The quotations from old Icelandic are printed with a Latin translation, presumably made by Magnússon. Another task that he undertook for Bartholin during this period, along with other Icelanders, was to provide source material for a history of the Danish Church that Bartholin planned to write. All this material was collected in thick folios, most of which are still preserved in the Royal Library in Copenhagen. They contain copies from numerous manuscripts and all manner of documents from Denmark, Norway and Iceland. Among other things the Bartholinian volumes are valuable in that they preserve copies of manuscripts and printed books from the Danish University Library destroyed in the Great Fire of 1728. Alongside his work for Bartholin, Magnússon copied manuscripts privately, assisted by Icelandic students in Copenhagen; the copies included texts from Icelandic manuscripts in the University Library and from manuscripts from Danish officials' private collections, many of which he acquired on their deaths. This work greatly augmented Árni Magnússon's growing private collection.

In August 1689 Magnússon went to Norway on Bartholin's behalf to look for old manuscripts and copies of them in preparation for his ecclesiastical history, travelling as far north as Trondheim. On his way back he spent more than three months on the island of Karmøy just off Stavanger, staying at the manor Stangeland owned by Torfæus, whom he had first met in Copenhagen. The visit marked the beginning of a friendship and collaboration that would last for the rest of their lives. Magnússon provided Torfæus with immeasurable assistance in preparing and publishing his books over the next few years. After being appointed Royal Historian of Norway in 1682, Torfæus had taken with him most of the chief Icelandic vellums from the Royal Library in Copenhagen: the *Codex Regius* of the eddic poems, *Flateyjarbók* and many other manuscripts of sagas of kings. Furthermore, Torfæus owned a sizeable private collection. Magnússon studied the manuscripts that Torfæus had with him and copied extensively from his books. He returned to Copenhagen in February 1690, having acquired several more manuscripts for his collection.

The same year, Magnússon's work for Thomas Bartholin came to an abrupt end when Bartholin fell seriously ill and died on November 5, aged only 31. Magnússon spent the following winter in the service of Bartholin's brother Caspar, preparing Thomas's library for sale by

Left: Bishop Brynjólfur Sveinsson.
Illustration by Benedikt Gröndal, printed in the Collected Works of Torfhildur Hólm, 1949, prefacing her account of Bishop Brynjólfur.

auction the following summer. The collection contained several Icelandic manuscripts that Bartholin had owned, and Magnússon acquired them instead of having them auctioned. Among them was *Möðruvallabók*, the greatest medieval collection of Sagas of Icelanders, some of which are not preserved in their entirety anywhere else. These manuscripts were a valuable addition to his collection, which he sought to augment by every means at his disposal, and he never tired of asking the whereabouts of manuscripts in Iceland.

Subsequently, Magnússon came under the patronage of Matthias Moth. Moth was the brother of Soffia Amalia Moth, who became the mistress of King Christian V of Denmark in 1671 and had three daughters and two sons by him. One son was Ulrik Christian Gyldenløve, whom the king appointed Governor of Iceland when he was only six years old – a position he held until his death in 1719 although he never visited Iceland. Matthias Moth also benefited from his sister's connections. He abandoned a career in medicine in 1675 at Soffia Amalia's urging and in the following years was awarded numerous offices and sinecures, and proved to be a highly capable official. One office was that of Chief Secretary to the Danish and Norwegian departments of the Government of Denmark, making him a highly influential figure in the realm. Magnússon spent the next few years working as a librarian for Moth, although little else is known about what he did then. However, it is fair to assume that the connection with Moth marked the beginning of Magnússon's growing influence behind the scenes in various matters concerning Iceland over the next few years, for example when public offices were conferred. Magnússon also apparently undertook to publish the first volume of Bartholin's ecclesiastical history and earned some income for doing so for some years, even though nothing came of its publication.

In June 1694 the Council of the University of Copenhagen selected Árni Magnússon to visit Stettin in Germany to examine and assess a library there which orientalist Andreas Müller Greiffenhagen had invited the University to buy. Although the library was never purchased, Magnússon stayed longer in Germany than was originally planned, spending more than two years there and apparently mostly at the expense of Matthias Moth. From Stettin he went to Berlin and Frankfurt, and in the autumn he arrived in Leipzig, where he stayed almost without interruption until Christmas 1696, examining the city's library and manuscript collection and gathering written and historical information that he thought would prove useful for his antiquarian studies later.

Shortly after Árni Magnússon set off for Germany, on July 14, 1694, Moth secured him a letter from the king promising him a professorship at the University of Copenhagen, which was tantamount to a number in the queue for one of the posts that would later fall vacant. To improve his chances in the competition for a professorship, during his stay in Leipzig Magnússon published a slender volume containing *Incertis auctoris Chronica Danorum et præcipue Sialandiæ* or *Chronicle of Zealand*, one of the few works that he published in his lifetime. He had copied it, while still in Bartholin's service, from an old vellum which later perished with the rest of the University of Copenhagen Library in the fire of 1728.

Copenhagen 1697–1702

On returning to Copenhagen, Árni Magnússon had neither property nor income and accepted Matthias Moth's invitation to stay with him. Moth stood him in good stead as ever and secured him a post as secretary in the confidential document archive which was housed in the vault beneath Rosenborg Palace, an office which he retained for the rest of his life. Initially this was an unpaid appointment but undoubtedly entailed few duties. Despite his slender means in these years, Magnússon continued to add to his manuscript collection, with assistance from various quarters. His connection with Moth and thereby with the government of the realm unquestionably made people in Iceland more willing to acquire manuscripts on his behalf or provide him with vellums, in the hope of his support if they had cases to present to the authorities in Copenhagen. One example was Þórður Jónsson, the son of Jón Vigfússon, Bishop of Hólar. Jónsson travelled to Copenhagen in 1697 with a view to securing the bishopric of Skálholt which had fallen vacant then on the death of Bishop Þórður Þorláksson. He undoubtedly sought Árni Magnússon's support for his application and gave him manuscripts which included two noteworthy folios. One was the *Skarðsbók* version of *Jónsbók*, written around 1363 and the most ornately illustrated of all medieval Icelandic manuscripts. The other was the *Kálfalækjarbók* version of *Njal's Saga*, thought to have been written around 1300 sometime before *Skarðsbók* and now in a dirty and dog-eared condition. Þórður Jónsson did not become Bishop of Skálholt, but was granted the headmastership of the school there and held the post for three years. It was Jón Vídalín who obtained the episcopate in 1697 and Árni Magnússon was almost certainly instrumental in that appointment. At least, Vídalín had only been bishop for two years when he had all the vellum books and fragments found in the possession of the diocese of Skálholt sent to Árni Magnússon in Copenhagen. Among them were such treasures as the great manuscript of *Stjórn* (AM 227 fol.), which ranks with the most beautiful Icelandic medieval vellums, and both *Skálholtsbók* versions of *Jónsbók*.

Árni Magnússon corresponded with a number of people in

Þormóður Torfason - Torfæus.

Jón Vídalín, Bishop of Skálholt.

Iceland, seeking their assistance with his inquiries about old books and manuscript fragments, letters and documents, wherever they could be found, that he could buy or have donated, or borrow for copying if they were not for sale. In May 1698 he wrote to his friend Björn Þorleifsson, Bishop of Hólar:

> I thank you dearly for assenting to having copies made of such letters older than 1560 as you may chance upon in your visitations, and for giving me notitie of pergament books, both good and bad, or such fragments wherever and howsoever obtained, if this might befall. If any are found in the churches, Monfrere may safely take them on the mere pledge to the churches that they shall be returned meo periculo. En Fin, I am so meek in my demands that anything older than 1560, of whatever name, I shall regard as a thesaurum, no matter how little worth each item may be.

By this stage Magnússon had gained extensive knowledge of the books and documents that had been preserved in Iceland and a considerable number of them had come into his possession. In a letter to the Swede Johann Peringskiöld in 1699 he mentions that there was hardly a larger private collection of Icelandic vellums than his to be found anywhere in Europe. This was no exaggeration.

Christian V died in 1699 and was succeeded by his son Frederik IV. With the change of ruler Matthias Moth was removed from all his offices, costing Árni Magnússon a powerful supporter. Nonetheless, the new king provided well for Árni Magnússon. He was paid a fixed salary for his work at the confidential documents archive from 1700 and on October 22, 1701 the king appointed him to the Chair of Danish Antiquities at the University. As fate would have it, however, Magnússon spent most of the following ten years back in Iceland, as a special envoy of the king.

Land register 1702–1712

Tough farming conditions and persistent hardship had severely impoverished Iceland by the end of the seventeenth century. In 1700 the Althing petitioned the king and in autumn 1701 one of the two Lawspeakers, Lárus Gottrup, obtained a royal audience to present proposals for improving living conditions in Iceland. Among the measures that the king decided in consequence was to send envoys around Iceland with extensive powers to examine the situation and present further proposals for improvements. He selected Árni Magnússon and Páll Vídalín, deputy Lawspeaker, for the mission. They were issued with a letter of appointment dated May 22, 1702 and listing 30 duties. The main task assigned to them was to compile a land register for the whole of Iceland.

Árni Magnússon set off for Iceland immediately and on arriving in Hofsós on June 24, 1702 he went straight to meet Vídalín in Víðidalstunga. On July 18 both men were at the Althing and the following day their announcement of the land register was read out at the Law Council. They ordered landowners to make records of their property stating its value, rent and chattels, with a copy of deeds of ownership for the land, signed by witnesses. Records were to be submitted to the sheriff, who would deliver them to the next session of the Althing. The envoys were expected to finish compiling the register within two years or so. But it soon transpired that it would be impossible to compile a reliable land register in such a short time. They had planned to travel around the country themselves, summoning farmers and writing the register from their statements. With no roads, travel was only possible in the summer, and even then it was difficult and uncomfortable. Although they soon opted to work separately and employ assistants to gather material for the register in various districts, the task remained much more extensive than they had ever imagined and collection of source material for the register was not completed until June 1714, thirteen years after they had begun. The job was not made any quicker by a smallpox epidemic which raged in Iceland from 1707-1709 and claimed an estimated 18,000 lives – an enormous loss, amounting to 35% of this small nation's population. According to a census taken by Árni Magnússon and Páll Vídalín in winter 1702-1703 Iceland had just over 50,000 inhabitants. After the epidemic, only 32,000 were left in the whole country.

Once the collection of source material for the land register was completed in 1714, a great deal of work still remained to be done; it had to be put into presentable form and translated into Danish for the benefit of the authorities who had commissioned it. They expected Árni Magnússon to do this at his own expense but he repeatedly dodged the duty, and after his death his estate could not be disposed of until the dispute with the Exchequer was settled. This finally came about when the trustees had the register translated in 1742-1750.

Árni Magnússon and Páll Vídalín's land register is a remarkable source of information on conditions in Iceland in the beginning of the eighteenth century. Regrettably it is no longer preserved intact, because the registers from the Múli and Skaftafell districts perished in the fire of 1728. It was not until 1913-1943 that the register was published by the Society for Icelandic Studies (*Hið íslenska fræðafélag*) in Copenhagen, in eleven large volumes.

The land register and census were only two of many duties assigned to Árni Magnússon and Páll Vídalín in their royal letter of appointment. In effect there was virtually no aspect of conditions in Iceland and the royal administration that was not of concern to them. Their remit was to inspect the living standards of tenant farmers, investigate charges brought by ordinary people against officials of all ranks without discrimination, supervise trade and propose improve-

ments in the arrangements for conducting it, inspect the cathedrals and bishoprics, examine the conditions of schools, look at monastic properties, make a study of sulphur mining, prospect for workable minerals and metals, consider fishing reforms, and other matters too numerous to mention.

Their sweeping mandate to intervene in the affairs of Iceland and its people kindled widespread hopes that they could rectify much of the injustice that was rife, and they were swamped with complaints, charges and pleas from all directions. They tried to resolve the problems of as many people as possible. Their intervention in the functions of Lawspeakers and sheriffs, and their investigations of old criminal cases which had not been appropriately handled and efforts to conclude them as prescribed by law, aroused the opposition and enmity of local officials, leading to protracted legal proceedings which proved burdensome for the two envoys. The officials introduced complications into these cases and complained about Magnússon and Vídalín to the highest national authorities in Copenhagen, gradually undermining the confidence they had enjoyed there.

The criminal proceedings against farmer Jón Hreggviðsson from Rein are well known from Halldór Laxness' novel *The Bell of Iceland*. Suspected of manslaughter, Jón Hreggviðsson had been sentenced to execution in 1684. He escaped to the Netherlands and went from there to Denmark where he obtained a letter of passage from the king to return to Iceland, along with permission to take the case to the Supreme Court. However, the authorities in Iceland did nothing further about the matter. Magnússon and Vídalín reopened the case twenty years later, in 1708, in order to investigate the part played in it by Lawspeaker Sigurður Björnsson and bring it to a conclusion. Eventually, after prolonged disputes, the Supreme Court in Copenhagen cleared Jón Hreggviðsson of the murder charge in 1715, almost thirty years after he first came under suspicion. Nonetheless, the Supreme Court rejected the sentence passed by Magnússon and Vídalín against the Lawspeaker for official misconduct and found him not guilty as well.

While working on the land register in Iceland, Árni Magnússon stayed at Skálholt with his friend Bishop Jón Vídalín. Magnússon had taken virtually his entire manuscript collection with him to Iceland and he had plenty of time during the winters to work on it, write letters and inquire about old books and documents all over the country. One provision in their letter of appointment granted the envoys access to all documents in Iceland, without a doubt at Árni Magnússon's instigation. He had full-time scribes at Skálholt who copied out books and documents which he borrowed from all over Iceland. On his travels he was able to visit farmers whom he knew or believed to own books and fragments. In this way he sought out and saved many scraps of manuscripts which their owners considered worthless and would otherwise have been lost. From Dýrafjörður in the West Fjords, for example, he received two pages from a manuscript that had been written and illustrated in 1200, containing a fragment of a twelfth-century Icelandic translation of a Greek work of natural science, the *Physiologius*. The pages had gone astray in the West Fjords and been used for a meal sieve. They would hardly have lasted for long in that role, but today they rank with the Árni Magnússon Institute's greatest treasures.

Árni Magnússon left Iceland twice during the period he was working on the land register. His first trip was in winter 1705-1706 when he was called back to present his and Vídalín's proposals for trading arrangements in Iceland. The other occasion was when he spent the winter of 1708-1709 in Copenhagen in connection with various matters and legal cases in which the envoys were involved. On that trip he married a Danish woman, Mette Jensdatter Fischer, on May 16, 1709. Árni Magnússon was 45 when he married, and his bride 19 years older. She was the widow of the Royal Saddlemaker, Hans Wichmand, who had died in 1707; the couple had lived by the square near the royal palace. Jón Ólafsson from Grunnavík recounts that Árni Magnússon knew the couple and sometimes called in to drink morning tea with them on his way to the archive. Little else is known about Mette Magnússon, but she owned a considerable amount of property when they married.

In the autumn of 1709 Árni Magnússon returned to Iceland and did not see his wife again for more than three years. Two letters that he wrote to her from Iceland have been preserved, mainly dealing with their finances and errands that he asked her to undertake for him: to buy paper and ink, shoes and shirts, coffee, tea and sugar, French spirits, medicinal preparations and rosewater, shaving soap, a peruke and hair powder. From Iceland he sent eiderdown, barrels of salted meat and woollen socks for his wife to give to his friends in Copenhagen. One letter from Mette to Árni Magnússon has been preserved, dated April 4, 1712. In it she tells her husband about the epidemic that raged in Copenhagen from the summer of 1711 to the following spring and sent 30 thousand people – one-third of the city's population – to their graves, including two of their maidservants: "God on high has visited us with a merciful and goodly pestilence," she wrote to him.

By 1712 the authorities felt that the land register had taken long enough and called Árni Magnússon back to Copenhagen. Yet another war had broken out between Denmark and Sweden, making it dangerous to sail there. Unwilling to risk taking his manuscript collection

King Frederik III of Denmark.

King Frederik IV of Denmark.

by sea during the hostilities, Árni Magnússon stored it along with the land register documents in chests which were kept at Skálholt for the next eight years. In September 1712 he left Iceland, never to return. It was a difficult crossing and Magnússon only got as far as Norway. He spent the winter there with his friend Thormod Torfæus and finally reached Copenhagen in March 1713.

1712–1728

Magnússon's return to Copenhagen marked the beginning of fifteen years in which his life followed a fairly regular routine. His days were spent on official duties and studying manuscripts, and he and his wife were well off and they were able to live in the style appropriate to their rank and station. In 1714 they moved into one of the university's professorial residences on Store-Kannikestræde. Árni Magnússon's house was probably a two-storey timber-framed house, set in large grounds where there were outhouses that served as homes for the household staff and as a food store, since the university paid part of the professor's salary in kind with produce from its farmland.

In Copenhagen, Magnússon resumed his former work that had been waiting for him while he was in Iceland. This included his secretarial duties at the confidential documents archive, which was transferred from the vault beneath Rosenborg palace to a new building on Castle Island in spring 1720. Just over four years later, in the New Year of 1725, Frederik Rostgaard, the keeper of the archive and Árni Magnússon's good friend, fell from royal favour and was immediately stripped of all his offices. Árni Magnússon was given the keys to the archive and supervised it for the rest of his life without being formally appointed its keeper.

At the university, Magnússon could finally devote himself to his professorial duties. Little is known about his teaching and there are no records that he ever gave lectures at the university. But he did give tutorials to almost two hundred students, a form of teaching that probably suited him better. He appears to have avoided administrative duties on behalf of the university, although in 1720 he was appointed supervisor of the Ehlers student residence which is two doors down Store-Kannikestræde from where his own house stood.

Magnússon was already familiar with the University Library but in 1721 he was appointed deputy librarian and he may have been assigned to run it in 1725. This meant he was a frequent visitor to the library in the loft of Trinity Church until it burned down in 1728.

Furthermore, Árni Magnússon resumed collecting and studying manuscripts and employed scribes as before to copy books and documents from other collections while waiting for his own to arrive from Iceland. In the autumn of 1720, all the land register documents and the private manuscript collection that had been stored at Skálholt after he left Iceland in 1712 were transported, in fifty-five chests carried by thirty horses, to Hafnarfjörður. There the chests were put on board a Royal Danish Navy frigate under the command of the new governor of Iceland, Admiral Raben, who took them to Copenhagen. Various formalities delayed the manuscripts from being delivered to Árni Magnússon until February 1721, when at long last he was able to arrange them in his residence on Store-Kannikestræde. The best known of Magnússon's scribes in Copenhagen was Jón Ólafsson from Grunnavík, who joined him in 1726. He was his scribe until Magnússon's death, whereupon he worked at the Arnamagnæan Institute for most of the time until his death in 1779.

The Great Fire of 1728

At this time Copenhagen was a fortified city enclosed by walls and canals, accessible only through the four gates of Vesterport, Nørreport, Østerport and Amagerport. Inside the walls, the city was crowded with narrow streets. The oldest part was around Gamletorg where the City Hall stood; above Nørregade was the Church of Our Lady with the university campus opposite it. Most buildings were largely timber-framed. The summer of 1728 was warm and dry and the good weather lasted until well into the autumn. On the evening of Wednesday, October 20, a fire broke out in a building by Vesterport, setting off a conflagration which lasted until the following Saturday and destroyed a large part of the city, including the entire university campus and professorial residences in the vicinity, several of the main churches including the Church of Our Lady and Trinity Church – and with the latter the University Library in its loft – as well as hundreds of other buildings and houses. Jón Ólafsson wrote an account of the fire shortly after the catastrophe struck, describing how many aspects of the fire-fighting were apparently bungled at first. The fire brigade had difficulty in bringing in pumps through the crowds that filled the narrow streets in the quarter. Water was also scarce; the supply had been cut off in the parts of the city where the fire blazed, due to work at Peblings Lake. When an attempt was then made to fetch water from the canals outside the city walls, the military commander in the city had the gates closed to prevent this from being done, because he feared desertion by conscripts. There was a strong southwesterly wind and the timber-framed buildings were parched after the warm summer. Everything combined to make the conflagration spread quickly. Eventually, the fire-fighting was reorganized and, with the help of thousands of soldiers and sailors from the city garrison and fleet, the authorities managed to extinguish the fire early on the Saturday morning. Jón Ólafsson writes that Árni Magnússon's residence burned down around four o'clock on the Thursday afternoon. When Magnússon heard on the Thursday morning that the spire of The Church of Our Lady had collapsed and the fire would clearly not be contained he began trying to rescue his library with the help of his servants and two Icelanders: his scribe Jón Ólafsson, and Finnur Jónsson, who later became bishop at Skálholt but was then a student in Copenhagen. They piled books and furniture into a carriage and eventually his coachman managed to force his way through the crowds in the streets with three or four loads across the town to the house of Hans Becker, a timber merchant who had worked as a scribe for Magnússon while the land register was being compiled in Iceland and for several years afterwards, and who now provided his old master with a roof over his head.

Árni Magnússon's last days

The full extent of the damage to Árni Magnússon's manuscript collection will never be known. He never took the time himself to make exhaustive inventories of his manuscripts, documents and books, so the size of his collection before the Great Fire is not clear. For the short remainder of his life he lived in straitened circumstances and could never arrange his collection to gain a picture of what had been rescued. He believed the damage was greater than subsequent studies have suggested, and he made frequent reference to this opinion in the letters he wrote back to Iceland in the year after the fire. In one of them, however, he admitted that he had managed to rescue most of his books of sagas, and it is now held for certain that the oldest and most valuable core of the collection, the ancient vellum books, escaped with only a handful perishing. Nonetheless, a great assortment of documents were destroyed, paper copies from older books and various writings by Árni Magnússon himself, which he had spent a long time compiling from sources that are now lost. The greatest damage was to his printed books, the majority of which were lost in the fire. Most professors at the University of Copenhagen lost all their books in the fire and the entire University Library perished as well. The rescue of Árni Magnússon's collection from the conflagration on those dark autumn days in 1728 was therefore a unique event in more than one sense.

Árni Magnússon lived only just over a year after the Great Fire. The ensuing winter was harsh, with heavy frosts at the same time as housing and all necessities were scarce. Like many others, Magnússon was homeless and had to move three times in that single year. On Christmas Eve 1729 he fell ill and it was obvious that he would not survive. On January 6, 1730 he was so weak that when State Counsellor Thomas Bartholin, the grandson of the namesake Árni

Magnússon had worked for during his first years in Copenhagen, and Assessor Hans Gram visited him to write a will for him and his wife, he could not sign it unassisted.

On the morning of January 7, 1730, at a quarter to six in the morning, Árni Magnússon died in his sixty-seventh year. On January 12 he was buried in the north choir of the Church of Our Lady, which was still a gaping ruin after the fire. His wife Mette died in September that year and was laid to rest by her husband's side.

RUNIR
Seu
DANICA
LITERATURA
ANTIQVISSIMA,
Vulgò GOTHICA dicta
luci reddita

Opera

OLAI WORMII D.
Medicinæ in Academia
Hafniensi Profess. P.

Cui accessit

DE PRISCA DANORUM POESI
DISSERTATIO.
Editio secunda auctior & locupletior.

HAFNIÆ,
Imprimebat Melch: Martzan, *suis &* Georg: Holst *sumptibus,*
ANNO, M.DC.LI.

The Nordic demand for Medieval Icelandic manuscripts

MATS MALM

In the 1600s an intensive interest arose in Nordic countries in the medieval Icelandic manuscripts. While there had been continuous contact between Iceland and Norway throughout the Middle Ages, it was now primarily in Denmark and Sweden that the spotlight was focused on these manuscripts. These were the two major political actors with the needs and resources to promote their nations' supremacy. Interest in the manuscripts was, if the truth be told, to a great extent motivated by nationalistic interests. It was in the interest of both Denmark and Sweden to show that their respective nation was the most "genuine", the one most closely related to the ancient Goths – the people who once had brought the mighty Rome to its knees. While at the same time jointly endeavouring to re-establish the Nordic reputation in the surrounding world, they competed with each other as to what extent Denmark or Sweden was true heir to the Nordic heritage. The conflict could at times become quite heated, especially since Denmark and Sweden were repeatedly at war with one another.

The Nordic historical source which was most accessible for learned Europeans was the *Gesta Danorum* written by Saxo Grammaticus near the beginning of the thirteenth century. His chronicle of the Danes' exploits was written in a Latin which was clearly more stylistically polished than the usual medieval Latin, and drew the praise of Erasmus of Rotterdam himself. *Gesta Danorum* was printed for the first time in Paris in 1514 and translated into Danish in 1575. This made *Gesta Danorum* learned Europe's first encounter with a Nordic source on Nordic history. During the 1600s, however, Danish and Swedish scholars eagerly studied the Old Icelandic writings.

While Saxo himself had praised the Icelanders' great knowledge of Nordic history, the picture of Iceland presented in learned works during the 1500s was less flattering. Arngrímur Jónsson, one of the Icelanders studying in Copenhagen during that century, felt compelled

Left: Title page of Literatura Runica, 2nd ed. 1651.

Ole Worm.

to present a more positive picture of Iceland and published his reply, *Brevis commentarius de Islandia*, in 1593. This work, together with several others by Arngrímur, contributed greatly to awakening interest in Iceland and Icelandic manuscripts as historical sources – not least when Arngrímur in a later work presented an Icelandic runic alphabet and maintained that people in Iceland had preserved the language which once had been shared by all the Nordic countries. Sections of Snorri Sturluson's history of the Norwegian kings, *Heimskringla*, appeared in Danish translation as early as 1594 and another translation was published in 1633. Danish scholars and statesmen had realised that the Icelandic manuscripts were of national interest and the contacts between Copenhagen and Iceland were intensified. In Iceland it was primarily the bishop Brynjólfur Sveinsson who collected manuscripts, many of which he passed on to Copenhagen. In 1640, the Dane Stephanus Stephanius received a manuscript of *Snorra Edda*, and around 1660 Bishop Brynjólfur sent the Danish King Fredrik III works including the compendium of kings' sagas *Flateyjarbók*, the collection of laws known as *Grágás* and the manuscript *Codex Regius*, containing the poems of the *Elder* or *Poetic Edda*.

A central figure in this activity was Ole Worm, the man behind the 1633 translation of *Heimskringla*. He worked closely with both Arngrímur and Brynjólfur, who sent him a number of manuscripts, not the least of which was a version of the *Snorra Edda* and related works now known as *Codex Wormianus*. Worm expected the Icelanders to be able to help him in interpreting the Danish runic inscriptions, but runes were not the writing system in which the Icelandic literature was preserved. The language of the runic inscriptions did, however, resemble very closely that of the Icelandic manuscripts, so that the co-operation did bring results. Worm was very determined to link the runes with the Old Icelandic literature and his great work *Runer* or *Literatura Runica* of 1636 includes Egil Skallagrímsson's *Head Ransom* (*Höfuðlausn*), and the death song of Ragnar Loðbrók in the snake pit (*Krákumál*), printed in runes, something which never occurs in any manuscript. Contemporary Europe of the time was fascinated by Egyptian hieroglyphics, to which magical import and occult knowledge were ascribed. For Worm this was one way to promote the highly developed culture and knowledge of the ancient north. He explained the runes in a manner which made them a Nordic variant of the hieroglyphs.

Literatura Runica would become highly influential. Even in our time we still see pictures of Vikings drinking mead from a human skull – an image dating back to a misinterpretation of a passage in *Krákumál*, stating that men drank *ór bjúgviðum hausa*. Worm's translation of this was *concavis crateribus craniorum*: "hollowed-out goblets of skulls", while the meaning is actually that men drink from the "bent trees of heads", in other words, drinking horns. *Literatura Runica* was of major significance for contemporary culture, partly because it was the first major work on runes, and partly because it presented the runes and ancient Nordic culture as a specifically Danish phenomenon, greatly provoking Swedish antiquarians.

Brynjólfur Sveinsson had also made a present to the Danish king of a manuscript of *Snorra Edda* and arranged the editing of a more easily accessible version of *Snorra Edda*. This was published in 1665 by Peder Resen, with a Danish and Latin translation, as *Edda Islandorum*. The publication was prefaced with a long introduction where Nordic ethics were given a position in the world's culture. Resen also concurrently published the *Sibyl's Prophecy* (*Völuspá*) and the *Words of the High One* (*Hávamál*), the latter translated as *Ethica Odini*, "Odin's ethics". In other words, it was not the search for historical facts which prompted this publication, but rather an interest in the world view and morals of the ancient northerners. A similar interest lay behind Thomas Bartholin's major work on the causes of the ancient Danes' scorn of death, *Antiqvitatum danicarum de causis contemptae a danis adhuc gentilibus mortis libri tres*, in 1689. This work too can be understood in the light of the enmity of the time between Denmark and Sweden: in it Bartholin highlights a Danish fighting spirit which almost certainly was intended to strengthen Danish courage against the Swedish enemy.

It was partly in co-operation with Bartholin that Árni Magnússon managed to undertake his invaluable collecting and copying of Icelandic manuscripts. From 1620 onwards Icelanders had been in frequent contact with Danish scholars and passed on manuscripts, but Magnússon's appointment as amanuensis for Bartholin would lay the foundation for the magnificent Arnamagnaean Collection. The great fire of Copenhagen in 1728 destroyed significant portions of his life's work, but most of it could be saved.

Bartholin was, in other words, seeking the ancient northmen's character and outlook on life, which he wanted to portray as typically Danish, but Árni Magnússon dealt with the quality of the Icelandic sources as sources for historical events. An important partner in this discussion was Þormóður Torfason, who for many years worked on a royal register of the Danish rulers, *Series Dynastarum et Regum Daniae*. When this work was finally available in print in 1702, a balance had been achieved between Magnússon's demands for historical criticism, on the one hand, and patriotic interest on the other, since the temptation was to use even sagas whose content was of doubtful veracity to exalt Denmark's prominence over Sweden.

The publication of Old Icelandic texts in Denmark during the

Title page of *Nordiska kämpa dater*, 1737.

EDDA SÆMUNDAR HINNS FRÓDA.

EDDA
RHYTHMICA SEU ANTIQVIOR,
VULGO SÆMUNDINA DICTA.

PARS I.

ODAS MYTHOLOGICAS, A *RESENIO* NON EDITAS,
CONTINENS.

EX CODICE BIBLIOTHECÆ REGIÆ HAFNIENSIS PERGAMENO, NEC
NON DIVERSIS LEGATI ARNA-MAGNÆANI ET ALIORUM
MEMBRANEIS CHARTACEISQVE MELIORIS
NOTÆ MANUSCRIPTIS.

CUM INTERPRETATIONE LATINA, LECTIONIBUS VARIIS, NOTIS,
GLOSSARIO VOCUM ET INDICE RERUM.

HAFNIÆ 1787.

SUMTIBUS LEGATI MAGNÆANI ET GYLDENDALII.
Lipsiæ apud Proftium in Commiſſir.

Title page of *Saemund's Edda* (*Sæmundar Edda*), Vol I, 1787.

1600s was thus not especially comprehensive. There were translations of the sources of leading importance for Danish history and they were used for historiography, but the emphasis was to a great extent on investigations of the language, runes and culture. A strong interest in the history of mentalities is given expression in works by Resen and Bartholin – it is the ancient northerners' character and world views which are dealt with.

In Sweden developments followed a different route. The political successes of Sweden's era as a great power demanded an historical legitimation, and Sweden's role in *Gesta Danorum* and *Heimskringla* was neither as illustrious nor as prominent as that of Denmark. The need for other sources for Swedish history was great, and it was in Sweden that the publication of source texts really made progress.

Leading the way in the 1600s was Johannes Bureus, a mystic who at an early age was fascinated by runes and the ancient "Gauts". Bureus, however, was not just an enthusiast. He laid a scholarly foundation for later times and his investigations have earned him the name "the father of Swedish philology". "The father of Swedish poetic art", Georg Stiernhielm, inherited his inspiration. Stiernhielm's efforts in language history were directed at showing how Swedish was the language most closely related to the ancient Nordic language and how this was, in fact, the most original of all languages, the one closest to the true, God-given, designations. It was this programme he was implementing in practice with his poem *Hercules* in 1658, while little of his scholarly production was ever printed. Its patriotism was strikingly evident, and would set its mark on subsequent Swedish scholarship.

It was in the 1660s that Icelandic sagas began to be published in Sweden. The sagas then translated were mythical-heroic sagas (*fornaldarsögur*), which were significantly less well anchored in reality than the sagas of kings or Sagas of Icelanders. The reason would seem to have been that Sweden figures more prominently in the mythical-heroic sagas. They thus served as sources for Swedish history, despite the fact that Sweden is often presented as a slightly backward region, full of supernatural occurrences. The first saga to be printed was *The Saga of Gautrek* (*Gautreks saga*), which appeared in 1664 and to start with is a pure parody of the people of the Västergötaland area of Sweden. But it is here that the description of a family suicidal precipice occurs, a description which recalled Plato's report on how the people of ancient Atlantis sometimes committed suicide by throwing themselves off a cliff. The Atlantans had done so because they felt satisfied and finished with their lives, while the West Gauts did this because they were miserly idiots, intending to avoid losing so much as an ounce of their riches, but the similarity was great enough. The saga could serve as proof that Sweden during its era of great power was in fact the great world power Atlantis, which had not sunk into the ocean at all – Atlantis had in fact not been flooded by the ocean's waves but by migrating hordes.

Since Iceland was under Danish rule, the Swedish scholars did not have the same opportunities to acquire manuscripts, but they did eventually acquire a significant number. Not least significantly, Magnus Gabriel de la Gardie managed to purchase the library of Stephanius. The latter's widow had been instructed not to dispose of his manuscripts, but was clearly suffering financial difficulties, and as a result the manuscript of *Snorra Edda*, now known as the 'Uppsala Edda', ended up in Sweden. In 1658 a vessel on its way to Copenhagen was captured, aboard which was the young Icelander Jón Rúgmann. He was first taken to Visingsborg and then to Uppsala, where he became a very important figure in Swedish publication activity. On his voyage he had taken the manuscripts of several of the sagas which would be published in the 1660s and 1670s, such as *The Saga of Herraud and Bosi* (*Herrauðs saga og Bósa*) and *The Saga of Hervor* (*Hervarar saga*).

It was Olof Verelius who would be responsible for the first Swedish saga publications. He was aided by Olof Rudbeck in drawing a map for *The Saga of Hervor*. The saga was published in a magnificent folio edition in 1672, but Rudbeck had been captured for life by Sweden's glorious past. During the final three decades of the 1600s he published what is unquestionably the greatest monument to Gothicism: *Atland, eller Manhem*. Its core concept was that Sweden was the cradle of civilisation, the country that had once, for example, been known as Atlantis. In support of this Rudbeck interpreted Greek mythology as a twisted retelling of Swedish history: the original name of the hero Hercules was Här-kuller, the renowned Thebes was in fact Täby near Uppsala and the Peloponnessos took its name from Pelle på näset. Naturally, Rudbeck does have some difficulties in justifying his interpretations but he uses Old Norse poetry in a highly creative fashion for help, not as a source but as a guide to method. He points to Snorri Sturluson's definition of the *kennings* of skaldic poetry. A kenning is usually a circumlocution, with a characterisation which explains what the actual meaning is. It is impossible to understand that the word "horse" is a poetic image for "ship" until you have the entire kenning: "horse of the waves". Then the circumlocution can be interpreted in its proper context, enabling us to understand what it actually means. The myths, claims Rudbeck, function in the same way. Plato says that there were elephants in Atlantis, which could be regarded as evidence that Sweden and Atlantis are not the same thing, since no elephants are found in Sweden. But if we, following Snorri's instructions, treat an elephant as a circumlocution and interpret it properly based on the context (Swedish nature), one must realise that an ele-

Title page of *The Saga of Herraud and Bosi* (*Herrauðs saga og Bósa*), 1666.

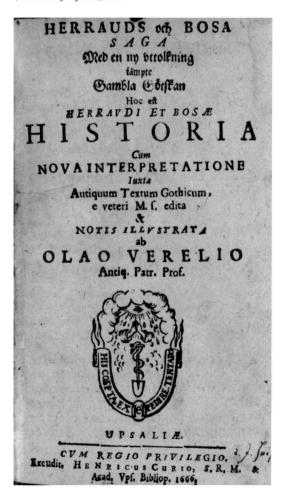

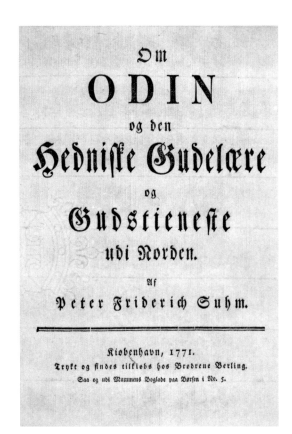

Title page of *Om Odin og den hedniske Gudelære*
(Odin and the heathen mythology), 1771.

phant actually means a wolf – which are of course found in Sweden! Thus Sweden is Atlantis, and Snorri Sturluson's poetical principles have been developed into historiographical principles.

In Rudbeck's treatment a number of other remarkable contributions to Sweden's glorious past are developed. The most spectacular is perhaps a saga forgery, which was printed in 1690 and again in 1710. The manuscript of *Hialmars och Ramers saga*, as it was called, was said to have been written in runes and the publication recreates the "original" in runic letters with Swedish translation. Hialmar and Ramer are conquered in Sweden by a powerful Olaf, reminiscent of Olaf Skautkonung who liberated Sweden from idolatry. The falsification, in other words, authenticates Sweden's importance for the establishment of Christianity in the Nordic countries, while at the same time the runic writing is to be understood against the background of Worm's claim that the runes prove that Denmark's culture is the most original. A contemporary commented on the saga as: "a prize document against the Danish, who claim for themselves the first occurrence of runes and [maintain] that our stories have never been written in runic scripts."

In Sweden, historiographers such as Johannes Loccenius and Johannes Messenius had made good use of Danish translations of *Heimskringla*, but in 1670 a Swedish translation was published thanks to Jón Rúgmann. Oddur the Monk's *Saga of King Olaf Tryggvason* was also published, but Johan Peringskiöld's splendid two-volume edition of *Heimskringla* in 1697-1700, translated by Guðmundur Ólafsson, far outshone all previous works. Quite a number of other sagas were also published in the early 1700s. Olof Rudbeck seems to have been planning to issue a collection of sagas, a *Corpus historiarum islandicarum*, but the fire in Uppsala in 1702 put a stop to his plans.

Publication of Old Icelandic texts in the 1600s was thus dominated by Sweden, but during the 1700s the situation changed. The most forceful Swedish chauvinism was not entirely compatible with Enlightenment ideas. When Erik Julius Biörner published a major collection of translations of mythical sagas, *Nordiska kämpa dater*, in 1737, his attempt to promote the northerners' heroic temperament was regarded as ludicrous. With the romantics of the early 1800s the picture changed once more. Erik Gustaf Geijer wrote Old Norse-inspired poems and Esaias Tegnér retold *Frithiofs saga* in poetic form. He had discovered the saga in Biörner's *Nordiska kämpa dater* and employed a number of Old Norse verse forms in this romantic undertaking, which would become highly popular even beyond the borders of Sweden.

In the Danish area, the Romantic era meant a similar upswing for Old Norse. The central figure here was N.F.S. Grundtvig, who made

Old Norse culture a central pillar of folk education. But in Denmark publication gained speed during the latter half of the 1700s. The Arnamagnean Commission was established in 1772 and a series of editions and translations of such varied texts as *Njal's Saga*, *The Saga of Christianity*, *The Saga of Gunnlaug Serpent-Tongue*, *Hungurvaka*, *The Saga of the Orkney Islanders*, *Rímbegla*, *The Saga of Hervor* and *Viga-Glum's Saga* were now published. During the years 1787-1818 the Commission published its large edition of the *Poetic Edda* and the philology was developed substantially.

The passion of the Romantic era for Old Norse was thus well grounded in scholarship, both through publishing and the refined philology. It was during the Romantic era that Old Icelandic culture came to exert a serious influence on literature written in the Nordic countries. The Eddas had been translated several times and their style as well as their spirit and content would inspire poets. Nevertheless, the Nordic countries were, when it came down to it, slower than England, Germany and other countries to see Old Norse as a literary ideal. During the closing years of the 1700s the "Nordic renaissance" had, in fact, swept across Europe. In England James Macpherson wrote fake Old Celtic works and Thomas Gray composed poems inspired by Old Norse, while in Germany J. G. Herder launched Old Norse poetry as a truly important poetic form. Not until this had happened elsewhere in Europe was the time ripe for Nordic poetry to become really inspired by the Old Icelandic literature.

The Danish and Swedish hunting for Icelandic manuscripts was an imperialist phenomenon and caused no small amount of loss, primarily through the Copenhagen fire and the loss of a ship on its way to the Danish capital with manuscripts. But it also meant that the manuscripts were collected and preserved to an extent which can be assumed to be greater than would have been the case if people had not, at that point in time, become interested in sources of historical knowledge on the Nordic countries and peoples.

Ár var alda
þá er endurborin
fold in fjall setta
í fyrsta sinn
velkast bók vol
um vegu ókunna
at orði alvalds,
sem all um skóp –

2. Sveipud saman
in hvasa Nótt
í ægisfaldi
þá er alfröðull
hvíglega höfst
um of heiðar brún,

helón hlífar
við himin-ljósi.

3. Þá var gaman
er um grænan dal
fella fagrar ær
fiskum hvísar
en itur fagur
í eirar-boð
saung svanaflockur
sa tum rómi.

4. Unap óþecktum
oc undran fylltur
magur in fyrsti
und meibi ham
en saman flód,

Eddas, sagas and Icelandic romanticism

SVEINN YNGVI EGILSSON

Antiquarian romanticism

The medieval Nordic literary heritage was extremely important to nineteenth-century poets in Iceland and Scandinavia, especially the romantics. The term *antiquarian romanticism* has been used to describe this literary movement in the form it appeared in Iceland. Admiration of the medieval age had been a strong element in European romanticism from the outset, especially the German branch that evolved in Heidelberg in the first decade of the nineteenth century. In many places it was synonymous with a "return to the roots" in various forms. People felt they could come closer to themselves and their own origins by going back in time or venturing into pristine nature, or both. Romanticism was inherently an individualistic philosophy, but the individual was invariably defined in terms of the concept of nationality, and a romantic poet's genius was measured by how intensely he managed to lend his nation a voice and produce a collective human view of the world. The Volksgeist, or spirit of the nation, was considered to be embodied in popular poetry and stories that had been preserved over the course of the centuries. People therefore looked towards popular poetry of later centuries and medieval European stories in equal measure. In Germany, admiration of the Middle Ages was often conservative, while in Scandinavia and not least in Iceland it assumed a very different and more progressive form.

Romanticism reached Scandinavia with the poem *Guldhornene* (*The Golden Horns*) in which the Danish poet Adam Oehlenschläger (1779-1850) portrayed a splendid picture of Nordic antiquity that had been lost for ever. Oehlenschläger wrote this poem after listening to one of the influential lectures that Henrik Steffens (1773-1844) delivered on romanticism in Copenhagen during the winter of 1802-1803, when he had just returned from Germany. Nor did the romantic message escape a young Icelander who was in the Danish capital at that time. Bjarni Thorarensen (1786-1841), poet and later sheriff general, was a keen enthusiast of ancient poetry. After graduating in law from the University of Copenhagen he received a stipend from the Árni Magnússon Commission which was then producing an academic edition of the eddic poems. Thorarensen's original compositions widely reflect this

Left: *Juvenilia* by Jónas Hallgrímsson, a poem to his friend Gísli Ísleifsson. It opens with the words "In days of yore", an allusion to *The Sybil's Prophecy* (*Völuspá*), and marks the revival of the ancient metre (fornyrðislag) in Jónas Hallgrímsson's verse. KG 31 b. Árni Magnússon Institute in Iceland.

Upper portrait: Bjarni Thorarensen.

Lower: Grimur Thomsen.

interest. Many are written in the eddic metres, *fornyrðislag* (ancient metre) or *ljóðaháttur* (poetic metre). He also revived the poetic diction of the Eddas and adopted many of their themes and ancient motifs.

In *The Poems of Sigrun* (*Sigrúnarljóð*, written c. 1820) Thorarensen adopts a Gothic voice and has the speaker of the poem declare to his beloved that he will love her no less when she is dead than alive. He makes a wish that she will visit him as a revenant on a cold autumn night and crush him in her arms. The name of his beloved and other aspects of the poem echo the eddic *Second Lay of Helgi, the Slayer of Hunding* (*Helgakviða Hundingsbana II*), which describes the love between the hero Helgi and the valkyrie Sigrun. Helgi dies but revisits his beloved, bloodstained and frozen. She welcomes him and they spend their final night in Helgi's mound, he a ghost but she alive. In the eddic poem the viewpoint is mainly that of Sigrun, but Bjarni Thorarensen reverses this and lets the male lover speak. The roles are also reversed in his poem, because it is the dead woman who visits the male.

The Fjölnir group and antiquity

Although Nordic antiquity was championed by Bjarni Thorarensen in his poetry, it did not acquire a proper political and historical content until the 1830s, in the writings of the *Fjölnir* group, which was associated with a journal of the same name published from 1835-1846. Its best known members were poet Jónas Hallgrímsson (1807-1845) and clergyman Tómas Sæmundsson (1807-1841), who was its leading ideologist. Both men had attended Bessastaðir School where they were introduced to the Icelandic medieval heritage by teachers such as Sveinbjörn Egilsson, who was a translator of Homer and a scholar of Old Icelandic. Jónas Hallgrímsson was deeply moved by the eddic poems and a volume of his juvenilia has been preserved written in this vein, in which he even resorts to archaic idioms to imitate the genre as closely as possible. Hallgrímsson and Tómasson later studied at the University of Copenhagen and launched the journal *Fjölnir* there.

The *Fjölnir* group wanted Iceland to reclaim control over its own affairs from its Danish colonial masters and have its own parliament, as it had in the Commonwealth period. Antiquity became almost a myth or metaphor in Hallgrímsson's poetry, as demonstrated by his famous *Iceland, fortunate isle!* (*Ísland, farsældafrón*, 1835) and *Gunnar's Holm* (*Gunnarshólmi*, written 1837). The former is reminiscent of Oehlenschläger's approach. After presenting a splendid image of Icelandic antiquity, the poem ends by reiterating that this is lost forever. The poem is not devoid of all hope, however, because it can be read as implying that Icelanders still have the chance to attain the dignity they enjoyed in the past, since "Comely and fair is the country, crested with snow-covered glaciers". The country has potential, if the nation can regain its bearings.

In *Gunnar's Holm* Hallgrímsson expands upon chapters 74-77 of *Njal's Saga* which describe how Gunnar Hamundarson from Hlidarendi is sentenced to three years' outlawry from Iceland for slayings. He sets off to fulfil the sentence but on the way to the ship his horse stumbles, and Gunnar looks up to the slopes of Fljotshlid and says the classic words: "Lovely is the hillside – never has it seemed so lovely to me as now, with its pale fields and mown meadows, and I will ride back home and not leave." Gunnar's decision not to leave Iceland may be read as the heroic ideal of maintaining his honour by refusing to yield to his enemies, but Hallgrímsson's romanticism interprets his motivation as patriotic: "For Gunnar felt it nobler far to die / than flee and leave his native shores behind him." He remains loyal to his country, and the country preserves the memory of this remarkable event: its site is still covered with grass on the deserted sands of the River Markarfljót: "but here some hidden favour has defended / the fertile holm where Gunnar's journey ended."

In Tómas Sæmundsson's writings in *Fjölnir*, Icelandic antiquity becomes a kind of social model, a blueprint for the organization of the Althing and a framework for the reclamation of national liberty. Furthermore, the old literature is a manifestation of the true *Volksgeist* which, in the group's view, could revitalize the latter-day Icelanders and inspire their campaign. The only possible option that they entertained was to hold the Althing at Thingvellir, its site in the golden age. Such ideas were widely challenged and *Sunnanpósturinn*, a rival journal to *Fjölnir*, criticized them as unrealistic nostalgia, since the Commonwealth was not exemplary in all respects: for instance in the custom of exposing new-born babies, and in performing executions without trial. For a while, however, it looked as though the Althing question would be resolved in the *Fjölnir* group's favour: King Christian VIII of Denmark proposed in 1840 that the Althing should be restored at Thingvellir. *Fjölnir* applauded this idea and Jónas Hallgrímsson wrote *The New Althing* (*Alþing hið nýja*) in honour of the king, drawing on the Edda tradition and employing its two main metres. In the event, the parliamentary question was settled differently. It was decided to hold the Althing in Reykjavík and the choice of venue disappointed the *Fjölnir* group intensely. But eddic poetry and the medieval tradition retained its appeal to Icelandic poets for much of the nineteenth century (see further Sveinn Yngvi Egilsson: *Arfur og umbylting*. Rannsókn á íslenskri rómantík. Reykjavík 1999).

The modern age and Nordic Middle Ages

One of these poets was Grímur Thomsen (1820-1896). He studied aesthetics and literature at the University of Copenhagen and later

Halldór Pétursson's illustration to The Battle of Hell-Path (Heljarslóðarorrusta), 1971.

Jón Sigurðsson.

held an office in the Danish foreign service. In the mid-nineteenth century he gave lectures on the characteristics of Nordic literature and published articles on this subject in newspapers and journals. He adhered to the Scandinavist movement, which regarded the Nordic countries as a single entity and their inhabitants as one nation. Grímur Thomsen believed that Nordic poets should seek inspiration from the riches of medieval literature, and that this was the only way for them to become national poets in the pan-Nordic sense of the term. He practised this himself with poems based on the sagas of kings and legendary sagas. These include *Glaesivellir* (*Á Glæsivöllum*) – freely based on *The Tale of Thorstein Mansion-Might* (*Þorsteins þáttur bæjarmagns*) – a swashbuckling account in the style of the legendary sagas which he uses to reflect his own precarious existence in the Danish foreign service. Historical integration of this kind became one of the chief characteristics of Icelandic romanticism. Poets in that era were particularly deft at striking up a dialogue between past and present in what they wrote.

Gísli Brynjúlfsson (1827-1888) was international in outlook, like Grímur Thomsen. A passionate believer in liberty, he was particularly stirred by the nationalist awakening in Hungary in the mid-nineteenth century. He wrote the inspired *Magyar Poems* (*Magyaraljóð*) about the struggle there, bathed in the light of medieval Nordic literature. Brynjúlfsson's work illustrates how extensively Icelandic poets drew upon medieval tradition. To their way of thinking, Eddas and sagas had strong contemporary relevance not only for the Nordic identity but equally for the uprisings in Eastern Europe.

Benedikt Gröndal (1826-1907) was exceptionally versatile. He was the son of Sveinbjörn Egilsson, whose pupils at Bessastaðir School would later found the *Fjölnir* group. Gröndal was a polymath, taking Nordic studies at the University of Copenhagen but also studying natural science and art as well as being a prolific author. He was one of several poets who wrote heroic eulogies of Jón Sigurðsson (1811-1879), the leader of Iceland's campaign for independence; they tended to idealize him by comparing him with the brave heroes of the Edda. Jón Sigurðsson himself cited the medieval *Ancient Lay of Bjarki* (*Bjarkamál hin fornu*) in his famous essay *Exhortation to the Icelanders* (*Hugvekja til Íslendinga*) in *Ný félagsrit* 1848.

Gröndal drew upon medieval literature in a variety of ways. In 1851 he wrote *Arrow-Odd's Drapa* (*Drápa um Örvar-Odd*) about the eponymous hero of the legendary saga. This was the first attempt by an Icelandic poet to write a modern narrative poem based on a saga. Later, Grímur Thomsen wrote *The Ballad of Bui Andridsson and Frid Dofradottir* (*Rímur af Búa Andríðssyni og Fríði Dofradóttur*, printed in 1906 but written earlier) based on *The Saga of the People of Kjalarnes*

(*Kjalnesinga saga*) and Matthías Jochumsson produced *Grettir's Poem* (*Grettisljóð*, printed in 1897 but written earlier) based on *The Saga of Grettir the Strong*. Jochumsson had previously translated the Swedish poet Tegnér's *Fridthjof's Saga* (1866), which enjoyed great popularity in Iceland and other countries. It may also be mentioned that Gröndal wrote a comedy based on the eddic poems and other old texts in 1866. Titled *The Witches' Ride* (*Gandreiðin*), this was a scathing satire on his contemporaries in the guise of medieval characters and gods. Gröndal also wrote sagas in the old style, like other nineteenth-century authors.

The saga tradition and nineteenth-century novels

The extent of the influence that the saga style had on the evolution of the narrative in the eighteenth and nineteenth centuries is disputed. However, it seems probable that the realistic and broad narrative technique of the Sagas of Icelanders had some significance for the development of the novel, while romances were another important influence. Both the chivalric and the legendary sagas of the Middle Ages are representatives of the romance tradition; stories of a similar type continued to be written in later centuries. Scholars such as Matthías Viðar Sæmundsson in the third volume of *Íslensk bókmenntasaga* (1996) have recently demonstrated that the modern Icelandic novel originated as much in the eighteenth century as in the nineteenth. Jón Thoroddsen's *A Boy and a Girl* (*Piltur og stúlka*, 1850) had previously been regarded as the starting point of the modern Icelandic novel, although a number of experiments had certainly been made with a kind of novelistic form before this was written. Authors included Eiríkur Laxdal (c. 1743-1816), who wrote *The Saga of Olaf Thorhallason* (*Ólafs saga Þórhallasonar*) and Jón Oddsson Hjaltalín (1749-1835), who composed many stories in the spirit of romance, e.g. *The Story of Hinrik the Wise-of-Counsel* (*Sagan af Hinriki heilráða*).

Benedikt Gröndal made a deliberate attempt to tell a modern story in the old romance style. His *Battle of Hell-Path* (*Sagan af Heljarslóðarorrustu*, 1861), surely one of the funniest stories ever written in Icelandic, playfully represents contemporary events and familiar characters in the guise of legendary and chivalric sagas. Queen Victoria, Napoleon III and other contemporaries of the author are scathingly parodied with repeated allusions to the Icelandic saga tradition. In one sense Gröndal's story is a precursor of Halldór Laxness' *Happy Warriors* (*Gerpla*, 1952), another satire based on medieval heroics, although the Nobel laureate models his work on the Sagas of Icelanders and sagas of kings – *The Saga of the Sworn Brothers* and *The Saga of King Olaf the Holy* (*Ólafs saga helga*) – rather than the romances.

Gísli Brynjúlfsson.

Matthías Jochumsson.

The sagas on stage

Júlíana Jónsdóttir (1838-1917) was the first Icelander to write a drama based on a saga. *The Slaying of Kjartan Olafsson – A tragedy in one act* (*Víg Kjartans Ólafssonar – Sorgarleikur í einum þætti*) was staged in Stykkishólmur in the winter of 1878-79, with the author cast in the leading role as Gudrun Osvifsdottir. Helga Kress has published the play in 2001 with an informative introduction in which she points out that Júlíana Jónsdóttir does not base her work on *The Saga of the People of Laxardal* as a whole, but rather focuses on one of its main episodes, the account of the slaying of Kjartan Olafsson and the events leading up to it (chapters 48 and 49 of the saga). Earlier in the nineteenth century Adam Oehlenschläger had written a tragedy in five acts, *Kiartan and Gudrun*, loosely based on the same saga, which may have drawn Jónsdóttir's attention to it as promising material for dramatization.

The closing scene in Jónsdóttir's play is particularly interesting. Until this point, she has followed the familiar plot of *The Saga of the People of Laxardal*: Gudrun and Kjartan fall in love and she is betrothed to him while, as was the custom among the sons of chieftains then, he goes abroad. But Kjartan spends longer abroad than had been agreed and Gudrun, believing that he has lost interest in her, marries his foster-brother Bolli Thorleiksson. When Kjartan eventually returns to Iceland, he is still in love with Gudrun, but the match cannot be unmade and their love turns to hatred. Kjartan marries Hrefna Asgeirsdottir and disputes between the two households escalate. Since Gudrun cannot suffer another woman to enjoy the man she loves, she wishes him dead. She urges Bolli to slay his foster-brother, and he does so with the help of Gudrun's brothers.

The ensuing final scene of the play is pure fabrication on Jónsdóttir's part with no foundation in the saga. In a monologue, Gudrun Osvifsdottir confesses her love for Kjartan. On the verge of being overcome by sorrow, she sits down to rest and falls asleep on the stage. The play continues:

THE GHOST OF KJARTAN enters, he has wrapped his cloak around him, but as he looks all around and walks over to GUDRUN, he opens his cloak to reveal an open wound to his heart; his face is pale and his hands are covered with blood, he clutches the wound with his left hand, places his right hand on GUDRUN'S shoulder, and speaks in a tearful but heavy voice.

GHOST OF KJARTAN: Gudrun! Gudrun! I have kept your memory *here*, and here is the wound that you will remember forever with hot tears .... But now we are reconciled. (*He rests one hand on GUDRUN'S cheek, and holds her hand with the other that had been resting on his wound, leaving a bloodstain on GUDRUN'S hand. – Then he slowly glides away the same way. – GUDRUN is startled from sleep, suddenly stands up and clutches her cheek*).

GUDRUN (*frightened*): What hellish cold .... Kjartan! You were *here* .... Are you still alive .... no, this must have been a dream or a figment of my imagination (*pensively*) – Now I remember my dream .... O, what a vision it was! – Kjartan has loved me passionately (*in a tearful voice*) – Now my sorrows are too great to bear. (*Takes a white cloth and puts it to her face, but as she does so she looks at her hand and sees the bloodstain*) – What is here on my hand? .... blood? .... blood .... Kjartan's blood .... I have often dreamt mighty things, but this is more than a dream .... Kjartan! Kjartan! How may I wash your blood from my hand! .... (*in a melancholy voice*) – With my tears .... yes, with my tears, Kjartan, I shall wash this stain, so that my hand will be pure and white, and then I shall be able to offer it to you, when we meet ...

Bolli then enters the stage and he and Gudrun exchange fairly cold words, but at the finale Gudrun stands alone on the stage again and says:

GUDRUN (*alone*): My counsels have been cold and hard, – but every fault can be redeemed, and I shall remember this longest of all, if I manage to do penance for my deeds .... (*louder*) – But the heavy judgements of men will always rest upon me.

The curtain falls.

Júlíana Jónsdóttir.

The passion and gruesomeness that appear in the final scene, with the loved one returning from death to visit his beloved, is reminiscent of the Gothic atmosphere in Bjarni Thorarensen's *Poems of Sigrun*. One difference, however, is that in the play it is the woman who speaks and the action is seen through her eyes. Furthermore, she is responsible for his death; he has an open wound to the heart. Gudrun's hands are besmirched with his blood and only her tears – the tangible image of suffering – can purify them.

Other Icelandic dramatists based works on the sagas towards the end of the nineteenth century, as Sveinn Einarsson has described in his *Íslensk leiklist* I (1991). Sigurður Guðmundsson (1833-1874), known as "the painter", the leading advocate of establishing a national theatre in Iceland at that time, considered medieval literature as a great resource for writers. A talented scenographer, he arranged his own exhibitions of "live images" or illustrated episodes from the sagas with actors in costume amidst painted scenery. Matthías Jochumsson (1835-1920) wrote *Helgi the Lean* (*Helgi hinn magri*), "a history in four acts", which was performed in Akureyri in 1890. However, this play lacked drama and focus, with a dramatis personae of more than 30 characters besides its hero, who was the first settler of the Eyjafjörður district. The sagas did not seem destined to give Icelandic drama the impetus that had been hoped.

Sigurður Guðmundsson also urged his compatriots to draw upon

Title page of *The Slaying of Kjartan* (*Víg Kjartans*). In the hand of Ólafur Thorlacius, (Lbs. 1784 4to). From the edition by Helga Kress.

Right: A seventeenth-century vellum, an almanac (Rím) with notes, AM 466 12mo. On the label inside the front cover, Árni Magnússon has written: from the Reverend Skúli from Grenjaðarstaður.

Overleaf: Belgdalsbók, AM 347 fol (left), and illuminated initials from Flateyjarbók. Árni Magnússon Institute in Iceland.

Icelandic folktales for the same purpose. The customary distinction between folktales and sagas was probably not as clearly made at that time. Both genres were examples of a native storytelling tradition and were inextricably connected with the landscape, regardless of whether they described heroes of old or latter-day outlaws. Matthías Jochumsson had risen to this challenge with his *Outlaws* (*Útilegumenn-irnir*, 1862) or *Skugga-Sveinn*, as he named the play in a revised version (1898). It earned a brilliant reception. Indriði Einarsson (1851-1939) also drew on the world of folktales with his popular *New Year's Eve* (*Nýársnótt*, 1872). Folktales provided a richer source than the sagas for playwright Jóhann Sigurjónsson (1880-1919), whose *Eyvind of the Mountains* (*Fjalla-Eyvindur*, 1911) earned him a reputation in several countries and *The Wish* (*Galdra-Loftur*, 1914) is still performed in Icelandic theatres. Sigurjónsson wrote *Mörður Valgarðsson* (1917), based on *Njal's Saga*, but it did not enjoy great popularity. Indriði Einarsson's play *Swords and Croziers* (*Sverð og bagall*), based on episodes from *Sturlunga saga* (1899), was never even performed.

Stage adaptations of the sagas have not achieved widespread popularity, so far at least. On the other hand, filmmakers have shown a growing interest in the sagas. They have either adapted individual sagas, as Ágúst Guðmundsson did with *The Outlaw* (*Útlaginn*, 1981), which is based on *Gisli Sursson's Saga*, or drawn freely on the saga tradition in more general terms, as Hrafn Gunnlaugsson has done in his films *Flight of the Raven* (*Hrafninn flýgur*, 1984) and *In the Shadow of the Raven* (*Í skugga hrafnsins*, 1988). These works seem to show that the narrative technique and mindset of the sagas is more suited to the artistic approaches and world of the cinema than of the theatre. In this respect they are more akin to the American western than to Shakespeare, notwithstanding their literary value. The sagas may return to the stage at some time, but they appear to have a much brighter future on the silver screen.

The eddic poems have also found a new relevance more recently. They have proved well compatible with contemporary rock music in *Odin's Raven Magic* (*Hrafnagaldur Óðins*, 2002), by Hilmar Örn Hilmarsson and Sigur Rós. As long as the medieval heritage manages to appeal to successive new generations, it will remain the living tradition that it has been hitherto.

ᵹeꝼ vmaga eyri
u é hn tekr vortu
allt ſua tiunda e̅
u ætti hialꝼr ſeldr
unda þe ſitt · enut
eꝼ þr koma vthi
t tiunda h̅ þe ſitt
h̅ þa vætr ſampt
hu þiꝛt · en þat
d ᵹa e̅ þr ᵹa hu ⁊
t · en eꝼ vaꝛ land
ok eᵹu þr þe epter·
allda tiund aꝼ er
i þe · en aꝼ hu þe
ed ſer · e̅ hn eᵹ ſky
nund · þo at hn ſe

hvartueggia · ſa t
hut er logradandie
tube und men aꝼ þe
ok ſkal hn þat þe ſu
ba vud hn aꝼ vma
mund gialda i þei
temuh ſau muſeri
at ſetraꝛ a tiundar
ſui vm · þo er rou e
eꝼut teum ok ſkal
la alaᵹaꝛa en hm
mui ſam en ſuiar
þggna inka ſekt ol
tiund gelldꝛ eᵹ het
eᵹ ſteꝼut vm þa er
ta ſumar ept mal

po tu baei turnu up

zt godzar hlwar e

m�; lið sir z þaurd a

han auftr til þa e

te̅ of· e̅ r· s· þulat

te̅ azmm̅ lange ap

z spurdu h' þir þau

ve non ar vp̅g te̅

WALKYRIEN

The "Germanic" heritage in Icelandic books

ÓSKAR BJARNASON

It was the romantic movement which discovered Old Icelandic literature in Germany. At the end of the eighteenth century the philosopher Johann Gottfried Herder, one of the pioneers of romanticism,
began championing the view that the world of Norse mythology was
closer than Greek mythology to the German national character and
therefore deserved a higher place in German culture. Herder, who had
translated Snorri Sturluson's *Deluding of Gylfi* into German, urged his
fellow-countrymen to explore the Norse myths and cultivate the
virtues extolled in them, such as keeping one's word, loyalty and heroism. His belief in the need for every nation to have a mythological
background would become one of the principles of romanticism
throughout the whole of the nineteenth century and in fact well into
the twentieth. Herder also aired the idea that the role of artists was to
give the gods a new lease of life and present them to their nations.

Defeats in the Napoleonic Wars in the beginning of the nineteenth
century gave a firm impetus to the German nationalist movement and
kindled a desire to unite all Germans in a single state. To strengthen
the sense of national identity, a great quest was launched to identify a
German and Germanic cultural heritage. The brothers Jakob and
Wilhelm Grimm held similar views to Herder about old Icelandic literature and pioneered Norse scholarship in Germany in the first half
of that century. They also underlined even more strongly the kinship
between Germans and Scandinavians and made no attempt to conceal
the fact that the motivation behind their scholarship was to promote
patriotism, German unification and the closest possible political solidarity among Germanic peoples. By and large, the Brothers Grimm
did not distinguish between the concepts "Germanic" and "German".
This confusion of terms, which exemplifies German efforts to usurp
the cultural heritage of other nations, dominated their attitudes
towards old Icelandic literature until the mid-twentieth century. Thus
Jakob Grimm gave his book, which largely dealt with the mythologi-

Illustration from Walhall, *Die Götterwelt der Germanen*, early twentieth
century.

Cartoon satirizing the premiere of Wagner's Ring, 1876.

cal world of the eddic poems and *Snorra Edda* and was published in 1844, the straightforward title *German Mythology*. In his preface he airs the view that the ethics of the sagas were superior to those of Christianity, which divided the world into good and evil with no middle ground. This was a viewpoint that many admirers of old Icelandic literature would later adopt.

The composer Richard Wagner subscribed to the romantic notion of the need to look back to the earliest antiquity in order to find life at its most untarnished and noble. According to this concept, the overlay of later, external influence had to be removed from ancient stories to reveal their pure essence. Ideas for producing an opera based on the German *Nibelungenlied* had been around for some time. Wagner embraced this view but soon came to the conclusion that the subject matter was inadequate for a major operatic work. He therefore began examining the eddic poems and *The Saga of the Volsungs* in depth, as well as consulting *The Saga of Thidrek of Bern*, Snorri Sturluson's *Heimskringla* and other works; he already had some acquaintance with Norse mythology from his childhood. Wagner regarded the sagas as a Germanic heritage and the words "Iceland" or Icelandic" never occurred in his writings. The outcome was that he drew heavily on these sources for an independent creative work about love and jealousy, heroism and revenge, greed and the lust for power. He wrote four operas in all – *Das Rheingold, Die Walküre, Siegfried* and *Götterdämmerung* – under the collective title *Der Ring des Nibelungen*. As Árni Björnsson has demonstrated in his book *Wagner and the Volsungs. Icelandic Sources of der Ring des Nibelungen*, Wagner modelled his work much more closely on Icelandic than German sources. For example, the sole models for Wotan (Odin), Fricka (Frigg) and other deities were to be found in Icelandic literature. The same applies to his prophetesses and valkyries, Valhalla, the apples of eternal youth, and key scenes such as where Brünhilde throws herself onto Sigfried's funeral pyre at the end of the work. The character of Siegfried has features from both German and Icelandic sources. His revenge for his father is Icelandic in provenance, as are his sharp glaring eyes which have become renowned in German visual art. Finally, *Götterdämmerung* is a translation of the word form *ragnarökkr* in *Snorra Edda*, meaning "Twilight of the Gods". When the Ring premiered in Bayreuth in 1876, five years after the establishment of the German Empire, it earned immediate respect and acclaim, and Kaiser Wilhelm and other leading figures attended the performance. By that time the Bayreuth Theatre had already been criticized as an institution for the glorification of the Empire and the Germanic race.

It was the enormous popularity of Wagner and his Ring Cycle that propagated general knowledge of the myths in Germany. The view became established that they were pedigree German and the gods were often invoked to underline German nationality. Wagnerian Societies were founded after the composer's death, combining an interest in music, radical nationalism and worship of "German" gods.

When Eugen Diederichs, owner of a publishing company in Jena and a champion of neo-romanticism, decided shortly after 1900 to launch a series of old Icelandic literature, a turning point was reached in the reception of these works in Germany. Over the period 1911 to 1930, twenty-four volumes were published under the title *Thule. Altnordische Dichtung und Prosa*, the most extensive translation project for this literature up to that time in any language.

Diederichs commissioned thirteen translators, most of them professors of Germanic studies, including Felix Genzmer, Rudolf Meißner, Gustaf Neckel, Andreas Heusler and Felix Niedner. While Heusler, a Swiss-born professor working in Berlin, had the greatest influence on Nordic studies in German in the long run, the most prolific translator was Niedner. He also wrote a detailed introduction, *Icelandic Culture in the Viking Age*, which made him one of the strongest presences in the *Thule* edition. Individual translators were given a fairly free hand in their translation and introduction for each volume, and they clearly did not all have exactly the same ideas about the task. For example Heusler, who translated *Njal's Saga*, and Meißner, who translated *The Saga of the People of Laxardal*, regarded the sagas as largely fictive authorial works, while others such as Niedner, the translator of *Egil's Saga*, hardly questioned their historicity.

There is no question that the principle behind the *Thule* edition was racism, in the sense that it was assumed that the characters of the sagas and their prospective readers were of the same race – Germanic – and that people of this stock were supposed to be superior in certain ways. Niedner conjectured that the Nordic peoples possessed a special "life force" that equipped them to perform uniquely heroic deeds. For example, the creation of the British Empire and even the military victories of the French throughout the centuries were claimed to be due to miscegenation with Vikings. The Nordic "force" was supposed to seek outer expression, but unfortunately could turn inwards if not channelled into "war for the fatherland". This was said to have been the case in the Saga Age, when "there was a berserk streak in every Icelander."

More mundane people such as Heusler did not stray into such fantasies, although he did agree with Niedner and Diederichs that the sagas demonstrated how Germanic people were by nature farmers rather than city-dwellers, and how farming was healthier and more noble than urban life, which made modern man rootless and decadent. As Julia Zernack has pointed out (*Geschichten aus Thule. Íslend-*

Valkyries, artist's depiction of the premiere of Wagner's Ring, 1876.

Title page of the German Thule edition.

ingasögur in Übersetzungen deutscher Germanisten. Berlin 1994), the farmer comes under special focus in many places in the *Thule* translations. It is also interesting that many members of the *Thule* group, including Heusler, Neckel and Diederichs, admired Friedrich Nietzsche and emulated him in seeking an ancient ethics free from the submissiveness of Christianity.

Very few of those engaged in the *Thule* project ever actually set foot in Iceland. In those days such travel was fairly exclusive, but undoubtedly their limited interest in modern Iceland was also to blame. The few who did visit Iceland set off with a preconceived image of the heroic Germanic stock and must surely have been disappointed when they arrived. This was Heusler's experience on his trip to Iceland in 1895. He was "shocked" at rarely seeing people with Viking or heroic characteristics, which he explained as a decline caused by poor external conditions, compounded by the modern Icelanders probably being a more mixed race than, for example, the residents of northern Norway and north Germany. By comparison, he claimed to have seen a Viking air about Faroese seamen, even "the splendid figure of the blond beast" from Nietzschean philosophy. Diederichs made a five-week journey to Iceland in summer 1910 to experience it for himself in preparation for his *Thule* project. There he found that Icelanders "in no way behaved like Vikings"; they struck him as rather base, shy and quietly spoken, and dirty as well. He concluded that the Icelanders could not be considered a "model Germanic nation" but would rather "always live on their ancient renown".

By the outbreak of World War I in 1914, nine volumes of the *Thule* edition had been published: the main Sagas of Icelanders and the first volume of eddic poems. Diederichs was one of those who saw the war as a cultural crusade, hoping that it would not only strengthen and steel their nation, but could also raise it to a higher cultural plane with publishers in a prominent role. His publishing house made its contribution in the form of booklets for soldiers describing German life, faith and heroism. They were printed in small typeface in a volume that fitted into the pocket of an army jacket. Neckel wrote a booklet on *The Germanic Heroic Spirit* containing excerpts from the Sagas of Icelanders. Soldiers could read in it about the burning of Njal, the death of Grettir and Illugi in Drangey and the end of the Jomsvikings, along with verses from The Sayings of the High One such as "Cattle die, kinsmen die ..." which were supposed to "shed light on the warrior spirit of life in ancient times". In his introduction, Neckel discussed the ethics of the sagas and presented Christian and Germanic morality as opposites. The Christian message, originating in Asia and advocating peace and forgiveness, was valid only in times of peace, he claimed, but this was a time to champion

Germanic values of unconditional vengeance, loyalty to leaders and the existence of values higher than life, "and the life of others too". The reader was left in no doubt that he was being prepared to face death: "They went to their deaths as if of their own free will. They defied the enemy in all respects, so that their own hope of living had to be weakened too, and in word and gesture they rejected that death was a curse. This is Germanic pride!" At the same time, advertisements for *Thule* were rephrased to match the new age: "The ancient Teuton was always prepared to sacrifice his life for higher values. In the vanguard are the stories of three lives: the masculine man of action Egil, the calm Njal, the reckless young Grettir – three fundamental types of German manhood." It is not known how popular the Sagas of Icelanders proved in the trenches, but the military volume does bear witness to shrewd salesmanship and ideological extremism in promoting the ancient literature.

As the war dragged on, the intoxication with it wore off. On the fourth centenary of the Reformation, in 1917, Diederichs found out about the Christianization of Iceland at Thingvellir and wrote articles using it to illustrate that, ultimately, Germanic people had to reject an ethics that caused incessant family feuds and was bound to end in catastrophe. Worship of Valhalla, warfare and unbounded worldly pleasures would surely have to run their course. However, this insight on the part of the publisher does not appear to have had any effect on the *Thule* edition and the way in which it was promoted and advertised.

Under the Weimar Republic, Diederichs aligned himself on the political and cultural right wing, and rejected Western democracy and excessive foreign cultural influences which he felt would smother the German national identity. His firm shifted its stance from all-round publishing where different movements united, to producing literature which was tainted by nationalism and racism. In the 1920s the remaining fifteen volumes in the *Thule* series were published. The extremist Neckel was assigned the task of compiling an anthology from *Thule* under the title *Germanisches Wesen in der Frühzeit*, which was published in 1924 and targeted in particular at the younger generation. Steadfastness in the face of death was supplanted as the predominant theme by the pure Germanic stock. His preface, which is only four pages long, contains 33 instances of the words "Teuton" or "Teutonic" (*Germane/Germanisch*), Icelanders are referred to as "Icelandic Teutons" and Norwegians as "Norwegian Teutons". The racially purest modern Teutons, on the other hand, were supposed to be found in north Germany and the inland parts of rural Sweden. Neckel warns against "racially corruptive cultural influences" from the east and south and has no doubts that the reader will sense his blood relationship with Sigurd the Dragon-Slayer, Gudrun Gjukadottir,

Gunnar from Hlidarendi and Gisli Sursson, who are all closer to him than "Achilles dragging the body of his enemy around the walls of Troy or Althaea beating the earth to charm the underworld into taking vengeance."

Diederichs remained eager to rear his nation on old Icelandic literature, but he complained bitterly about the reception. Judging from his print figures, he failed in his mission to introduce the sagas into German homes. Only his eddic poems sold well, and Felix Genzmer's translation became "a kind of national book, at least among a certain group of people" in the publisher's view.

Societies of esoteric nationalists had been active since before 1900; they were opposed to Jewry and foreign influences and sought to create a new German or Germanic religion. To a large extent the content of this religion was taken from the *Edda* myths, which were very whimsically interpreted. The societies adopted various symbols from them, such as Odin with his spear and ravens, and Thor's hammer. Undoubtedly the most important group was the *Thule* society in Munich which was active from 1918 and played a major role in the insurrection there which led to the fall of the left-wing government a year later. The society's chairman, Rudolf von Sebottendorf, put extremely eccentric interpretations on the myths, and was convinced that the last heathen Teutons had fled to Iceland to preserve their ancient heritage there. While the significance of the *Thule* society and esoteric nationalism in general have been overstated, the roots of the Nazi party lie partly in such societies, and a similar kind of mysticism continued to be practised within the SS under the aegis of Heinrich Himmler. At the end of the 1920s Diederichs became a vehement supporter of Hermann Wirth, who advocated very similar theories. Diederichs published Wirth's books and founded a society to support him. Wirth, who had been involved with the Nazi party in the 1920s, later became president of Himmler's eugenics institute. The scholars engaged with the *Thule* edition did not associate themselves with this kind of pseudoscience (apart from Neckel) and Heusler rued that his publisher should go astray in such a direction.

The publication of volume 24 of the *Thule* edition, *Sturlunga saga*, in 1930, coincided with Iceland's celebrations of the millennium of the Althing. This provided the publisher with an occasion to launch an advertising campaign. Describing the edition as a "gift to the people of Iceland", he sent a copy to the speaker of the Althing. Diederichs arranged a kind of opinion poll among well known German cultural and political figures about the value of old Icelandic literature for the German people. The survey is interesting in two respects. Firstly, it shows Diederichs' boundless ambition to come to the rescue of German national culture, as he saw it, at a critical juncture. Secondly, it

FOR DANMARK! MOD BOLCHEVISMEN!

is interesting how many people were prepared to echo his sentiments and describe the sagas and eddic poems as part of the German renaissance.

The survey presented leading questions: "What significance does *Thule* have for the future development of the German spirit?" The 107 respondents included professors of Germanic studies, pedagogues, historians, literary scholars and theologians, German ambassadors to the Nordic countries, the mayors of the cities of the Hanseatic League and four ministers in the German government, along with the Chancellor himself, Heinrich Brüning. Naturally they were not all able to answer

World War II propaganda poster aimed at encouraging Danes to support the Nazis on account of the common Germanic heritage and Viking culture.

(the Chancellor, for example, seems to have been otherwise engaged) but replies from half the sample were printed in the publisher's brochure.

Most respondents agreed that the sagas dealt in some way with German history. The literary critic Hermann Bahr rebuked his compatriots for having forgotten "the spirit of the *Edda*, Wayland the Smith, the myths" and rued that a new, young generation should have grown up "without even knowing the poet Egil by name" – just as if Egil Skallagrimsson had been a German. Ernst Jünger, author of war books, described the *Thule* edition as "characteristic of modern attempts to state what is German and make it flourish." Some responses were in the spirit of "cultural pessimism" and saw Thule as opposed to the decadence of modern times, an instrument against materialism, worship of Mammon and blind faith in technological progress. Several made no attempt to conceal their racist views and regarded Thule as a weapon in the battle between the races. Thus Count Börries von Münchhausen warned against racial infiltration in Germany and Schmitt-Wodder, a member of the Danish parliament for north Schleswig, saw the German character in danger of being smothered by the Roman, Greek, Jewish and Christian tradition for once and for all.

Of course it is not surprising that most respondents championed nationalism and even racism. This makes it all the more interesting to read answers from several people who saw reason to protest against the use of old Icelandic literature on behalf of a doubtful cause. Heinrich Getzeny, a Catholic, warned against eulogizing the Germanic past at the expense of Christianity, which ought not to be seen as an enemy of the German *Volksgeist*. Clergyman Johannes Mumbauer went further and criticized the arrogance and narcissism implied by focusing on one's own race and rejecting all foreign influences. It could be imagined that arguments about racial issues had little relevance for a brochure advertising the Sagas of Icelanders, but it typifies the cultural situation at the end of the Weimar Republic that they appear to have been taken for granted.

The respondents made little mention of the Icelandic Althing – except one, member of parliament Theodor Heuss, later President of the German Federal Republic. He pointed out that the history of the Althing indicated that parliamentary democracy was not alien to the Germanic character; rather, it was fascinating from the perspective of jurisprudential history. Heuss was rather out on a limb with his views, because admirers of the Germanic past tended at the same time to oppose modern parliamentary democracy.

It is interesting how many well known writers took part in Diederichs' survey and praised the *Thule* series. This suggests that even though old Icelandic literature had not achieved a widespread general readership, it nonetheless had earned a place of honour with right-wing intellectuals and leading cultural figures during the Weimar period.

After the Nazis came to power in 1933 the eddic poems and sagas were unconditionally bracketed as "national" literature in Germany and although few new translations were made, many publishing houses produced anthologies and adaptations. The Sagas of Icelanders did not become bestsellers any more than before, but achieved much wider distribution. Diederichs reaped the fruits of his publishing strategy from the 1920s, although he was not one of the most passionate distributors of Nazi propaganda. He profited most from a handful of war books, but sales of *Thule* rallied as well. The anthology *Thule. Ausgewählte Sagas von altgermanischen Bauern und Helden* from 1934 reached a print run of 40,000 copies in 1944. Mythology held its ground and many rival translations of the *Edda* appeared on the market. *Die Edda. Volksausgabe*, an abridged version of Genzmer's translation, reached 127,000 copies in 1945. Some Nazi educators planned to incorporate the sagas into children's and young people's curricula, as Arthúr Björgvin Bollason has described (*Ljóshærða villidýrið. Arfur Íslendinga í hugarheimi nasismans*. Reykjavík 1990). The extent to which such plans were actually put into practice remains unclear. One thing is certain: the eddic poems were regarded as essential reading for a Nazi upbringing. The last 11,000 copies of *Die Edda. Volksausgabe* in 1945 were prominently labelled "Special edition for the Hitler Youth. Not for Sale."

The idea of the Old North in Britain and the United States

ANDREW WAWN

For the reluctant ninth-century settler Ingimund Thorsteinsson Iceland was an *eyðisker* [a desolate outcrop]; for an anonymous English poet, discussing the state of trade in the British Isles in 1430, there was no doubt that 'Of Yseland to wryte is lytill nede, / Save of stokfische'; while for Thomas Nashe in 1594 Iceland was 'one of the chiefe king-domes of the night', with 'sulphureous stinking smoak... that poysons the whole Countrey'. Yet by 1871 the writer and political reformer William Morris could claim that Iceland was 'a marvellous, beautiful and solemn place...where I have been very happy'; for the artist and scholar W.G. Collingwood, on a pilgrimage to the sagasteads in 1897, Iceland was 'the glory of the North'; while W.H. Auden, recalling his return to Iceland in 1967, thirty years after his first visit, noted: 'In my childhood Iceland was holy ground...at fifty-seven it was holy ground still, with the most magical light of anywhere on earth'.

What had led to this remarkable change in sensibility over the centuries? Why should celebrated nineteenth- and twentieth-century writers in the English-speaking world express such enthusiasm and reverence for the land, light, and literature of a remote North Atlantic island, previously associated only with stockfish, sulphur and sea-weed? Why, not least, were so many British and North American enthusiasts drawn to Iceland at the end of the nineteenth century when so many Icelanders were emigrating to North America to escape the economic privations of their native land?

Nineteenth-century fascination with Iceland in the English-speaking world was driven in part by a variety of non-literary reasons. Those (mostly British) travellers who risked life and limb in Iceland-bound sailing ships did so in order to fish for salmon, to study the fabled geothermal wonders (the volcanoes, the hot springs of Haukadalur), to investigate indigenous diseases (tetanus, leprosy), to explore the potential for commercial exploitation of minerals (kelp, sulphur), to climb mountains (Hekla, Snæfellsjökull), to study

Left: First night in Vinland, from R. M. Ballantyne, *The Norsemen in the West*, 1872.

Title page of a French translation of *The Saga of Frithiof the Bold*, 1904.

ornithology and botany, to examine customs of crop and animal husbandry, and, not least, to maintain a close watch on French efforts to secure a permanent naval base in north-west Iceland. At the beginning of the nineteenth century there was even talk in London of making Iceland a British protectorate, leading one ambitious young English diplomat to dream of becoming the Earl of Iceland, or Baron Mount Hekla!

The breadth of intellectual sympathies among these Enlightenment-Age explorers, however, ensured that research into birds, basalt and barometric pressures sometimes went hand in hand with an interest in Iceland's unrivalled medieval literary culture. Scientific sense and literary sensibility often marched side by side. The young British baronet John Thomas Stanley who explored Iceland in 1789 is a telling case in point. As a student at Edinburgh University, he had attended discussions on Old Norse mythology with Sir Walter Scott; he then organised a geological expedition to Iceland, returning home with an Icelandic *au pair*, two dogs, many rock samples and an intensified interest in Old Icelandic history and literature. Stanley, like his friend Scott, proceeded to fill his library with the latest Scandinavian editions of eddas and sagas, many of these volumes with facing-page Latin translations that greatly facilitated access to the respective worlds of Odin, Thor and Frey, and Njal Thorgeirsson, Gunnlaug Serpent-Tongue, Viga-Glum and other saga heroes. By 1847 the dying octogenarian Stanley could still be found copying out (in a faltering hand) verses from *Balder's Dreams* (*Baldurs draumar*), an eddic poem which tells of the impending death of the god Balder, and of the apocalyptic conflict which that tragedy portended. Stanley's protégé Henry Holland followed his Cestrian mentor to Iceland (in 1810), having first read widely in those same Latin translations of Old Icelandic texts. On his return he contributed an influential essay on medieval Icelandic literature to Sir George Mackenzie's *Travels in the Island of Iceland…in the Summer of the Year 1810* (1811). Holland's summary of *The Saga of Gunnlaug Serpent-Tongue*, a tale of destructive rivalry in poetry and love, encouraged Mackenzie to write *Helga*, a ham-fisted drama based on the saga. The play ran for just one (disastrous) performance in Edinburgh in 1812. It was the first of many halting nineteenth- and twentieth-century attempts to transfer Icelandic saga narratives to the British and North American stage.

Stanley, Holland and their Enlightenment-Age contemporaries were not quite the first generation of Britons to engage with old northern literature. The late eighteenth-century literary culture into which they were born was already familiar with and fascinated by the gothic exoticism of Norse myth and legend. Such stories first became readily available to 'the common reader' in Bishop Thomas Percy's

pioneering English translations of key primary and secondary works
(*Five Pieces of Runic Poetry Translated from the Islandic Language*, 1763;
*Northern Antiquities: or, A Description of the Manners, Customs, Religion
and Laws of the Ancient Danes, and other Northern Nations*, 1770).
Forensic summaries of or literary responses to material from such volumes subsequently appeared in leading periodicals. Anna Seward, 'the
Swan of Lichfield', and a friend of Scott, Stanley and Holland, was just
one of many poetasters of middle England who produced blood-cur-
dling verses based on these myths and legends. Other devotees, more
soundly grounded in old northern philology, engaged more soberly
with the primary texts. Scandinavian-based British diplomats such as
James Johnstone translated Old Icelandic texts relating to the British
Isles, as in *The Norwegian Account of Haco's Expedition against Scotland;
A.D. 1263* ([Copenhagen], 1782), derived from *The Saga of King
Hakon* (*Hákonar saga Hákonarsonar*). At this time those with knowledge

Frithiof kills two sea-witches, painting by Carl Peter Lehman, 1826.
Bergen Art Museum, BB. M. 385.
Photograph: Geir S. Johannessen.

of the Old Icelandic language had often studied George Hickes's authoritative compendium of antiquarian lore and grammatical learning, *Linguarum vett. septentrionalium thesaurus grammatico-criticus et archaeologicus* (Oxford, 1703-5).

The gods and myths of northern Europe never lost their popularity in nineteenth-century Britain and North America. They came to face stiff competition, however, from a group of previously unfamiliar Old Icelandic heroes and heroines, as English translations of prose sagas gradually became available. It was in the 1820s that enthusiasts of the old north finally found their first fully-fledged popular saga hero. Our modern canon of such figures is dominated by the noble Njal, the luckless Grettir, the four times married Gudrun Osvifsdottir, and the widely travelled Gudrid Thorbjarnardottir. For much of the nineteenth century, however, none of these characters could hold a candle to the hugely popular – and now largely forgotten – lovers, Frithiof Thorsteinsson (Friðþjófur Þorsteinsson) and Ingibjörg Beladóttir. The fourteenth-century Icelandic *Saga of Frithiof the Bold* (*Friðþjófs saga hins frækna*), was virtuosically paraphrased in verse by the Swedish Bishop

Esaias Tegnér, and reborn as *Frithiofs saga* (1825). Almost at once that poem, translated into English and many other European languages (including Icelandic), enjoyed enormous popularity. Set in Sognefjord in Norway, the story tells of the love affair between Frithiof, the promising son of a worthy yeoman, and his royal fiancée: its passionate beginnings, the opposition of Ingeborg's brothers, the plots against Frithiof, Ingeborg's dutiful marriage to the avuncular but aged King Ring, and the eponymous hero's patient pursuit and eventual recovery of his bride. The nineteenth-century popularity of this decorous tale was such that by 1900 there were at least fifteen English-language translations of the Swedish poem. In their wake came numerous *Frithiof*-related poems, plays, paraphrases and pictorial representations. Artists responded eagerly to the famous scene in which Frithiof confronts and defeats the gruesome sea-witches sent to destroy his Orkney-bound ship.

It was no accident that Bishop Tegnér's tale found such an enthusiastic response in and beyond the English-speaking world. Many British enthusiasts of the old north sought to explain their nation's imperial pre-eminence in terms of the Viking blood still coursing through Victorian veins, and the ancient Viking spirit still animating the modern Victorian soul. It had, though, to be the right sort of Viking spirit. *Frithiofs saga* offered no glimpse of the bloodthirsty old north constructed by morose monastic chroniclers and ghoulish post-medieval gothicists. Instead its hero was a gifted and inspiring poet, an individual whose nobility derived from nature rather than nurture, a righteous pagan whose natural faith awaited fulfilment in the Christianity that was soon to reach his Sognefjord home, and eventually the elected leader of his proud community. The poem thus seemed to endorse the kind of constitutional monarchy and consultative democracy that was emerging in Victorian Britain, not to mention the kind of nautical bravado to which every spirited schoolboy aspired. In turn, the exemplary Ingeborg was the most demure and dutiful bride-to-be. The first English translation of Tegnér's poem was undertaken in 1834 by the young Princess Victoria's chaplain at Windsor Castle. In his dedication, the Reverend William Strong loyally underlines the parallels between the medieval Norwegian princess and the modern British Queen-in-waiting. Thereafter the Victorian royal court promoted many aspects of old northern culture, encouraged perhaps by fanciful claims that the entire Hanoverian dynasty was descended from Ragnar Shaggy-breeches, a formidable Viking chief who had met a gruesome end in a Northumbrian snake-pit.

The Viking Age depicted in *Frithiofs saga* was essentially Norwegian, as was that represented in a second nineteenth-century translation which also came to represent the substance and spirit of

Watercolour by W. G. Collingwood of a rune stone on the grave of Kjartan Olafsson. National Museum of Iceland.

the old north for many British and North American readers: Samuel Laing's ground-breaking 1844 English translation of Snorri Sturluson's early thirteenth-century *Heimskringla*. Laing, a man of Orkney with an unquenchable enthusiasm for all things Norwegian, and working from Jakob Aall's 1838 Dano-Norwegian translation, translated Snorri's seventeen sagas with their panoramic view of the medieval Scandinavian kings. Many nineteenth-century readers acknowledged Snorri as a chronicler worthy to be named alongside Homer, Herodotus, Froissart, Pepys, Macaulay and Clarendon. They relished the sweep of his narrative as mighty dynasties rose and fell, monarchs were made and broken, and Things gathered and dispersed. Sturdy farmer stands alongside savage berserker; the solidity of great halls, fine ships, and famous swords shares the spotlight with the mysteries of sorcery, sacrifice and strange dreams. British readers could relish Snorri's references to Caithness, Cleveland, Scarborough, London, the Isle of Man and the Menai Straits; while Scandinavian communities in North America could reconnect with the stirring history of their ancestral homelands. Laing's peppery Introductory Dissertation promotes his very personal and politicised version of Viking values: agrarian self-sufficiency, coherent spirituality, commercial energy, cutting-edge naval technology, and representative democracy. Laing's translation reappeared in a lavish subscription edition in 1889, promoted by the indefatigable Norwegian-American scholar Rasmus Anderson, whose journalistic pen-name was (inevitably) 'Frithjof'. Anderson subsequently arranged for the 1889 text to be incorporated in his Norrœna Society set of canonical old northern texts (mythology, legend, chronicle, saga) published in New York in 1906.

In the nineteenth and early twentieth centuries the most popular of Snorri's *Heimskringla* sagas was that which narrated the life of King Olaf Tryggvason – from his adventurous formative years through to the triumphs (and cruelties) of his Christian missionary period in Scandinavia and Iceland. Popular British novelists such as Robert Leighton (*Olaf the Glorious*, 1895) retold incidents from the saga as parables of virtuous living for teenage readers. Henry Wadsworth Longfellow, who travelled widely in Scandinavia after graduating from Harvard, devoted one of his *Tales of a Wayside Inn* (1863-73), that of the Musician, to a Tegnér-style verse paraphrase of sections from Laing's 'King Olaf Tryggvesson's saga'. In 1896 it was a real musician, Edward Elgar, who created the cantata *Scenes from the Saga of King Olaf*, shortly before his triumph with *The Dream of Gerontius*; the Olaf text was based on Longfellow's poem. So it was that by the end of the nineteenth century choral societies all over Britain and its empire were lustily serenading the charismatic Christian king of Norway.

It was another of Rasmus Anderson's Norrœna Society texts that helped to promote a major paradigm shift in the reception of old northern literary culture in Britain and North America. The work in question, a pioneering translation of a mighty Icelandic saga, encouraged a switch of focus towards early Icelandic history and fable, and away from both the noble Viking-Age Norway of Frithiof (and of Samuel Laing), and the seductive post-Viking-Age Orkney as dramatised so influentially in Sir Walter Scott's popular novel *The Pirate* (1821). As its title implies George Dasent's *The Story of Burnt Njal; or, Life in Iceland at the End of the Tenth Century* (1861) was much more than just the first English-language translation of *Njáls saga*, the longest and finest of the Sagas of Icelanders. Following the example of Laing's *Heimskringla*, Dasent provided a 200-page Introduction in which the principal social and cultural elements of the early Icelandic commonwealth were described in authoritative detail. *Heimskringla* was a chronicle of Scandinavian kings, and *Frithiofs saga* a Viking-Age romance; now Dasent's *Burnt Njal* provided readers with an epic-scale account of the death of two heroes and the birth of a nation – and did so in a way which attracted favourable comparisons with the epics of Greece and Rome. The saga's broad narrative canvas offered memorable images of law and lawlessness, taunt and truce, Christianity and paganism, heroism and villainy, sin and saintliness, fate and free will. Nineteenth-century readers were familiar with lengthy naturalistic novels set in recognisably British settings, whether ancient or modern: and now Dasent's *Burnt Njal* provided them with a kind of medieval Icelandic *Middlemarch*, to be followed swiftly by *The Story of Gisli the Outlaw* (1866: Dasent's translation of *Gísla saga Súrssonar*). Other translators were stirred into action: among them Sir Edmund Head (*The Story of Viga-Glum,* 1866), William Morris and Eiríkur Magnússon

(*The Story of Grettir the Strong*, 1869; *Three Northern Love Stories*, 1875 –
Friðþjófs saga, Víglundar saga, Gunnlaugs saga ormstungu), and Benjamin
Thorpe (*The Edda of Sæmund the Learned from the Old Norse or
Icelandic*, 1866).

As assistant editor of The Times newspaper, moreover, George
Dasent was a well-placed propagandist for Old Icelandic culture in
general and *Burnt Njal* in particular. He helped to promote a cultural
'trickle-down' effect, as the saga gradually found its way into popular
consciousness at home and abroad. During the fifty years following its
1861 publication *Burnt Njal* was artfully repackaged for a variety of
different readerships. Shorn of its Introduction, Dasent's clear-voiced
translation was reprinted twice at the end of the nineteenth century,
and was still available as an Everyman Library paperback in the 1970s.

Individual poems and poetic sequences based on key moments from the saga began to appear in print, though none of these works matched the remarkable popularity of William Morris's epic poems *The Lovers of Gudrun* (1869: based on *The Saga of the People of Laxardal*) and *Sigurd the Volsung* (1876: based on *The Saga of the Volsungs*). Attempts were even made to transfer *Njal's Saga* to the London stage. Moreover the *Burnt Njal* sagasteads of southern Iceland soon became places of pilgrimage for cultural tourists, their well-thumbed copies of Dasent's translation in hand. Visits to the Hlidarendi site of Gunnar's death, or the Bergthorshvoll site of the burning of Njal and his family became obligatory: the traveller's 'very toes [would] tingle and his pulse beat higher...if he has any soul in him'. W.G. Collingwood's *A Pilgrimage to the Sagasteads of Iceland* (1899) included reproductions of several of the 150 accomplished watercolours which he painted from his own *in situ* sketches, each one an atmospheric glimpse of a location that had by this time 'been rendered sacred ground'.

While sagastead exploration in Iceland attracted scholars and antiquarians from North America, many of these enthusiasts believed that there were even more exciting saga locations to be investigated much nearer home. 1837 had seen the publication in Copenhagen of *Antiqvitates Americanae*, a folio-sized collection of literary-historical and archaeological sources for the study of Viking-Age Vinland. Reliable archaeological confirmation of the thirteenth-century saga accounts of Leif Eiriksson and his fellow explorers in North America did not emerge until the mid 1960s, through the excavations of Helge and Anne-Stine Ingstad at L'Anse aux Meadows in Newfoundland. But for much of the nineteenth century, despite the restraining influence of fastidious scholars such as Arthur Middleton Reeves, North American cultural wish was often father to archaeological fancy and (even) forgery. Cultural wish there certainly was. Protestant members of eastern seaboard communities eagerly embraced *Eirik the Red's Saga* (*Eiríks saga rauða*) and *The Saga of the Greenlanders*, texts which appeared to confirm that their nation's founding father had not been the fifteenth-century Italian Roman Catholic Christopher Columbus but rather the tenth-century Icelander (or Greenlander) Leif Eiriksson, a Christian convert. On the other hand, reliable archaeological evidence there certainly was not – which left all the more room for the exotic fantasies of wealthy zealots such as Eben Horsford of Boston. In a series of privately printed volumes he claimed to have located the site of Leif Eiriksson's landfall (on the Charles River in Boston) and of the lost city of Norumbega, allegedly inhabited until the late middle ages by Leif's descendants who had intermarried with native Americans. In no time, tours of the newly-excavated saga sites were instituted, and a pocket guidebook was published; poets celebrated the discoveries in soaring verse; and novelists such as the Swedish-American Ottilie Liljencrantz of Chicago reimagined the great events in *The Thrall of Leif the Lucky: A Story of Viking Days* (1902) and *Randver the Songsmith: A Romance of Norumbega* (1906).

As the Liljencrantz novels suggest, the twentieth century began as if the popularity of old northern texts and images would develop along essentially nineteenth-century lines, promoting familiar socio-political and cultural agendas on both sides of the Atlantic. Laing's *Heimskringla* achieved renewed popularity in Britain through its republication in the Everyman Library series; *Frithiofs saga* enjoyed a run on the London stage via Frederick Winbolt's pallid *Frithiof the Bold: A Drama Based upon the Scandinavian Legend* (1902); and Kaiser Wilhelm II's *Frithiofs saga*-based 'Song of Ægir' featured prominently in the coronation entertainment for King George V in 1911. These and other Old Icelandic texts were by this time being taught in major universities in both Britain and the United States, as part of English or Germanic Studies programmes. Indeed, at the turn of the century, William Carpenter was almost certainly the first scholar of Old Norse to achieve high university office in the English-speaking academic world: he became President of Columbia University in New York. Moreover, by 1917 scenes from Dasent's *Burnt Njal* could be found in a textbook prepared for teenage pupils throughout the British Empire by a schoolmaster in India. A list of suggested essay topics encouraged students to reflect on the poignant links between medieval Iceland and modern war-torn Europe: 'Contrast sea-fighting in the tenth and twentieth centuries', and 'Does civilisation make men less cruel?'

The Great War certainly cast a shadow over old northern and Germanic enthusiasms. When the young J.R.R. Tolkien returned to Oxford at the end of hostilities, and sought to pursue his interest in Anglo-Saxon and Old Norse language and literature, he was told sternly that philology was an essentially German branch of scholarship which had contributed significantly to the arrogance of Britain's 1914-18 foes. Undeterred, Tolkien later found supportive colleagues and willing pupils in the English Department at the University of Leeds before returning to Oxford. For Tolkien's students in both institutions *Beowulf*, the *Poetic Edda, The Saga of the Volsungs* and other works doubtless represented 'set texts' to be mastered effortfully, whereas for Tolkien himself the same texts served as a philological and narrative treasure hoard around which he coiled himself like some dragon of old northern legend, and from which he drew powerful imaginative sustenance. These were the kinds of works, suitably re-imagined and re-fashioned, which helped in due course to substantiate and animate the Middle-Earth of *The Hobbit* and *Lord of the Rings*. The

fairy-tale world created by Tolkien out of Old English, Middle English and Old Icelandic philology provided the fictional space in which familiar Viking- and Saga-Age notions of heroism, faith, community, treasure, and quest could be redefined for the mid twentieth century. Specific borrowings are not hard to identify, as in *The Hobbit* with the names of the dwarves (from the eddic *Sibyl's Prophecy*), and the 'Misty Mountains' (from *The Words of Skirnir*). Similar sources for broader Tolkienian themes and emphases can also be traced. Thus, the combination of pride, ferocity and sadness to be found in *Lord of the Rings* and *The Silmarillion* recalls the poetic treatment of conflicts between the Huns and the Goths that found its way into *The Saga of Hervor*. In addition, in its laconic humour and respect for antiquity Tolkien's fictional vision recalls that of Snorri Sturluson, notably in his *Snorra Edda* collection of mythic lore. Though nineteenth-century old northernism found a successful literary champion in William Morris, the current world-wide popularity of Tolkien's fictions is on a wholly different scale, and the box-office success and critical acclaim of the films based on *Lord of the Rings* suggests that the phenomenon is in little danger of decline in the foreseeable future.

Nor have the Viking and Saga Ages lost their power to inspire more historically realistic fiction. In the Canadian-Icelandic immigrant communities of Manitoba accomplished poets and novelists (such as Laura Goodman Salverson, *The Viking Heart*, 1923) responded creatively to their medieval Icelandic literary legacy. The Vinland sagas in particular have offered a potent cultural reference point for writers exploring the ties that once bound and the gulf that now separates Canadian 'New Iceland' from its ancestral homeland. The same sagas have also attracted modern novelists from well beyond Gimli, albeit that imperialist agendas have yielded to a range of post-heroic, post-modern, feminist and native-American perspectives. Thus, Ottilie Liljencrantz gave way to Neville Shute (*An Old Captivity*, 1940; *Vinland the Good*, 1946), and, more recently, to Thomas Pynchon (*Vineland*, 1991), George Mackay Brown (*Vinland*, 1992), Joan Clark (*Eiriksdottir: A Tale of Dreams and Luck*, 1994) and others. Recent non-Vínland novels of comparable vigour and deftly concealed scholarly insight include Stephan Grundy, *Rhinegold* (1995), and Harry Harrison and John Holm, *The Hammer and the Cross* (1992) and *The King's Way* (1995). Moreover, old northern images and notions have found memorable expression in the work of some of the twentieth century's finest English language poets – amongst them W. H. Auden, Ted Hughes and Seamus Heaney.

Indeed, there seems every chance that these flourishing traditions of novelistic and poetic response to Old Icelandic literary tradition will be further nourished by the recent and forthcoming publication by Penguin Books of new translations of many of the Sagas of Icelanders. It was the post-1770 publication of Latin and English saga translations that underpinned nineteenth-century interest in medieval Icelandic culture. The current Penguin series may be viewed as an appropriate vote of confidence in the present and future capacity of these 'tales of the Northland of old' to intrigue and inspire new generations of devotees.

Right: *Hauksbók*, AM 371 4to. Árni Magnússon Institute in Iceland.

Parliament, sagas and the twentieth century

JÓN KARL HELGASON

Sagas as the property of the nation

At the end of 1941 Iceland's parliament, the Althing, passed a law stipulating that the Icelandic state had the exclusive right to publish Old Icelandic literature, i.e. works written before 1400. The law was based on the idea that this literature, like the fishing grounds around Iceland, is the common property of the entire nation, and the proprietary right to it should be vested in the state on behalf of the citizens. However, this did not imply that the state alone should handle all the publication of the literary heritage. Just as the Ministry of Fisheries is in charge of allocating quotas to fishing vessel operators, the Ministry of Education should authorize the private publication of individual works, on condition that it adhered to a particular orthography, the "standardized old spelling." The law also stipulated that The Old Icelandic Texts Society (*Hið íslenzka fornritafélag*) had unlimited authorization to publish this literature.

It may seem surprising that Iceland's parliament was pondering the publication and spelling of medieval literature at this time. World War II was raging, Iceland was under foreign military occupation and the future of the crown union with Denmark was uncertain. Society was in the process of transformation. The economy was recovering after the depression of the 1930s, but cultural life was in upheaval, partly as a result of stronger foreign influences and rapid urbanization. Such turmoil created anxieties about the future of Icelandic culture. There was a broad consensus on the need to preserve native traditions and establish continuity between past and future, the rural and the urban. But the best way to establish such a continuity was fiercely disputed.

Legislation granting the state the exclusive right to the sagas was one aspect of this conflict. Not only did it provoke fierce clashes in parliament, but the first and only court action brought on the basis of it ended with the Supreme Court ruling that the law was unconstitutional. At face value it appeared to be an issue of protecting national

Left: They found Hoskuld slain. Illustration by Þorvaldur Skúlason in Halldór Laxness' edition of *Njal's Saga*, 1945.

Halldór Laxness.

treasures – no one should treat the sagas exactly as he or she pleases. Essentially, however, it hinged upon conflicting attitudes towards the literary heritage, political control over culture and one of Iceland's most controversial authors at the time, Halldór Laxness.

Sacred sagas

The reason the controversial law was passed in December 1941 was that, two months previously, a newspaper had reported that publisher Ragnar Jónsson intended to produce an abridged version of *The Saga of the People of Laxardal* with modern spelling, and had commissioned Halldór Laxness to undertake the task. It had been the custom for some time then to publish the old literature with a spelling which was supposed to resemble the orthography of the oldest manuscripts and had been standardized by Icelandic and foreign scholars in the nineteenth and twentieth centuries. Among the differences were vowel spellings - thus modern *ö* was written either *ø* or *ǫ* in the old spelling, and *æ* either as *œ* or *æ*; word forms, such as *ek* and *ok* for *ég* (I) and *og* (and), and endings, with *maður* (man) written *maðr*.

Ragnar Jónsson's plan produced a fierce reaction, at first in the newspapers and later in parliament. The express aim of the law granting the state the exclusive right to publish the sagas was to prevent the announced edition of *The Saga of the People of Laxardal*. However, Ragnar Jónsson, Halldór Laxness and printer Stefán Ögmundsson were quick off the mark and managed to publish the saga before the law was passed by parliament. A year later they published *The Saga of Hrafnkel Frey's Godi (Hrafnkels saga Freysgoða)*, this time in defiance of the law, and were sentenced by a lower court to pay a fine or serve forty-five days imprisonment. They appealed on the grounds that the law on which the sentence was based was in breach of the constitutional freedom of expression in writing. While the case was being heard by the Supreme Court in the spring of 1943 they managed to obtain permission from Einar Arnórsson, the then Minister of Education (and Halldór Laxness' ex-father-in-law), to publish *Njal's Saga*. This time parliament responded with a resolution recommending that the state-run publishing division of the Cultural Fund and "Friends of Iceland" (*Þjóðvinafélagið*) should publish its own edition of the saga. The aim was to sabotage Halldór Laxness' pending edition.

The parliamentary resolution on an official edition of *Njal's Saga* was tabled by MPs Helgi Jónasson, Ingólfur Jónsson and Sveinbjörn Helgason. In a report accompanying their proposal they said: "As admirers of *Njal's Saga*, we aim with this parliamentary resolution to ensure that the nation has the opportunity to acquire it in an inexpensive, quality edition, unbesmirched by those who wish to drag everything down into the gutter and who do not spare even our most precious works of art such as *Njal's Saga* from such a fate." The imagery suggests they are condemning an act of gross defilement or the profanation of holy relics. Similar ideas lay behind the legislation on the sagas which, when it was passed in 1941, was described by Minister of Finance Jakob Möller as being presented by people "who regard the old literature as something sacred which must not be debased."

Precious sagas

When the Cultural Fund and Friends of Iceland published the official edition of *Njal's Saga* in 1944, the year the Republic of Iceland was established, Vilhjálmur Þ. Gíslason wrote in his introduction that the Sagas of Icelanders were "among the greatest and most precious relics of Icelandic culture," and of these, *Njal's Saga* was not only the largest and most comprehensive but also "the richest in many ways." These words echo the speeches of the MPs who proposed the resolution on the saga publication, in particular Helgi Jónasson. "The point about us Icelanders," he said, "is that we are poor and few in number, and we have little worldly wealth, but we have one treasure, namely our old literature. It is almost unexampled for a nation as small as ours to own such jewels as the old literature." Imagery of this kind has long typified cultural dialogue in Iceland and takes such forms as the fossilized concepts of "the literary heritage" and "cultural value."

On the same occasion Helgi Jónasson criticized Halldór Laxness' edition of *The Saga of the People of Laxardal* for being badly printed on poor quality paper. "It is obvious," he said, "that this was done to make money, and not to enhance the value of Icelandic literature." There seem to be two underlying notions here. Firstly, it is implied that it is unnatural if individuals make money from the property of the nation such as the old literature. This point, which is reminiscent of criticism of the fishing quota system today, had also surfaced when parliament debated the 1941 legislation and Jakob Möller described one of its aims as ensuring "that the old literature will not be disfigured for commercial purposes."

Secondly, Helgi Jónasson also implies that saga editions should preferably reflect what treasures these books are. In this context it is interesting to note that when Laxness' edition of *Njal's Saga* appeared in 1945, publisher Ragnar Jónsson stated "that no expense would be spared to produce an edition of the highest possible quality," as Laxness phrased it in his postscript. The work is exceptionally large, with quality binding and lavish illustrations. Laxness underlines that in this respect the publication was supposed to pay tribute to the ancient manuscripts, which were certainly expensive to produce and are still considered priceless treasures. Ragnar Jónsson clearly did not intend to open himself to criticism for "devaluing" *Njal's Saga*.

Title page of the Cultural Fund's edition of *Njal's Saga*, 1947.

NJÁLS SAGA

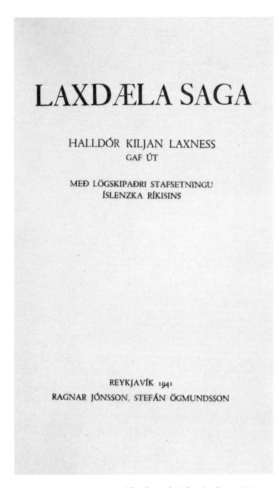

LAXDÆLA SAGA

HALLDÓR KILJAN LAXNESS
GAF ÚT

MEÐ LÖGSKIPAÐRI STAFSETNINGU
ÍSLENZKA RÍKISINS

REYKJAVÍK 1941
RAGNAR JÓNSSON, STEFÁN ÖGMUNDSSON

Title page of Laxness' edition of *The Saga of the People of Laxardal*, 1941.

This aspect of the attitude towards old literature in the twentieth century overlaps with the campaign for the return of the manuscripts themselves from Denmark. That process was an extension of the campaign for independence; it hinged upon Iceland's rights to its cultural crown jewels.

Sagas as local stories

In the debate on the old literature act, Þorsteinn Þorsteinsson, district magistrate in Dalasýsla, gave his opinion of Halldór Laxness' newly published edition of *The Saga of the People of Laxardal*. "The district with which I am associated has now had the misfortune to see its main saga, *The Saga of the People of Laxardal*, published with new-fangled spelling, without introduction, index or notes, and more or less disfigured in all respects," he said, and voiced his support for the State's exclusive right to publication so that other districts would not end up "in the same gutter." His argument highlights the way that although the saga corpus was regarded as the property of the nation, individual districts had a special claim upon the sagas connected with them.

It may be worth pointing out that the three MPs who tabled the proposal for an official edition of *Njal's Saga* in 1943 all lived in Rangárvallasýsla district, where the saga is set. Helgi Jónasson was district physician at Stórólfshvoll in Fljótshlíð, Sveinbjörn Högnason was a clergyman at Breiðabólsstaður in Fljótshlíð, and Ingólfur Jónsson lived at Hella in Rangárvellir. Helgi Jónasson and Ingólfur Jónsson represented the district in parliament, and Sveinbjörn Högnason West Skaftafell. Although it was never said in so many words, a probable explanation for their involvement in the matter was the interests of their constituents and neighbours.

However, the matter hinges no less on the historicity of the Sagas of Icelanders; among the criticisms that the MPs levelled against Halldór Laxness was distorting the sagas as historical sources. Þorsteinn Þorsteinsson regretted various omissions from Laxness' *Saga of the People of Laxardal* including "family ties and places of residence. I think this is inappropriate and I do not consider this the proper way to treat old and classical authorities." Helgi Jónasson voiced a similar view in 1943 and pointed out that the genealogies in the Sagas were necessary for understanding why the characters of the sagas feuded.

Helgi Jónasson himself lived at Stórólfshvoll in Fljótshlíð. A genealogy in chapter nineteen in the unabridged version of *Njal's Saga* relates that a certain Storolf Haengsson (presumably from Stórólfshvoll) was the great-grandfather of Gunnar of Hlidarendi - he was the father of Hrafnhild, who was the mother of Gunnar's father Hamund. Helgi Jónasson from Stórólfshvoll was presumably loath to see this information omitted from the official editions.

The opening of Búi Kristjánsson's comic strip based on *Egil's Saga*, from *Zeta* 2/1 (2001).

Sagas as public property

The attitudes expressed here are typical of the standpoint towards the sagas that Icelanders held in the first half of the twentieth century. Halldór Laxness' publications in the 1940s clashed with these views in various ways. Firstly, Laxness felt that if the Sagas of Icelanders were to retain their value in the modern age, they would need to be made as accessible to the public as possible. He aired this view as early as 1935 in a short newspaper article prompted by the recent publication of *Egil's Saga* and *The Saga of the People of Eyri* by The Old Icelandic

The district of Reykjavik with streets named after saga heroes. In the first half of the twentieth century many street names were taken from the sagas, sometimes arranged to represent their plots. From Njal's Saga, Skarphedin's street runs southeast to his parents Bergthora and Njal. The location of Barónsborg playschool between the couple recalls the burning scene in which they meet their deaths in bed, with their grandson Thord Karason between them. Gunnar's road intersects Skarphedin´s and to the west is an allusion to the episode involving Kari and Bjorn from Mork in the last part of the saga. Similarly, the plot of The Saga of the People of Laxardal can be traced along Aud's street to those of Bolli, Gudrun, Kjartan and Hrefna. The street layout reflects the love affairs in the saga, with Gudrun situated between Bolli and Kjartan. The streets southwest of Skarphedin's street are named after Karl, Vifil, Mani and Skeggi, all figures from the district claimed by the first settler of Iceland (and Reykjavik), Ingolf Arnarson. Flókagata is named after Raven-Floki, discoverer of Iceland.

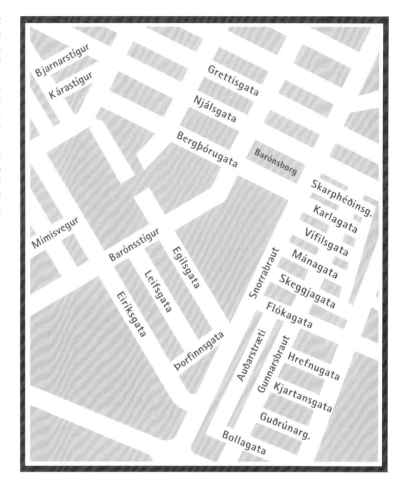

Texts Society. Laxness protested against Icelandic scholars using the standardized old spelling in their publications, which he described as an act of hostility towards the sagas, serving only to repel ordinary readers.

On this point, some MPs shared Laxness' views and opposed the old literature act. One was Magnús Jónsson, a professor of theology at the University of Iceland, who considered it unwise to publish the sagas with standardized ancient spelling, since this perpetuated the fallacy that medieval and modern Icelandic were two different languages. "This must not be handled like a drug that can only be obtained with a prescription," he said in a parliamentary debate in 1941.

Two years later, a similar viewpoint was expressed by Sigfús Sigurhjartarson, who advocated publishing the sagas and re-creating them as diversely as possible. Scholars had to have their academic editions with old spelling and detailed introductions, but the general public also needed quality editions in modern Icelandic and children needed anthologies of key passages from the main sagas. Other art forms would follow in their wake, he claimed: "Our poets and com-

posers will later create immortal works from the Sagas of Icelanders. ...
We shall have paintings of Kolskegg and Gunnar going their separate
ways, and other memorable scenes from the saga [*Njal's Saga*]. ...
Sculptors will also appear on the scene and commit the saga to metal
and stone."

As it happens, a number of Icelandic artists had been following
such a manifesto. Poets over the centuries had taken their subjects
from the old literature and in the first half of the twentieth century
painters, dramatists, novelists and composers drew upon the same
source. In the latter half of the century other artists followed, including Halldór Laxness himself with his novel *The Happy Warriors*, in
which he went even further in demythologizing the sagas.

Sagas as fiction

Laxness also campaigned fiercely against the "misunderstanding," as
he called it, that the Sagas of Icelanders were historical works. He
regarded them as fiction. This perspective is presented with an interesting analogy in the introduction to *The Saga of the People of Laxardal*,
in which Laxness compares the author to a gifted pianist: "It is as if
the virtuoso spends a long while finding his way around the keyboard,
and chances upon various melodies and fragments of tunes, some lofty,
others mystical or capricious, but in a loose casual relationship with
each other, sometimes even none, only occasionally striking a few
contrapuntal notes from the main theme, which nonetheless covertly
dominates his thoughts behind all the other themes, until it breaks
forth in the second part of the work with unstoppable momentum,
and captivates its creator completely."

Such descriptions irritated parliamentarians, in particular Jónas
Jónsson from Hrifla who wondered whether Laxness would talk next
about "the counterpoint in Gudrun Osvifsdottir or Kjartan or Bolli."
On the same occasion he criticized Laxness for implying that the saga
was fictional: "This is tantamount to alleging that the whole of *The
Saga of the People of Laxardal* is one big lie." In reply to this remark,
Magnús Jónsson pointed out that Laxness' ideas were not without par-
allels: "Sigurður Nordal has demonstrated that *The Saga of Hrafnkel
Frey's Godi* is fiction, and opinions are divided about how much of the
Sagas of Icelanders is fiction and how much real events."

The fact of the matter is that Laxness' arguments conformed with
those of the scholars who often go by the name of "the Icelandic
school" in Old Icelandic studies, not least Sigurður Nordal and Einar
Ól. Sveinsson. In contrast to those who regarded the sagas as historical
works, products of oral tradition, the Icelandic school emphasized that
they were the works of authors, the pinnacle of a unique form of literary creation in the late Middle Ages. These ideas gradually gained

supremacy in the saga dialogue in Iceland – interest shifted from the heroes of the sagas to their authors.

Sigurður Nordal gives a memorable description of this change in his study of *The Saga of Hrafnkel*, in which he points out that the Icelandic school's theory by no means diminishes the value of the sagas as national treasures: "In terms of nationalist ambition, it can be said that any breach that may be hewn into the renown of Saga Age warriors and men of strength has been filled by new heroes who hitherto have been hidden away in the shadows: the authors of the sagas. Do we lose anything by that exchange?"

Sagas as a political weapon

While the parliamentary debates in 1941 and 1943 reveal a number of key attitudes towards the sagas at that time, it must be pointed out that in its broadest sense this issue was political as much as literary. The chief opponents of the old literature act and the resolution to publish *Njal's Saga* were MPs of the Socialist Party. They argued that both these issues were engineered by one Progressive Party member, Jónas Jónsson from Hrifla, and that his motive was to discredit leftists, in particular the most prominent writer in their ranks, Halldór Laxness.

Jónas from Hrifla – who had in fact retold passages from the sagas himself in his perennial textbook on Icelandic history – stated in 1941 that the act had been passed in order to prevent "communists" from being able to publish the old literature in "slang" for the "rabble." "We can put up with various things from the communists, but not that," he said. In his powerful post as chairman of the Education Council, Jónas Jónsson had entertained the idea that the Cultural Fund should begin publishing the sagas for the general public and he was far from pleased when Halldór Laxness pipped him to the post. He and Laxness clashed over many questions at this time, including the Council's controversial stipends for Icelandic artists. Jónas Jónsson was hostile towards all proponents of "un-Icelandic" artistic movements and towards those who held political views that he did not approve of.

Behind these conflicts lay the belief on both sides that "control" over Icelandic culture – including the sagas – would bring control over the people of Iceland at the same time. It is a telling reflection of the political atmosphere at the time that both sides compared their adversaries with German Nazis. The Reverend Sveinbjörn Högnason, who proposed the official publication of *Njal's Saga* in 1943, said he knew "about one edition of the holy scriptures, which should not be emulated but Hitler's archbishop has permission to publish, in which the Sermon on the Mount is completely turned on its head." In the same way, presumably, Halldór Laxness would alter *Njal's Saga*. Two years previously, Socialist MP Einar Olgeirsson had compared the act on the sagas to Nazi censorship: "The same kind of book burnings are to be made law here as those practised by Hitler. It is astonishing that this should be proposed to parliament." He added that the only motivation was Jónas Jónsson's animosity towards Halldór Laxness: "Our old literature must not be allowed into people's homes except in Jónas Jónsson's interpretation of it, as put forward in his history of Iceland."

Sagas as a challenge

Various commentators have pointed out that Halldór Laxness' position towards the old literature was persistently ambiguous: a combination of admiration and challenge. Steingrímur J. Þorsteinsson talks about Laxness' "filial role" with regard to the old authors, the problem faced by "a man of outstanding accomplishments who has a world-famous parent." Laxness was not alone in wrestling with this problem. In the first half of the twentieth century, many Icelandic artists pursued their "campaign for independence" through the creative reworking of material from the saga world. Suffice it to mention Jón Leifs' *Saga Symphony* or the Cubist influences in Ásmundur Sveinsson's sculpture *Sæmundur on the Seal's Back*.

It is interesting to read Halldór Laxness' remarks about the illustrations to his *Njal's Saga*, which were by Gunnlaugur Scheving, Snorri Arinbjarnar and Þorvaldur Skúlason. "I feel convinced," he wrote in his postscript, "that some of the drawings presented here for the first time will prove to be lasting artistic achievements, as respected as the immortal text they were created to serve." A similar notion is found in an article by Kristinn E. Andrésson, one of the Socialist MPs, written to commemorate the seventh centenary of the death of Snorri Sturluson: "We can rejoice and delight in acknowledging, when we remember Snorri now, that Iceland today has achieved cultural triumphs fully worthy of the Saga Age."

As the century wore on, this first generation of professional Icelandic artists assumed the paternal role that the old literature had played towards them in their own day. The sagas do not have as absolute a value for culture and everyday life in Iceland in the beginning of the twenty-first century as they had during World War II when there was a parliamentary majority for granting the state a legal copyright to them. More recent controversies over "natural property" have involved the fishing grounds around Iceland, natural resources in the highlands and information in medical records. Nonetheless the old literature still accompanies the Icelanders as they venture forth into the future, both in its own right and as an echo from the twentieth century. The national wrestling champion is awarded *Grettir's Belt*; a district youth movement is named *Skarphéðinn; Lokastígur* is a street in Reykjavík; a trawler is named *Snorri Sturluson* RE 219; there is a

chocolate factory called *Freyja* and a brewery named after *Egill Skallagrímsson; Hótel Saga* is in Reykjavík; *Óðinn* is a coastguard vessel; The Saga Centre in Hvolsvöllur is known as *Njálusetrið*, after Njal's Saga; the three fates *Urður, Verðandi og Skuld* (Past, Present and Future) have become a genetics company ... In this way, the medieval literature is still the property of the nation – a stock of wealth from which individuals, businesses and local communities reap dividends in their respective ways.

The saga tradition and visual art

AÐALSTEINN INGÓLFSSON

In the first volume of his survey of Icelandic art, Björn Th. Björnsson relates how painter Ásgrímur Jónsson applied to parliament for a grant to travel abroad. This was in the spring of 1903. With his application, Jónsson submitted several of his works, including a painting based on *Njal's Saga* showing Gunnar and his brother Kolskegg taking their leave of each other on the Markarfljót river mudflats.

When the members of parliament began discussing the artist's application, their attention focused above all on this painting. One MP was worried that Gunnar's horse was unbridled and implied that nothing much could ever be expected from someone who did not know to bridle a horse. For a while it looked as if Jónsson's application would be rejected. Then MP Hermann Jónasson from Þingeyrar pointed out that the artist had actually presented a new and original explanation for Gunnar's decision to turn back instead of going into exile. The doubting voices were quelled and eventually Jónsson was awarded a grant of 600 krónur.

Exaggerated as this account may be, it nonetheless gives an insight into official attitudes to the sagas and Icelandic visual art at the beginning of the twentieth century. For members of parliament, and presumably the majority of educated Icelanders as well, the artist's loyalty to the main details of the saga counted for much more than his skills and artistic conviction.

If we bear in mind that, at the beginning of the twentieth century, literature had almost totally dominated Icelandic culture for centuries, while academic art had only recently sprung to life – Þórarinn B. Þorláksson held his first one-man exhibition in 1900 – it should not come as any surprise that visual art was regarded as a subordinate, or what would probably today be termed a "service provider", to literature. What is remarkable, though, is how long this attitude to the visual arts prevailed in Iceland, even among broad-minded scholars and writers. Well into the 1940s, long after Expressionism and other inter-

Left: Skarphedin glides across the ice on Markarfljot River. Painting by Otto Bache, 1862. National Gallery of Iceland.

national art movements had relieved Icelandic artists of the obligation to produce landscapes or portraits and thereby opened a path for them towards independent interpretation, they were still expected to show the letter of the sagas undivided loyalty and respect. But more of that later.

Conceivably, the sense of the sagas as being "inviolate" was one reason for the reluctance of Icelandic artists to use them as raw material for their art. Icelandic landscape, their main theme for most of the twentieth century, was of course free from all such cultural obligations. A look at the oeuvre of the five pioneers of Icelandic visual art – Einar Jónsson, Þórarinn B. Þorláksson, Ásgrímur Jónsson, Jóhannes Kjarval and Jón Stefánsson – reveals that only one of them, the sculptor Einar Jónsson, consistently looked to the saga tradition for inspiration, with noteworthy results. In particular I am referring to his monumental sculpture and the works he based on Nordic mythology. And to return to Ásgrímur Jónsson, it can be added that only about a dozen of his watercolours and drawings can be directly or indirectly linked with the saga heritage.

The lack of interest that Icelandic artists displayed towards this heritage is even more noticeable among the so-called "second generation", which reached maturity in the aftermath of World War I: Muggur (Guðmundur Thorsteinsson), Kristín Jónsdóttir, Júlíana Sveinsdóttir, Eyjólfur Eyfells and Nína Sæmundsson, for none of them produced noteworthy work on saga themes, excepting a single marble head of Njal, by Sæmundsson.

In the heat of Iceland's campaign for national independence, Einar Jónsson was the country's only artist of stature to embrace to his compatriots' veneration of the saga tradition. His *Ingólfur Arnarson* (1907, inaugurated 1924) and *Þorfinnur Karlsefni* (1916-18) are seen as battle-ready warriors, not unlike the superhuman heroes featured in today's computer games. In all likelihood it was Einar Jónsson's abiding interest in the saga heritage which ensured him both enduring popular acclaim and the goodwill of the authorities. In 1920 he was described in glowing terms in Morgunblaðið newspaper as the artist who "has been most Icelandic of all in his art and has had the resourcefulness and gifts to render the 'Icelandic character' in such a way that other nations have looked to it in veneration."

It must be said, however, that for a long time Icelandic artists were under no great pressure to make use of the sagas, neither as illustration nor in independent works. The editions of the Sagas of Icelanders familiar to most educated people were generally without illustration, or they contained at most photographs and drawings of saga sites. Thus there was no continuous Icelandic tradition of saga illustration.

Not until Iceland attained sovereignty in 1918 and began contem-

plating celebrations at Thingvellir to mark the millennium of the Althing in 1930 did the government begin considering ways to enhance Icelandic national awareness and people's knowledge of their cultural heritage. Incidentally, on the subject of the Althing celebrations, it may be mentioned that, unlike the custom today, people then took their time, in fact most of the 1920s, to organize them. For example, a special set of commemorative crockery for honorary guests was ordered from Copenhagen as early as 1923.

It soon became clear that the whole framework for the celebrations would be modelled upon what was thought to be known about the golden age of Icelandic culture. Booths in "the ancient style" – today termed "notional replicas" by archaeologists – were to be set up at Thingvellir with interior and exterior decoration reminiscent of old-style carvings and old textiles, actors in costume would perform familiar episodes from the sagas and a wealth of appropriate souvenirs would be produced: coins, stamps, statuettes, postcards, teaspoons, ashtrays and the like.

At this time, general knowledge of the saga culture mostly derived from the sagas themselves. Thus the organizers needed artists to produce a variety of visual material and decoration based specifically on descriptions in the sagas. Interestingly, except for Einar Jónsson none of the artists mentioned earlier took part in or was commissioned for this task; instead, it was largely assigned to a new generation of artists, all of whom had a background in handicrafts: woodcarver Ríkarður

Gunnar from Hlidarendi by Snorri Arinbjarnar.
Árni Magnússon Institute in Iceland.

Jónsson; his brother Finnur Jónsson, a painter and goldsmith; and
graphic designer Tryggvi Magnússon; and painter and goldsmith
Baldvin Björnsson.

But the sagas were short on detail about the Icelanders' clothing,
weapons and buildings during the Age of the Commonwealth. What
did they really look like, the "cloaks" in which their forebears
wrapped themselves, how long were they, what kind of lining and
trimmings did they have, and so forth?

Endless discussions took place about the exact dimensions of
Gunnar from Hlidarendi's famous spear and how he used it, and there
was no lack of self-styled experts on ancient weaponry. Little help was
to be had from the National Museum which was scarcely out of its
infancy and ill-equipped to provide detailed information about the
apparel of Icelanders 900 years previously. Such information could

mainly be gleaned from a handful of Nordic museums, and in the early 1920s Einar Jónsson was probably the only Icelandic artist familiar with such institutions.

In this context it is instructive to recall how the earliest Icelandic illustrators responded to this lack of tangible sources about people's appearances, clothing and weaponry in days of old. Although visual art and illustration in the professional sense of the term did not take root in Iceland until towards the end of the nineteenth century, interesting amateur depictions are widely concealed in old manuscripts and the earliest books. One of the most impressive of these saga illustrations can be found in *Flateyjarbók* (c. 1387), portraying the death of King Olaf the Saint. The illustrator positions the characters of the saga on a circular surface, showing attackers wielding swords and spears closing in on the defenceless king. But interestingly enough, the illustrator does not try to produce a historically accurate depiction of the events; instead he adopts the clothing and weapons that were closest to him in time, fourteenth-century cowls, chain mail and English and French headgear. In this way – and probably completely unintentionally – he brings his narrative closer to the reader.

Two other and equally well known illustrations from a seventeenth-century manuscript (AM 426 fol.) derive their effectiveness from the same kind of ahistorical approach. In the oldest known depiction of Egil Skallgrimsson the illustrator focuses entirely on his terrifying appearance, his gigantic frame and ugly features. The image is so convincing that we hardly notice that Egil is dressed like a seventeenth-century farmer and wields some sort of carving knife rather than a sword worthy of a Viking. A portrait of Grettir Asmundarson is also found in the same manuscript, but the inconsistency is quite noticeable there, because this supposedly great warrior is made to resemble a squat mercenary from one of the many religious wars that took place in the seventeenth century.

Another entertaining portrait by an unknown illustrator, from a manuscript of 1698, shows Njal Thorgeirsson. While *Njal's Saga* says that he was "well off for property and handsome to look at", the portrait, which looks quite professional, shows a young and portly dandy from the seventeenth century rather than the wise and shrewd man of law visualized by most readers. In the Skálholt version of *The Book of Settlements* from 1688 the illustrator – conceivably not an Icelander – clearly wants to emphasize the warrior temperament of Eirik the Red by dressing him in the only battle-gear he knows, a fifteenth-century breastplate and gauntlets, loin guards, armoured leggings and other accoutrements. By then, people had long stopped wearing such attire.

Some of the most charming of these early saga illustrations were made by Guðlaugur Magnússon, a farmer in west Iceland, in 1871-75

From Tryggvi Magnússon's saga card pack, produced in connection with the celebrations for the Millennium of the Althing in 1930.

to accompany several sagas which his brother Guðmundur had copied from old manuscripts. Guðmundur Magnússon named his anthology *Some Sagas and Tales of Icelanders in Olden Times (Nokkrar sögur og þættir af fornaldarmönnum Íslendinga)*. It contains passages from *The Book of Settlements, The Saga of the Confederates, Ölkofri's Saga* and 18 other sagas, and all the heroes and heroines are dressed like nineteenth-century farmers and their wives on trips to the town, the men wearing clothes of homespun cloth and the women in national costume. At the same time the men are armed with swords and shields in the time-honoured fashion.

Scrutinizing these old illustrations of the sagas in their entirety leads one to surmise that the illustrators' casual approach towards historical accuracy in the detailing of clothing and circumstances was not entirely due to a lack of source material, but rather because they simply felt no need for such accuracy if the stories themselves were vivid and enjoyable enough. For them, the illustrations serve as extensions of the sagas rather than reflections of them. This, I feel, is clear from a number of drawings made by Sigurður Guðmundsson, Iceland's first trained visual artist in latter times, based on saga texts.

Sigurður Guðmundsson can hardly be accused of ignorance about old Icelandic culture, because as a student in Denmark he specifically studied Nordic history, archaeology, various aspects of ethnology and even the history of costume. He also had a profound respect for the saga tradition and was one of the first Icelanders to realize that it could be employed as a symbol for national solidarity in the campaign for independence.

Thus it is surprising to see Sigurður Guðmundsson's red pastel drawing of Grettir Asmundarson from around 1860, in which we find Grettir looking like a Greek philosopher basking in the Mediterranean sun. Shortly afterwards Guðmundsson produced a pencil drawing of the meeting between Gudrun Osvifsdottir and Helgi Hardbeinsson, in which the figures are wearing costumes from different periods. Gudrun wears a variation on the Icelandic national costume that Guðmundsson was designing at the time, and the men sport headgear, cloaks and armour from various periods. Admittedly it can be argued that this was a deliberate ploy on Guðmundsson's part: thus he was able to stress that the saga heritage was both timeless and international.

In the early 1920s Icelanders above all sought confirmation of their glorious past which would stand them in good stead in their first steps towards independence. And since there was clearly a shortage of reliable local sources about this past, the obvious solution was to emulate their Norwegian cousins, who not only had extensive knowledge of their shared ancient culture – in 1880 they had unearthed the Gokstad Viking ship – but had also repeatedly invoked it with impressive results in their own campaign for independence.

There is no evidence that the artists working on the 1930 Millennium Festival were familiar with the Norwegian artists who had depicted Nordic heroes and mythology – Johannes Flintoe, Ole Peter Hansen Balling and Christian Krohg – but they were well acquainted with Andreas Bloch's romantic drawings of episodes from the sagas. In 1898 a book was published in Norway containing 50 illustrations by Bloch to *Njal's Saga, The Saga of the People of Laxardal, Egil's Saga* and *The Saga of Gisli Sursson*, which sold well throughout the Nordic countries. Not surprisingly, since Bloch embraced in all respects the notions that nationalistic Danes, Norwegians, Swedes and Icelanders entertained about their forebears.

Bloch's saga characters are mighty impressive in appearance: handsome, clad in finery and well armed. Their whole demeanour is noble and their vigour virtually superhuman. Even when their conduct is questionable, for example in the account of Egil Skallgrimsson's dealings with King Athelstan of England, Bloch tends to give them the benefit of the doubt. Bloch bases his topography on prints and photographs from Iceland and descriptions in the sagas, his costumes and weaponry on artefacts found in the Norwegian National Museum and traditional Norwegian national costume. His dwellings are mostly based on old Norwegian timber houses and stave churches.

Icelandic artists had immediate access to Bloch's pictures, since postcard reproductions of many of them were in circulation after 1910, probably in completely unauthorized editions. In the early 1920s when preparations for the Millennium Festival were well under way, an enterprising publisher produced a series of hand-coloured postcards after Bloch's illustrations, which can now be found in all antiquarian bookshops in Iceland. But still Icelanders had not had their fill of Bloch, because after the 1930 Millennium celebrations a series of collector cards of his pictures was included with a popular brand of cigarettes.

There is another foreign painter who may have had some influence on the Icelanders' ideas about the appearance of the saga heroes. Björn Bjarnason's donation of art works to the nation, which was sent to Iceland in 1883 and kept on exhibit in Parliament House for many years, includes the Dane Otto Bache's painting of Skarphedin by the river Markarfljót. Bache is more restrained in his interpretation than Bloch in terms of appearance, clothing and weaponry, but in no way plays down Skarphedin's heroism.

Bache's painting is specifically mentioned here because it was the only one in Bjarnason's donation based on the sagas, and because it was published as a postcard in the 1920s and widely distributed in Iceland. Also, painter Eggert Guðmundsson produced a variation on

Viking by Sigurjón Ólafsson, 1952. National Gallery of Iceland.

Then the ring slid from my hand, by Hringur Jóhannesson, illustration for Laxness' edition of *The Saga of the People of Laxardal*, 1973.

this painting in the 1920s, a postcard of which was also in circulation following the Millennium Festival.

It is obvious from the work produced for the festival that Icelandic artists primarily looked towards the romantic image of the Golden Age of which Bloch is the main architect. This is apparent from Ríkarður Jónsson's postage stamps, Tryggvi Magnússon's playing cards, Baldvin Björnsson's commemorative coins, Finnur Jónsson's prototype stained glass windows, (later installed in Bessastaðir Church), the assembly hall at Thingvellir designed by Tryggvi Magnússon, and not least the lavish costumes of the actors who performed a dramatization of the adoption of Christianity at the festival.

Even Jóhannes Kjarval, who until then had avoided this kind of subject matter, felt himself compelled to produce a painting – his only one on a Viking theme – celebrating the noble spirit of the saga heroes. Probably painted in the festival year, it shows two handsome warriors shaking hands to seal their loyalty to each other.

If Andreas Bloch was the main architect of the idealized and heroic image of the saga heritage that most Icelanders subscribed to for much of the twentieth century, Halldór Laxness surely was the great debunker of this image.

Laxness had an interest in the saga tradition from an early age. In 1924 he declared, with an arrogance typical of young and ambitious authors, that neither *Heimskringla* nor *Njal's Saga* in any way measured up to the contemporary Danish authors he was reading at the time. Later, all the hullabaloo surrounding the Millennium Festival in 1930 struck Laxness as a ridiculous caricature of Icelandic history and the saga heritage. He wrote a number of satirical verses about the festival, one of which, "Inauguration", opens with these words:

> A world-famous moment when the dapper police
> dressed in blue and white directed us to where
> the chieftains huddled in their booths to hear
> a solemn speech on Christ and old king Chris.

But by the 1930s Laxness' attitudes towards saga literature had changed somewhat. He had read the sagas thoroughly and become convinced of their importance. However, unlike various influential figures – and indeed the majority of the public – he maintained that they were largely fiction. In doing so he can be said to have killed two birds with one stone: liberated the saga tradition from the shackles of history, topography and other trappings of the theory of oral preservation, and augmented Icelandic literary history with material that modern authors, including himself, could measure themselves against.

It can also be assumed that Laxness's attitude towards the sagas was directed in particular against the conservative nationalist movement which was the real driving force behind the 1930 Millennium Festival, and its most influential spokesman in Iceland, Jónas Jónsson from Hrifla. Throughout the 1930s and well into the 1940s Jónsson levelled bitter criticism at a number of "decadent" modern visual artists, including Jóhann Briem, Jón Engilberts, Gunnlaugur Scheving, Þorvaldur Skúlason and Ásmundur Sveinsson. Broadly speaking, these artists were accused of disfiguring the "image of the true Iceland" in their works, outraging the "unpolluted" aesthetic sensibilities of ordinary people and importing anti-Icelandic attitudes to art.

Thus it was hardly a coincidence that when Halldór Laxness and Ragnar Jónsson decided to publish *The Saga of the People of Laxardal* with modern spelling in 1941, they commissioned one of these "decadent" artists, Gunnlaugur Scheving, to illustrate the saga, rather than an artist of whom Jónas Jónsson approved. Scheving's drawings are not entirely convincing, but their harsh simplicity does contain seeds of a new Icelandic vision of the sagas.

Halldór Laxness' and Ragnar Jónsson's next move was to publish in Iceland a Norwegian edition of *Heimskringla* from 1898, which contained black-and-white drawings by several of the leading Norwegian artists of that time, including Christian Krohg, Erik Werenskiold, Gerhard Munthe and Halfdan Egedius. In their day these drawings had generated considerable discussion in Norway, not least because of the artists' raw and blatant depictions of the violence contained in the sagas. Their drawings of the kings of Norway and other noblemen in their death throes provoked particular outrage. While Norwegian intellectuals and artists valued this edition, it did not enjoy general popularity in Norway and was not reprinted until 1934.

There is no evidence that Icelandic artists actually saw this book until it was printed by Ragnar Jónsson's publishing house Helgafell in 1944, not even the artists who had studied in Norway during the first half of the century. And even if they had, it is by no means certain that it would have had any influence on them. Jónas Jónsson's bogeymen, the modernists, were not keen on the subject matter, while more conservative artists would probably have been disturbed by the alleged disrespect shown by their Norwegian colleagues towards the sagas.

In 1944, when World War II was at its height and the brutality that civilized nations were prepared to inflict upon one another seemed boundless, Icelandic artists finally discovered the meaning of the carnage in these Norwegian drawings.

They were quick to respond. By then Halldór Laxness had already made plans for a new edition of *Njal's Saga* with modern spelling, and to the particular annoyance of Jónas Jónsson he commissioned not one but three "decadent" artists to illustrate the book: Gunnlaugur Scheving, Þorvaldur Skúlason and Snorri Arinbjarnar. Particularly interesting are Laxness' remarks in his postscript on their drawings, namely that they "will prove to be lasting artistic achievements, as respected as the immortal text they were created to serve" – in other words, the visual arts in Iceland no longer needed to rely on the literary tradition but could stand on their own, independent and strong.

The artists did not betray Laxness' trust. The *Njal's Saga* project and his discovery of the Norwegian edition of *Heimskringla* were a formative experience for Gunnlaugur Scheving. He seems to have immersed himself in the drawings of Egedius and Munthe; and in doing so his own style changed, becoming coarser, yet more efficient and dramatic. Interestingly, many of the most powerful drawings by Scheving, a man with a horror of bloodshed, are of slayings: the deaths of Gunnar, Grim and Svart.

In his illustrations to *Njal's Saga* Þorvaldur Skúlason sought inspiration not only from Norwegian artists but also from his French mentor, Marcel Gromaire, and other Post-Cubists. This combination

unleashed a primitive creative force that, until then, had largely eluded this highly cultivated artist: witness his powerful depiction of the battle by the River Rangá. It is instructive to compare this drawing with Andreas Bloch's elegant representation of this event.

The weakest link in this illustrated *Njal's Saga* is undoubtedly Snorri Arinbjarnar, because his talents primarily lay in the field of painting itself: he was never a natural draughtsman.

Halldór Laxness and Ragnar Jónsson had still not completed their mission of introducing the Icelandic public to a new angle on the sagas. In 1946 they published *The Saga of Grettir the Strong* with modern spelling and illustrations by Scheving and Skúlason. Here the visual element is not as successful as in *Njal's Saga*, mainly because by this time Skúlason was breaking free from the fetters of figuration and forging a more complex semi-abstract style, witness his drawing of the ghost Glam. Scheving's drawing of Glam, on the other hand, is characterised by directness and impressive dramatic power. Nonetheless, a handful of drawings by both artists in this book rank with the most impressive depictions of the saga tradition ever made.

It is fair to say that these portrayals by Icelandic and Norwegian artists which appeared before the people of Iceland in 1941-46, along with the publication of Halldór Laxness's *Happy Warriors* in 1952, radically transformed subsequent Icelandic artists' attitudes towards the sagas. Although nothing could change the engrained nationalism of artists such as Guðmundur Einarsson from Miðdalur, active until the early 1960s, since the end of World War II the majority of interpretations of the sagas, illustrations as well as individual artworks, have been unfailingly realistic, aggressive and critical. If we look in particular at illustrations from the 1970s, artists show a noticeable lack of interest in the heroic deeds of saga characters. They are more interested in the depiction of the tragic consequences of heroism and the everyday lives and fate of ordinary people, or they produce outright parodies of saga heroes and Nordic gods. This is true of, for instance, the illustrations by Gylfi Gíslason, Hringur Jóhannesson and Haraldur Guðbergsson. There are a number of exceptions, however, such as Jóhann Briem's delicate illustrations to ancient lays.

Sigurjón Ólafsson's sculpture *The Death of Grettir* (1947) shows Grettir and his killers as part and parcel of the same beast; the message is that blood invariably calls for more blood. In the same year as the publication of *The Happy Warriors*, 1952, Sigurjón Ólafsson also carved his *Viking*, which is as far from the old, idealized image of the Viking – let us say Einar Jónsson's Þorfinnur Karlsefni – as could be imagined. Ólafsson's *Viking* resembles more than anything else a primitive idol, howling and bloodthirsty.

In Icelandic three-dimensional art this revision of the saga tradi-

tion possibly reaches its apogee in the 1977 assemblage by Magnús Pálsson on *Njal's Saga*. In this work the artist puts together ten type-writers, one for each of the victims of the fire that killed Njal, the typewriters being an embodiment of the art of writing and therefore the real "authors" of Skarphedin, Njal and the other characters in the book. The typewriters are inscribed with the names of the victims of the Bergthorshvol fire, and they are all draped with dried chickweed, similar to that used to set fire to the farmhouse. In other words, the tragic fates of these fictional characters is their only – and greatest – creative work.

"Bring the manuscripts home!"

GÍSLI SIGURÐSSON ET AL.

After the landmarks in the campaign for independence from Denmark in the twentieth century, Iceland started to make claims for the return of all Icelandic documents and manuscripts, including the collection that Árni Magnússon (1663–1730) had bequeathed to the University of Copenhagen. In 1927 an agreement was made to hand over Icelandic documents from Danish archives and in 1961 a law was eventually passed in Denmark approving the return of the manuscripts. Because the law was challenged in court it did not take effect immediately and the first manuscripts were not returned until April 21, 1971. Delivery of the manuscripts to be sent to Iceland lasted for 26 years and was formally concluded on July 19, 1997. Relations between Iceland and Denmark improved with the successful resolution of the manuscript issue, which set a precedent in international relations for efforts to retrieve relics and cultural valuables from former empires and colonial masters – as outlined by Jeanette Greenfield in *The Return of Cultural Treasures*.

The day before his death on January 7, 1730, Árni Magnússon and his wife Mette made a will. It stipulated that all his manuscripts and printed books would become the property of the University of Copenhagen after his day, and on the death of both of them the interest on their assets would provide a stipend for one or two Icelandic students as laid down in a charter for the bequest. The charter was to be written by two of Magnússon's Danish friends, Thomas Bartholin and Hans Gram, who had the best idea of how he wanted to dispose of his belongings.

Bartholin and Gram drew up a draft charter, but this was not finalized until 1760. Two inspectors were to supervise the library and other belongings. The interest earned on just under half of the principal was to be paid out in the form of stipends, and the remainder shared between reinvestments, remuneration to the inspectors, scribes and librarian, and payments to have books published. In 1772 the Árni

Left: The Danish coastguard vessel Vædderen docks in Reykjavík, April 21, 1971. Photograph: Guðjón Einarsson.

Danish navy officers bring ashore two manuscripts, the *Codex Regius* of
the Edda poems and *Flateyjarbók*. Photograph: Gunnar V. Andrésson.

Magnússon Commission was established, and since then it has managed the bequest. There has always been one Icelander on the commission, and for a period from 1936 the University of Iceland
appointed a special representative to it.

Iceland obtained home rule in 1904, and parliament agreed in
1907, on the initiative of Hannes Þorsteinsson, to take steps to retrieve
from Denmark the documents and manuscripts that Árni Magnússon
had borrowed from episcopal sees and other Icelandic institutions.
These overtures were ignored by Denmark at the time, but after
Iceland had achieved sovereignty in 1918 they were repeated in 1924
and extended to cover documents in other Danish archives. The outcome was that in 1928 the National Archive of Iceland was presented
with some seven hundred old charters and four manuscripts from
Árni Magnússon's collection, in addition to a large quantity of documents from the Danish State Archive, which included the land register
compiled by Árni Magnússon and Páll Vídalín.

Following this strategic victory Iceland stepped up its demands to
reclaim the manuscripts, as described in an article by Páll Eggert Ólafsson in 1929. In 1930 and again in 1938, parliament passed resolutions
urging the government to begin talks with the Danish government on
the return of manuscripts and other documents from archives.

Although the matter was discussed in the Danish-Icelandic consultative committee, which operated under the Crown Union Act of 1918, the Danish representatives did not accede to an Icelandic suggestion that the governments of both countries should appoint a committee of experts to make proposals for handing the manuscripts over.

The establishment of the Republic of Iceland in 1944 and the end of World War II gave added impetus to Iceland's claims to have the manuscripts returned, among other things with a legal opinion delivered by Ólafur Lárusson. In 1947 the Danish government appointed a large committee of politicians and scholars, which was split several ways in the findings that it presented in 1951. All the members wanted to find some recourse for Iceland, but differed over how much to concede. The same year Professor Sigurður Nordal, the leading authority on Old Icelandic literature at the time, was appointed Icelandic ambassador to Denmark, showing the serious view that the Icelandic government took of the matter, and in 1954 the Danish Minister of Education put forward a compromise which would have declared the manuscripts the joint property of Denmark and Iceland and shared them appropriately between research institutes in Reykjavík and Copenhagen. While this idea was rejected by Iceland, in 1955 parliament set up a forerunner of a research institute by contributing some funds towards manuscript publication, and in Copenhagen the Arnamagnean Institute opened in 1956.

The manuscript issue was intensely debated in the 1940s and 1950s in both countries. Articles appeared in Icelandic newspapers and journals presenting historical, nationalist and academic arguments that the manuscripts belonged in Iceland, to which the scholars Sigurður Nordal and Jón Helgason made strong contributions. Denmark refused to recognize Iceland's legal claim to the manuscripts, although there was widespread support for acceding to its wishes in part or in full; this group was led by representatives of the "People's Schools" and Bjarni M. Gíslason was an energetic campaigner in his lectures and articles. On the other hand, most members of the university and library community who expressed an opinion at all were strongly opposed, for fear of unforeseen consequences. Politicians were sharply divided over the issue, but those who wished to make some concessions to Iceland were in the great majority.

In 1959 parliament appointed a committee of five chaired by Professor Einar Ól. Sveinsson to work with the government on moving the manuscript issue forward. This committee wanted to base Iceland's requests on the nationality of the scribes. In 1961 a list of the manuscripts that Iceland wanted to have returned was drawn up for the then Minister of Education, Gylfi Þ. Gíslason, to submit to the

Children were given a holiday from school to welcome the return of the manuscripts. Photographs: Kári Jónasson.

From the ceremony in the University Theatre to mark the return of the manuscripts. Photographs: Kári Jónasson (above) and Gunnar V. Andrésson.

Danish government. That spring the Danish and Icelandic governments agreed on a resolution. This involved dividing up Árni Magnússon's bequest, which had been in the custody of the University of Copenhagen. Broadly speaking, manuscripts containing material written or translated by Icelanders, which also mainly or entirely dealt with Iceland or Icelandic subjects, were to be presented to the University of Iceland for preservation and administration. Icelandic manuscripts could also be handed over from the Royal Library under the same provision. The Danish Parliament passed an act to this effect in 1961 and again in 1965. The two countries also agreed to allow up to a quarter of a century for the delivery of the manuscripts, from the date when the entry to return them went into effect, and the Icelandic government waived any further claims to national relics in Denmark. However, legal challenges after the law was passed delayed the treaty from being validated until a ruling by the Danish Supreme Court on March 19, 1971.

On the last day of winter in 1971 – April 21 – the Danish coastguard vessel Vædderen entered Reykjavík harbour with the first manuscripts on board, the *Codex Regius of the Elder Edda* and *Flateyjarbók*. Iceland had made a particular point of including these two manuscripts, and since they were considered to fall outside the provisions of the law their delivery was stipulated separately. A crowd of thousands gathered by the harbour when Vædderen moored, and others watched the event on the first outdoor live broadcast made by State Television. Representatives of the Danish government and parliament attended the ceremony at the University Theatre where Helgi Larsen, the Danish Minister of Education, handed over the manuscripts to his Icelandic counterpart, Gylfi Þ. Gíslason, who in turn passed them on to Magnús Már Lárusson, Vice-Chancellor of the University. *The Codex Regius of the Elder Edda* is now preserved, along with the other manuscripts from Denmark, as the crown jewel of northern culture at the Árni Magnússon Institute in Iceland.

Under the Danish manuscript act an ad hoc committee, comprised of two representatives of the University of Copenhagen and two nominated by the University of Iceland, was to assess which of the manuscripts in the Árni Magnússon collection and the Royal Library fell within the provisions of the law; the Danish Prime Minister had the ultimate authority to rule on these questions. The manuscript committee was comprised of Chr. Westergård-Nielsen and Ole Widding for Denmark, and Jónas Kristjánsson and Magnús Már Lárusson from the University of Iceland, while the secretary to the Icelandic committee members and their deputy was Ólafur Halldórsson. After the committee had made its first list of manuscripts to return and this had been ratified by the minister in 1973, regular consignments began. The committee held 42 meetings, the last in 1984, and agreed on most of the manuscripts unanimously, but some by a majority vote. In quite a few cases the vote was tied and a second committee was appointed to settle the matter. Its members were Ivar Kjær and John Kousgård Sørensen from Denmark and Jakob Benediktsson and Jónas Kristjánsson from Iceland. The final decision on how to share out the manuscripts was made in January 1986 and was marked with another agreement signed by the respective Ministers of Education, Bertil Haarder and Sverrir Hermannsson, to cooperate on photographing and repairing the Icelandic manuscripts that would remain in Copenhagen, and on manuscript research in the two countries. This agreement was ratified and the manuscript issue was formally concluded when the ministers signed a memorandum at Thingvellir on August 1, 1986. It provided for 1,666 manuscripts and fragments to be sent to Iceland, along with about 1,350 charters and 6,000 copies of them from the Árni Magnússon collection, and 141 manuscripts from the Royal Library.

The provision in the treaty that the delivery of the manuscripts might take up to a quarter of a century was justified by the need to keep them in Denmark in connection with the large Icelandic dictionary which was then being compiled and is now being published. Other preliminary work on returning the manuscripts took time as well. A photograph was taken of each manuscript to be returned, and then compared with the original, leaf by leaf. The condition of each manuscript was checked, leaves and bindings were repaired as necessary, boxes were made for some of the manuscripts, and the charters were specially packed in order to preserve their seals. Finally, each consignment of manuscripts was packed in such a way as to preclude any damage during transportation. All this work cost the Danish state something like the salaries of five to eight people per year for a quarter of a century, along with materials, equipment and facilities.

Most of the manuscripts that were returned deal with Icelandic subjects, as the Danish law had stated. From Árni Magnússon's collections, virtually all the manuscripts of Sagas of Icelanders have been returned, and also Ari the Wise's *Book of the Icelanders, Sturlunga saga*, Sagas of Bishops, annals, law books, genealogies, books of court rulings and charters, and individual old charters and copies of them. The extensive dictionary and other works by the prolific scholar Jón Ólafsson of Grunnavík were included. Manuscripts of ballads and other genres of poetry have also been returned, and chivalric sagas and younger sagas of saints which are definitely considered to have been written in Iceland, along with one of the two main manuscripts of *Stjórn*, Old Testament translations with exegeses. Most of these manuscripts are from the collection made by Árni Magnússon himself, but some are later additions from collections made by other Icelanders: Magnús Stephensen, Stefán Eiríksson and Konráð Gíslason. Manuscripts containing material of the same kind have also been returned from the Royal Library, as well as the *Codex Regius of the Elder Edda* and *Flateyjarbók*.

More than 1350 manuscripts remained in the Árni Magnússon collection in Copenhagen; roughly half of them are not Icelandic, as he also collected other manuscripts. Most are Danish, but others are from Norway, Sweden, Germany, the Netherlands, Spain and Italy, and the collection also contains old Norwegian and Danish original charters and copies. The remaining Icelandic manuscripts include the sagas of kings and translations of various foreign works, such as *The Saga of Alexander the Great* (*Alexanders saga mikla*), *The Saga of Charlemagne* and tales of saints; in some cases it is uncertain whether the work itself originated in Norway or Iceland, even though the manuscripts are Icelandic. The entire collection owned by Rasmus Rask remained in Denmark in the Árni Magnússon collection. The Royal Library also contains many Icelandic manuscripts of the same kind, and all the manuscripts it has acquired from private collections of Danes, some of which were copied out for them by Icelandic students in Copenhagen. The main collections of this kind were owned by the historians P. F. Suhm (d. 1798), A. Kall (d. 1821) and Count O. Thott (d. 1785).

Icelandic manuscripts are found in many collections outside Iceland and Denmark. However, not many of them are medieval, apart from those in the Royal Library in Stockholm; the Swedes collected Icelandic manuscripts as early as the seventeenth century, mostly at the instigation of Jón Eggertsson from Akrar in Skagafjörður, who also copied them for Swedes in Copenhagen. Outside Stockholm, the largest Icelandic collection in Sweden is in Uppsala University Library. In Norway there are many later Icelandic manuscripts, most of them in the Oslo University Library and the Library of the Royal Norwegian Academy of Science in Trondheim, and manuscript fragments from the thirteenth and fourteenth centuries are kept in the Norwegian State Archive in Oslo.

A large number of Icelandic manuscripts, most of them dating from later centuries, are preserved in Britain, especially in the British Library in London and the Advocates Library in the National Library of Scotland in Edinburgh; these libraries purchased many of their Icelandic manuscripts from the collection owned by Finnur Magnússon, keeper of the confidential document archive in Copenhagen (d. 1847). There are other Icelandic manuscripts in the

Right: Minister of Education and Culture Gylfi Þ. Gíslason presents Flateyjarbók to Magnús Már Lárusson, Vice-Chancellor of the University of Iceland, at the ceremony at the University Theatre on April 21, 1971. Photograph: Gunnar V. Andrésson.

Bodleian Library in Oxford and Trinity College in Dublin. Various museums in continental Europe outside Scandinavia contain a few Icelandic manuscripts, the oldest and best known being three vellums in Wolfenbüttel in Germany. In North America there are Icelandic manuscripts in a handful of places, led by the Fiske Collection at Cornell University, and in Harvard there are manuscripts from the collection of the German Icelandophile Konrad Maurer.

Finally, by far the largest collection of Icelandic manuscripts is housed in the manuscript department of the National University Library of Iceland. The bulk are paper manuscripts from later centuries, but among them are a large number of copies of medieval writings with independent textual value. Post-Reformation literature and other materials, however, form the core of this collection.

Melsted's Edda: The last manuscript sent home?

GÍSLI SIGURÐSSON

"Bring the manuscripts home" was a popular slogan in one of the only two matters on which Icelanders were in almost total agreement during the twentieth century. They were virtually unanimous about the return of the manuscripts from Denmark and the establishment of the republic at Thingvellir on June 17, 1944. Both issues were successfully resolved and in 1997, when the last manuscripts had been returned from Denmark according to the treaty on sharing them out, no one expected any further deliveries for the time being. Then, in 2000, the family of the Icelandic consul in Minnesota, Örn Arnar, bought an Icelandic manuscript from Kenneth Melsted, a Canadian-Icelandic farmer from Wynyard on the plains of Saskatchewan (known to the Icelandic community as Vatnabyggð), and he donated it to Iceland, to the Árni Magnússon Institute. This is a paper manuscript, named *Melsted's Edda* after its previous owners and written by Jakob Sigurðsson from Vopnafjörður in 1765-66 – Jónas Kristjánsson deciphered the scribe's name from extremely cryptic handwriting. Haraldur Bessason, then professor of Icelandic in Winnipeg, had heard about the manuscript in the early 1970s from Árni Bjarnarson, a book publisher in Akureyri, who had seen it in a bank vault at the Royal Bank in Wynyard. Kenneth Melsted took the manuscript by plane to Winnipeg and showed it to Haraldur Bessason, who called in Guðbjartur Gunnarsson to take the photographs which were sent to Jónas Kristjánsson in Iceland.

Although the manuscript was not delivered by a navy frigate with an impromptu official holiday and live TV broadcast – as was the case when the first consignment arrived from Denmark – its return still deserves to be welcomed. But what exactly is this manuscript? Is it remarkable? And – what is *remarkable* about manuscripts? The value of a manuscript has often depended on whether it contains the oldest text of a given work – a case in point is the *Codex Regius* of the eddic poems, which is remarkable for being our only source for most of the

Left: Odin. The ravens Hugin and Munin sit on his shoulders and bring him news from all over the world. From *Melsted's Edda*, SÁM 66. Árni Magnússon Institute in Iceland.

texts it contains. Or a manuscript has been valued in terms of its appearance and ornamentation, as with *Flateyjarbók*, a lavishly produced and illustrated collection of numerous texts, many of which exist in older and "more original" versions.

By these criteria, *Melsted's Edda* does not count for much, perhaps. The texts in it are based on older, known manuscripts or printed books, giving it little value for establishing an original text. All the same, it includes eight leaves which are beautifully illustrated with mythological scenes, the hallmark of this book, not unlike the illustrations in the manuscript written in 1760 by the Reverend Ólafur Brynjólfsson from Kirkjubær in Hróarstunga, now preserved in the Royal Library in Copenhagen. Brynjólfsson died in 1765, the year that *Melsted's Edda* was written, and his son Eiríkur probably sold his father's *Edda* manuscript to buy drink in Copenhagen – as Professor Jón Helgason in Copenhagen surmises in his *Handritaspjall.*

So is this just an unremarkable manuscript, of "absolutely no worth," as Finnur Jónsson, professor of Icelandic in Copenhagen in the early twentieth century, sometimes said of later paper manuscripts? The answer is no! While neither the text nor the art are original, *Melsted's Edda* bears remarkable witness to the cultural situation and attitudes of people towards the heritage it contains – and has possibly even played its own small part in linking the history of modern Icelandic art to the manuscript art tradition.

Jakob Sigurðsson wrote and illustrated numerous manuscripts in his day, when he was not busy moving with his ever-growing family between crofters' cottages in east Iceland. The National Library of Iceland has fourteen acquisition numbers for his manuscripts, the largest containing 339 leaves with fifteen romances and sagas of legendary heroes. He also wrote a manuscript of hymns which was donated to the Manuscript Institute, the predecessor of the Árni Magnússon Institute, in 1967. On that occasion, Benedikt Gíslason from Hofteigur wrote a long article about Jakob Sigurðsson in the Christmas edition of *Þjóðviljinn* newspaper. There he argues that Sigurðsson had probably been brought up by the Reverend Ólafur Brynjólfsson at Kirkjubær where he learned to read and write, so the affinity with the latter's manuscript is hardly surprising. Jakob Sigurðsson began farming at the age of just over twenty with his wife Ingveldur Sigurðardóttir in 1749, at Jórvík in Breiðdalur, after which they moved from one croft in Vopnafjörður to the next until he died at Breiðumýri in Vopnafjörður in 1779, just over fifty and the father of at least seven children. Sigurðsson knew neither formal education nor worldly wealth at any time in his life, but he was more than compensated in spiritual values, as may be seen from this verse composed about him on his death:

Jakob now has passed away,
from hardship's torments free.
A scribe and poet in his day,
Vopnafjörður's glee.

Left: High, Just-as-High and Third answer Gangleri's questions.
Right: The cow Audhumla licks away the stones to create the first man,
Buri. From *Melsted's Edda*, SÁM 66. Árni Magnússon Institute in Iceland.

Thus *Melsted's Edda* is a beautiful testimony to spiritual richness amidst
the abject poverty of the eighteenth century, which by itself would
suffice to earn Jakob Sigurðsson a place of honour in the great and as
yet unwritten roll-call of Icelandic scribes. But what does this manuscript contain and what does it tell us about the reception of old lore
and attitudes towards it?

2 leaves: Contents
216 leaves written in 1765
    80 leaves: eddic poems
    8 leaves: Mythological illustrations
    80 leaves: S*norra Edda*, copied from the *Resens Edda* printed in
    Copenhagen in 1665 (three prefaces before "Preface Authoris", the
    Fables of the Deluding of Gylfi, Names and Kennings, in
    alphabetical order)
    8 leaves: Alphabet and runes, various types
    40 leaves: *Calendarium* of Bishop Þórður Þórðarson of Skálholt

(published in Skálholt), Appendix and *Mensa Pythagorea* (multipli
cation table)
24 leaves written in 1766
6 leaves: arithmetic
18 leaves: A gloss of the *Sibyl's Prophecy* by Björn from Skarðsá
and a genealogy from Adam via Odin to Bishop Jón Arason
Total: 242 leaves

The prefaces to *Snorra Edda* written here follow the main version
known from the *Wormsbók*. They draw much closer parallels between
Nordic and classical mythology than was customary before – although
the connection with Troy has been there from the beginning. And
from what is said of this connection, it is clear that people were well
aware of how the classical myths were used to explain celestial phenomena, the planets Jupiter, Saturn, Uranus, Mars and Venus or Freyja,
and the constellations of the Zodiac; in traditional societies in many
parts of the world myths have precisely that double function as the
language of astronomy. Here we see a familiar notion at work, applied
to the Nordic myths. It is also interesting that these *Edda* texts should
be included in a book with an almanac, which also describes the position of celestial bodies, and with arithmetic – two kindred branches of
knowledge. *Melsted's Edda* is therefore a remarkable testimony to the
fact that in the eighteenth century the ancient understanding of the
link between myths and the heavens was still alive, and the *Edda* did
not serve solely as a fountain of poetic diction. It is highly apt that this
Edda should be returned from the Icelandic settlements in North
America, which spawned people like Björn Jónsson from Swan River
in Manitoba, who championed the idea that the old lore could be
read from the stars in the firmament (cf. his book *Star Myths of the
Vikings*).

On the last page of the manuscript, after Adam's line has been
traced to Odin in the forty-third generation from Adam and on to
Bishop Jón Arason of Hólar in the seventy-sixth generation, where it
ends, come three names, probably those of the owners of the book.
The first is Gísli Gíslason from Skörð who "rightly owns the book the
Edda." Gísli Gíslason lived from 1797-1858, a farmer, poet and book-
binder from Skörð in Reykjahverfi, who himself owned 68 books
when he died. He lived for a while at Auðnir in Laxárdalur, a tied
farm at Þverá, and the binding of the book uses a sheet torn from a
letter to Jón Jóakimsson from Þverá, the father of Benedikt from
Auðnir, written by independence movement leader Jón Sigurðsson -
thereby indirectly linking the manuscript with Iceland's campaign for
independence. Gísli Gíslason was the father of the painter Arngrímur
Gíslason (1829-1887) possibly providing a significant role for *Melsted's*

Edda in transmitting the manuscript illustration tradition to modern art. In Kristján Eldjárn's biography of "Arngrímur the Painter" (p. 83), the following account is attributed to Sigurjón Þorgrímsson from Hraunkot, who for some time was an innkeeper in Húsavík and heard Arngrímur describe his first artistic efforts:

> *It was in spring, good weather, most of the people at Skörð had gone to church, but Arngrímur remained at home. A book of drawings was on the shelf in the main room. The lad reached out for the book, ran outside with it and up to Skarðaháls hill, started drawing and became completely absorbed. When the people returned from church no one knew what had happened to him. A search was mounted and he was eventually discovered, absorbed in the first drawings that he ever tried to make.*

It is impossible to ascertain whether the young Arngrímur Gíslason forgot himself over the same illustrations that may be seen in *Melsted's Edda*, but is very tempting to toy with the idea that this book actually passed through his hands, and that the illustrations in it were thus his first initiation into the visual arts.

Some way farther down on the last page is the name "St. Petersen," who has not been identified, and at the bottom "Magnús Guðmundsson." Most probably this is the Magnús Guðmundsson who was a farmer at Sandur in Aðaldalur, since his daughter, Elín Sigríður, left Halldórsstaðir in Kinn for Canada with her six children in 1876, claimed land near Gimli and named their farm Melstaður. One of these children was Jóhannes Frímann Magnússon Melsted, born at Gvendarstaðir in Kinn in 1859. He later lived on a large farm at Gardar in North Dakota until he moved to Wynyard in 1910. His son was Leo Melsted, born in 1902, a farmer in Wynyard, the father of Kenneth Melsted, who was born on June 19th, 1931. Kenneth later became a farmer on his family's land and is described as follows in *Vestur-íslenskar æviskrár* (vol. 5, p. 180): "A great lover of good books and owns extremely rare Icelandic books in his library. He also owns a large and remarkable collection of postage stamps." This description can hardly be very exaggerated, and could equally have applied to Árni Magnússon had postage stamps existed in his day – because among these books was the manuscript which has now been returned to Iceland, not only a rare work but a unique one too, and so remarkable that in 1876 a mother of six, crossing the North Atlantic on her quest for a new life in an unknown country with all her children, could think of nothing better than to take it with her in the little luggage which she could carry. Such a book must surely be worth something, and hardly deserves to be considered "of absolutely no worth."

Hi flijg.r Oþin i arnar
ham med hvijt biga mia
var fillina. Jnum As
grind.r og fullting.r Jöt
un i Arn ham ept.r ho
nu. 3osm 61. dæmi 9:
Sþiи utvijsar þ þaru.m
mä lesa fä er vill

"Our lot"

PÉTUR GUNNARSSON

"Bring the manuscripts home" – this was the slogan of the 1950s and the 1960s. Denmark and Iceland had been separated for a quarter of a century when they finally underwent a formal divorce in the spring of 1944. As is common in divorces, a dispute arose afterwards about how to share out their belongings.

This is not to say that the Icelanders made a claim on the Circular Tower, Tivoli or the Little Mermaid; it was the manuscripts they wanted. Somehow the newly founded republic's very existence depended upon retrieving these pieces of calfskin that had been rounded up and sent abroad during Iceland's darkest hour in the seventeenth and eighteenth centuries.

The whole of Icelandic society, from professors at the university down to the youngest classes at kindergarten, was engulfed by this demand. And as is often the case when David finds a suitable Goliath, the former won, the manuscripts were sent home on board a Danish warship, crowds gathered on the harbourside, schoolchildren waving flags filled the streets.

A guard of honour took up its position on both sides, horns were sounded and – for a moment – it was as if the ceremony had strayed into a H. C. Andersen fairy tale: Sailors were seen walking down the gangway carrying two little packages, almost nothing!

In the packages were *Flateyjarbók* and the *Codex Regius* of the eddic poems, the vellums which Bishop Brynjólfur had offered up to the king in the seventeenth century in the hope of having them published. *A pars pro toto* that over the following years gradually made its way back to Iceland.

These manuscripts, which had resisted attack by the vandals Damp, Mould and Rot, survived misery, wretchedness and negligence, had floated under sail across the vast ocean and been rescued from fire in Copenhagen ... at last they had come home.

In some mysterious way they were the birth certificate of the

Left: Torn leaves in *The Life of St. Thorlak*, AM 382 4to. Árni Magnússon Institute in Iceland.

Icelandic nation and this is the reason that visiting heads of state are invariably driven straight to "look at the manuscripts" – instead of the traditional military parades which are routine in other countries. This is our guard of honour, our Colosseum and our Pantheon – it was on these pages that the spirit of the nation made its home in days of yore.

★★★

But when all the ceremonial speeches are over and the flagpoles have started babbling to themselves again, what do these manuscripts mean to us?

The Sagas of Icelanders in commemorative editions which once filled shelves as the hallmark of a cultured household, yes, the manuscripts are definitely to some degree what anthropologists call a "fetish": something to which man assigns magical powers and then worships.

And now that they have found a safe haven at last in a fireproof and earthquake-resistant bunker where they reside at exactly the right temperature and humidity in receptacles that not even the teeth of time can gnaw through, there is nothing that can threaten them except the brute force of indifference, the destructiveness of negligence, the erosive power of banality. Not even Árni Magnússon and Bishop Brynjólfur could rescue them from that.

The Church, which in those men's day operated the only printing press in Iceland, turned up its nose at these texts. Today it is up to the visual media to give this heritage a new, creative lease of life, but they are just as inept and reluctant as the Hólar printing press was during Iceland's darkest hour. Television makes do with broadcasting the mass-produced gospel of today: the soap opera.

★★★

But haven't the manuscripts already been given their due? Haven't they been printed and republished in splendid editions?

In much the same way that general ownership of 4WD vehicles has opened up once rarely travelled paths into the wilderness, land has been bestowed upon people today on a larger scale than upon earlier generations, who only had the chance to visit a handful of places – Thingvellir, Gullfoss and Geysir, Ásbyrgi.

The same should apply to the sagas. A Sunday drive to *Njal's Saga, Egil's Saga, The Saga of the People of Laxardal* and their sisters was fair enough, but there is more excitement about opening new paths, blazing new trails, not necessarily to experience the rural idyll, but just as much the wilds of Sprengisandur, Gæsavötn and Ódáðahraun.

King Olav V of Norway, King Gustav XVI of Sweden and Queen Silvia examine manuscripts at the Árni Magnússon Institute, accompanied by President Vigdís Finnbogadóttir. Photographs: Jóhanna Ólafsdóttir

To settle the land that lives in these texts, the whole swarm of characters and events that step forth from them. The medieval world view in its entirety.

★★★

What is the explanation for this deluge of creativity? Why did it take place on this island in the northernmost Atlantic? Why over this limited period? And then: end of story.

Journeys engender narratives, we have only to recall the first time we left home and thereby acquired two worlds: the one we left behind and the one we visited. And thereupon we were qualified to write the essay: "What I did in the summer" at school in the autumn.

This view of two worlds, which appears immediately in the book of Genesis when the Lord says to Abraham: "Get thee out of thy country, and from thy kindred, and from thy father's house, unto a land that I will shew thee" is the beginning of a story to which no end is yet in sight. Or the expulsion of Adam and Eve from Paradise, which at the same time represents the beginning of human history: If the Devil had not lured Eve to eat of the tree of knowledge, she and Adam would have lived for an uneventful and routine eternity. Which is surely a fine thing, but perhaps too insipid to be the making of a good yarn.

The Greeks' long journeys in the Trojan War spawn the epics of Homer, the national migrations yield us heroic poetry, the crusades deliver chivalric literature and the troubadours, whereas the discovery of Iceland, Greenland and Vinland bear fruit in the sagas ...

This last-mentioned act of creation was and is and continues to be the best-guarded secret of European cultural history. Even prodigies who set themselves the task of running through the entire literary history of the continent (Auerbach, Steiner, Kundera ...) run straight past the Icelandic chapter.

Which must not, however, lead us to regard these works as isolated phenomena instead of seeing them grow from a context which may never have been as unambiguous as during the Middle Ages in Europe when all Christians had one and the same mindset and obeyed one and the same dogmatic authority.

★★★

The medieval Icelanders are a part of a world view, but they also venture beyond it in the same way that an astronaut tears himself free from the Earth's gravitational field. They sail out of it by discovering new and uncharted lands, but also step out of the prevailing realm of

Mary Robinson, President of Ireland; Queen Elizabeth II of the UK; and US First Lady Hillary Clinton examine manuscripts at the Árni Magnússon Institute. Photographs: Jóhanna Ólafsdóttir

Manuscripts in storage in the basement of the Árni Magnússon Institute in Iceland. Photograph: Jóhanna Ólafsdóttir

Upper photograph: Leaves from the *Staðarhólsbók* manuscript of *Grágás*. Árni Magnússon Institute in Iceland.

Lower: Law books. Árni Magnússon Institute in Iceland.

thought with its typifying emphasis on the looming end of the world and the day of judgement. The rebirth of the mind and the world which accompanied the settlement of Iceland bestows the primal force of the origin upon them as their birthright. In this respect they resemble the ancient Greeks. Those who are at the beginning of a journey think differently from those who are at its end.

It was this primal fountain of youth that the poet and politician Grímur Thomsen offered to present to the Nordic nations in the nineteenth century, provided that they rediscovered the language which once had been at the root of their own tongues. He spoke of Iceland as the Nordic Provence, by which he meant that the Icelanders, like the troubadours of southern France, had begun to compose in the vernacular instead of Latin which was the predominant language of culture.

Grímur Thomsen's offer was not accepted.

On the other hand, modern Icelanders almost seem to heed that call when they flock to evening classes about the sagas year after year, the climax of which is a rendezvous with the saga sites. A kind of journey back to the starting point, a family reunion, where the heroes have taken it upon themselves to be our forebears and the land itself supplies the banqueting hall.

The sky is still the same and the mountains stand guard. Anything in the scenery that might not quite fit the picture is accounted for by the rivers' tendency to switch course and rearrange the topography. The wind and the birds in the moors see to the original soundtrack and the farm animals disperse around the meadow as in the days of old. Admittedly the raven has stopped scouring the bloody battlefields for carrion and has turned towards the containers of rubbish in the colonies of summer chalets, the horses have changed from chargers to ponies, cows are milked in computer-controlled sheds and the sheep have become welfare clients.

Not forgetting us.

★★★

Egil's Saga describes how Einar Skalaglamm sent Egil a splendid shield "adorned with legends". The recipient's reaction was unexpected: "That scoundrel. Does he expect me to stay awake making a poem about his shield? (...) I shall ride after him and kill him."

This is precisely the point. The magnitude of the gift makes demands of the person who accepts it. We are a obliged to "stay awake making a poem about it". Always imminent is the threat that the nation will drift away from its heritage, that it will become valueless in a kind of currency conversion, abandoned amidst the furore of the media, left to erode when the springs where language wells up are disturbed. There are so few of us on whom it depends for its value, there is no one else but us.

It has fallen to our lot to be creative recipients. The sagas show us a world which is departing, and we too are living in a world which is packing its bags. In the space of a very few years flourishing rural areas have been abandoned and farms which were in the last telephone directory no longer answer. The land is rapidly forsaking its memory and its memories.

In our day too a fierce battle for power is being waged, only the clashes are no longer over land but profit. They have left the stage for stock market trading which goes on in the invisibility of the Internet. People can fight to the death without ever meeting eye to eye.

And the settlement of the land is by no means over, the land is being overlaid with new people, some of them from far corners of the world, new settlers, new sagas according to the formula for the stimulating effect of moving on and beginning a new life.

The old new texts enable us to remain in the same place yet cross the abyss of the centuries from here to the days of old. To meet ourselves in other positions with another mindset, yet at the same time render visible the reality and the fate that we face now.

Overleafs: *Flateyjarbók*, the fall of King Olaf the Saint. GKS 1005 fol. Árni Magnússon Institute in Iceland.

Below: *The Life of St. Margaret* (*Margrétar saga*), AM 431 12mo. Árni Magnússon Institute in Iceland.

FURTHER READING:

Árni Björnsson: Wagner and the Volsungs: Icelandic Sources of Der Ring des Nibelungen. London: Viking Society for Northern Research, 2004.

Bekker-Nielsen, Hans & Ole Widding: Arne Magnusson. Transl. Robert W. Mattila. Odense, 1972.

Brown, Michelle P.: A Guide to Western Historical Scripts from Antiquity to 1600. London: The British Library, 1990.

Byock, Jesse: Viking Age Iceland. London: Penguin Books, 2001.

The Complete Sagas of Icelanders. Ed. Viðar Hreinsson. Reykjavík: Leifur Eiríksson Publishing, 1997.

Gísli Sigurðsson: The Medieval Icelandic Saga and Oral Tradition. Transl. Nicolas Jones. Publications of the Milman Parry Collection of Oral Literature 2. Harvard University Press, Cambridge MA, 2004.

Greenfield, Jeanette. The Return of Cultural Treasures. Cambridge: Cambridge University Press, 1989.

Gunnar Karlsson: Iceland's 1100 Years: The History of a Marginal society. London: C. Hurst & Co., 2000.

Hreinn Benediktsson: Early Icelandic Script as Illustrated in Vernacular Texts from the Twelfth and Thirteenth Centuries. Reykjavík: The Manuscript Institute of Iceland, 1965.

Jón Karl Helgason, The Rewriting of Njáls Saga: Translation, Ideology and Icelandic Sagas. Clevedon: Multilingual Matters, 1999.

Jónas Kristjánsson: Eddas and Sagas: Iceland's Medieval Literature. Transl. Peter Foote. Reykjavík: Hið íslenska bókmenntafélag, 1988. – : Eddas und Sagas: Die mittelalterliche Literatur Islands. Transl. Magnús Pétursson & Astrid van Nahl. Hamburg: Helmut Buske Verlag 1994.

Jónas Kristjánsson: Icelandic Manuscripts, Sagas, History and Art. Transl. Jeffrey Cosser. Reykjavík: Hið íslenska bókmenntafélag, 1993. – : Les miniatures islandaises, Sagas, histoire, art. Transl. Régis Boyer. Paris: La Renaissance du Livre, 2003.

Lindow, John: Handbook of Norse Mythology. Santa Barbara: ABC-Clio, 2001

Lönnroth, Lars: Skaldemjödet i berget: Essayer om fornisländsk ordkonst och dess återanvändning i nutiden. Stockholm: Atlantis, 1996.

Malm, Mats: Minervas äpple. Om diktsyn, tolkning och bildspråk inom nordisk göticism. Stockholm: Brutus Östlings Bokförlag Symposion, 1996.

Meulengracht Sørensen, Preben: Saga and Society: an introduction to Old Norse literature. Transl. John Tucker. Odense: Odense University Press, 1993.

The Poetic Edda. Transl. Carolyne Larrington. Oxford: Oxford University Press, 1996
.
See, Klaus von: Barbar, Germane, Arier. Die Suche nach der Identität der Deutschen. Heidelberg: C. Winter, 1994.

Sigrún Davíðsdóttir: Håndskriftsagens Saga - i politisk belysning. Overs. Kim Lembek. Odense: Odense universitetsforlag, 1999.

Shailor, Barbara A.: The Medieval Book. Illustrated from the Beinecke Rare Book and Manuscript Library. Toronto, Buffalo, London: University of Toronto Press, 1991.

Snorri Sturluson. Edda. Transl. Jean I. Young, revised by Julian Thorsteinsson. Gudrun, 2003.

Vésteinn Ólason, Dialogues with the Viking Age. Narration and Representation in the Sagas of the Icelanders. Reykjavík: Mál og menning, 1998.

Turville-Petre, Gabriel, Origins of Icelandic Literature. Oxford: Clarendon Press, 1953.

Wawn, Andrew: Vikings and Victorians. Inventing the Old North in Nineteenth Century Britain. Cambridge: D.S. Brewer, 2000.

Zernack, Julia: Geschichten aus Thule. Íslendingasögur in Übersetzungen deutscher Germanisten. Berlin: Freie Universität Berlin, 1994.